1
2

The research carried out by Mélanie van der Hoorn was made possible with funding from the Creative Industries Fund NL, the Van Eesteren-Fluck & Van Lohuizen Stichting and the Arts and Culture Division at the Austrian Federal Chancellery. The publication of *Serious Fun* was made possible by the Creative Industries Fund NL.

Author Mélanie van der Hoorn
Translation Billy Nolan
Design SJG/Joost Grootens, Julie da Silva
Printing and lithography NPN Drukkers, Breda
Publisher Eelco van Welie, nai010 publishers

nai010 publishers is an internationally orientated publisher specialized in developing, producing and distributing books in the fields of architecture, urbanism, art and design.

nai010 books are available internationally at selected bookstores and from the following distribution partners:
North, Central and South America—Artbook | D.A.P., New York, USA, dap@dapinc.com

Rest of the world—Idea Books, Amsterdam, the Netherlands, idea@ideabooks.nl

For general questions, please contact nai010 publishers directly at sales@nai010.com or visit our website www.nai010.com for further information.

Printed and bound in the Netherlands

ISBN 978-94-6208-689-0
www.nai010.com

Mélanie van der Hoorn

SERIOUS FUN

Architecture & Games

nai010 publishers

Contents

THE POWER OF PLAYFULNESS

Plunging into and Reflecting on Architecture Games

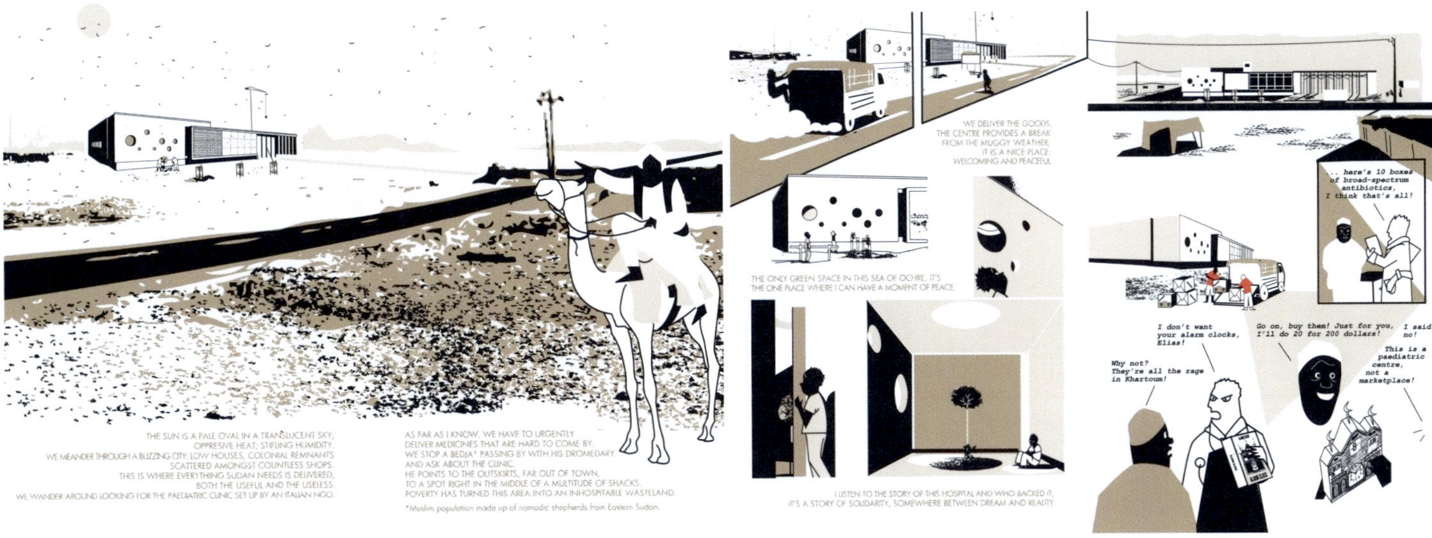

01

Building blocks used to construct spectacular skyscrapers, sleek doll's houses that make real houses pale by comparison, hexagonal cards that imitate the functioning of a complete city, joysticks that fill virtual streets with cars and people: games like these are full of architecture and urban design. They are analogue, digital, or both at the same time. Even the real city can sometimes become the field of play, for example when an app opens up a parallel world full of challenges and riddles to be solved in situ. Games are motivational, accessible, enjoyable and powerful. That can prove useful in architecture and urban design, which is why some designers have developed games specifically for their profession. They reveal hidden or underexposed issues, offer insight into complex relationships, foster discussion among relevant parties with varying points of view, and sometimes help to solve real problems.

How to reach a wider audience outside the profession of architecture and urban design? How to involve these people in design processes and exchange ideas with them? How to tell stories about the built environment—stories in which architecture consists of more than just material, construction and finishing? How to convey ideas, atmospheres and feelings? All these questions surfaced in *Bricks & Balloons: Architecture in Comic-Strip Form* (van der Hoorn 2012) and *Spots in Shots: Narrating the Built Environment in Short Films* (van der Hoorn 2018). Architecture games now complete the overview. They distinguish themselves from comic strips and films by their interactive character: Those who take part are not simply observers. They become part of the action and help determine how the game unfolds. That stimulates identification and involvement, curiosity and inquisitiveness.

ALL-ROUNDER TAM ASSOCIATI: THE START OF THIS PROJECT

The first incentive to write this book came from the Venice architecture office TAM Associati, which advocates social and ecological sustainability. The office attaches just as much importance to participatory processes and open communication as it does to concrete designs—and it has also published a number of comic books. For *Bricks & Balloons*, architect Simone Sfriso explained that they deploy comics not only to involve future users in a project but also to look back and explain their motives, concerns and doubts as designers. In a comic they can communicate with readers in a personal and engaging way.[1] A case in point is *Destinazione Freetown* (2012) →01, about the realization of five hospitals in Africa from the fictive perspective of Elias, a Sudanese truck driver, and Khalid,

1 See: van der Hoorn 2012:152-153 and van der Hoorn 2015.

02

a young nurse from Sierra Leone who, as a refugee in Italy, decided to return to his homeland after a negative experience. The book addresses in an accessible and enjoyable way serious questions like 'what it means to work on quality in architecture, and what it means to work with an NGO on the African continent, and to bring health care to these countries'.[2]

TAM Associati has also experimented with animation films on numerous occasions. One of them is *Le giraffe hanno il collo lungo… e sono curiose* (2005) →02 ('Giraffes Have Long Necks…. They Are Truly Curious Creatures'), the simple story of a little man who walks through the city at night and starts to read in the light of a lamppost. As soon as the lamppost notices just how much pleasure he derives from that activity, it bends over backwards to read along with him. But its laughter irritates the man, leading to mutual needling. In the film, 'life seems to be infused not only in human beings but also in the objects that populate the cityscape'.[3] The lamppost is a real design by TAM Associati and lamppost manufacturer Viabizzuno, which is presented here poetically and with lots of humour.

TAM Associati are not the only designers with both comics and films to their name; others include Wes Jones, Bjarke Ingels Group, Håkon Matre Aasarød, Studio Asynchrome and De Urbanisten.[4] But TAM Associati goes even further.

2 Interview with Simone Sfriso on 20 November 2014.
3 Cited from: https://www.architectureplayer.com/clips/giraffes-have-long-necks-they-are-truly-curious-creatures (last consulted on 3 July 2022).
4 See: van der Hoorn 2012 and: https://www.architectureplayer.com/strips/the-power-of-drawings-architecture-videos-borrowing-from-animated-cartoons (last consulted on 3 July 2022). For the work of Wes Jones, Håkon Matre Aasarød and Studio Asynchrome, see also: Berre, van der Hoorn & Lunde (eds) 2015, and for the film *Cohabitation* (2008) by Robert Cha, Caroline Dahl & Amir Lotfi supervised by Wes Jones, see: van der Hoorn 2018:116-119.

giocolaguna
barche e navigazione
giocolaguna
architettura
animali e piante della laguna

03

04

After a conversation about animation films for *Spots in Shots*, Sfriso pulled out a green-blue bag emblazoned with the name *Gioco Laguna* (2003) →03: 'Lagoon Game'. Similar to *Trivial Pursuit*, it is a knowledge game about the unique ecosystem in the expanse of water between the coast and sandspit in Venice. A throw of the dice determines how many squares you can move forward, after which you get a question about architecture, shipping, flora and fauna or history. If you answer correctly you can continue. It is a simple and classical game concept packaged in a strikingly attractive way. The side-pockets of the bag contain all sorts of additional material about the lagoon, such as a handbook by project mascot Alvise and his dog Aida, a children's book about the adventures of Gobius the fish, and a video game, called *Laguna Big Game* (2003) →04. That is an entertaining yet critical position against the 'motondoso', the damage to quays and buildings caused by the intensive motorboat traffic in Venice. In the game the captain of a simple boat powered by solar and wind energy bombards as many passing motorboats, pleasure yachts and cruise ships as possible.

The projects and explanations by TAM Associati confirm the impression that arose during the research for *Bricks & Balloons* and *Spots in Shots*: Architects and urban designers who experiment with alternative forms of representation and communication often do so on numerous fronts at the same time.[5] Whether they create architecture comics, films or games, they have comparable motives. They hope to reach more people than they do with floor plans, diagrams, models and computer renderings. They try to smoothen the exchange of views between professionals and people outside the discipline, and to encourage and facilitate participation. In terms of contents, they shift the emphasis to the stories 'behind' the architecture: the experiences, observations and memories of users and other parties involved, and the social or political significance of buildings and places. Comic strips, films and games can all contribute to that end, though they differ from one another in key ways. *Serious Fun* focuses on the unique potential—as well as the ambivalence—of games.

A PROVOCATION FROM THE THRIFT SHOP: THE (SUPPOSED) POWER OF ARCHITECTURE GAMES

At the start of this project the game *Provopoli: Wem gehört die Stadt?* (1972) →05 turned up in a thrift shop. The subtitle immediately captures the game theme: To whom does the city belong? The game is the work of a socio-critical collective headed by Carl-Ludwig Reichert. It is set in a fictive place called Grünstadt ('Greentown'), where two teams compete with each other: the Blues represent existing power relationships, the Reds seek change and evolution. Around half of the buildings belong to both parties: tax office, university, hospital, cafés, shops, apartments and so on. The other half mostly belongs to the Blues—town hall, police stations, prison, barracks, reformatory, etc.—while the Reds must make do with a party head office, three communes, a press building and a secret transmitting station. But they can block access to roads or buildings with barricades, or clear away such barricades or buildings with explosives. *Provopoli* is an 'Anti-*Monopoly*': it turns the capitalist discourse of *Monopoly* on its head. It is by far not the only game of its kind, though it is unique because of the designation on the packaging: 'INDIZIERT' ('indexed'). From 1980 to 2005 it featured on the list of 'Writings Harmful to Young Persons' drawn up by the Bavarian Ministry for Family

5 In 2007 the exhibition *Building Asia Brick by Brick* was shown in various places in China. It was a collaboration between the periodical *ArtAsiaPacific* and People's Architecture Foundation, for which fourteen Asian architecture offices realized a built manifesto using 7,800 white *Lego* blocks. Participants included Map Office (Hong Kong), Research Architecture Design (Hong Kong) and Yung Ho Chang with Lijia Lu (Beijing/Boston), all of whom have also worked with comic strips. See: van der Hoorn 2012:87-88, 202-205, Berre, van der Hoorn & Lunde (eds) 2015:42, Maerkle & Perlmutte 2006 and: https://web.archive.org/web/20080828201815/http://peoplesarchitecture.com/brickbybrick/architects.html (last consulted on 3 July 2022).

05

Affairs, Labour and Social Affairs. The committee deemed that its 'terrorist contents were hostile to the state' and could lead to 'social and ethical confusion (disorientation)' and 'morally endanger' children and young people. Irrespective of whether this response was justified or not, it illustrates the potential attributed to games. In other arts, most notably the art of comic books, such warnings and rejections have long been common. At best, comics were dismissed as a passing and superficial form of popular culture, but in the United States and Germany, full-blown campaigns were launched against this so-called inferior reading matter that could harm young people.

Games are an important part of our cultural heritage. Architecture games reflect the choices of material, forms of construction, prevailing ideas, and sometimes also counter-currents of the times in which we live. They represent in miniature and/or simplified form the world around us, with all its political and socio-economic dimensions. They exert a special power of attraction on young and old; participants can be completely absorbed by them as they explore, copy, imagine and/or change the built environment. Game developers draw on that valuable and powerful form of cultural transfer to convey concepts and ideas, but oppressive or stigmatizing world views can sometimes creep in, consciously or unconsciously: Games can open up perspectives, broaden knowledge and stimulate creativity, but they can also limit them. For example, many doll's houses are steeped in conservative gender relations and successful city building games are frequently rooted in rigid urban design models and narrow-minded suburban idylls.

A specific point of view or message from the game developer can often be detected in the scoring mechanisms and plans of games. A plan helps to better understand a location, and eventually to conquer and control it, but that assumes abstraction and simplification: some elements are omitted, while others are emphasized or enlarged. That influences our perception and determines the relationship and possible interaction between players and game space. Alex Gekker discusses this in '(Mini) Mapping the Game-Space: A Taxonomy of Control' (2016): '[M]aps have never been mere depictions of an existing place. […] [They] are better understood as guides for action, which dissect, order, colonize and produce "existing" space, making it available for use and consumption. […] Just

06

07

like the medieval cartographer's choice to highlight a certain aspect of the land over another illuminates various politics of visibility and access, so the game designer's choice in relation to mapping can be read as inscribing certain affordances into the game to be explored and experienced' (2016:134-135).

This book pays close attention to the choices, ideas and ideologies in the games discussed. Do they stimulate creativity, imaginative power, tactics, or critical thinking? How much freedom do participants enjoy and in which areas? If there is a scoring system, what actions does it reward or punish? What perception of and engagement with the built environment does the game express? Does it raise environmental or social issues? How critical and innovative are the underlying concepts?

HORN OF PLENTY: THE COLLECTION OF THE CANADIAN CENTRE FOR ARCHITECTURE

A logical starting point for this study of architecture games was the Canadian Centre for Architecture (CCA) in Montreal, which boasts one of the world's biggest collections and unique expertise in that area →06. Over three hundred specimens were collected within an eight-year period by architect, author and curator Norman Brosterman: 'building blocks; paper toys such as houses of cards and cut-and-assemble buildings; a set to design a garden parterre; miniature villages; and construction toys made from all manner of materials' (Hodge 1990:5). The CCA conducted exhaustive research starting in the late 1980s, and from 1990 on it made eight exhibitions and catalogues about parts of the collection of construction toys.[6] In the first of those, exhibition coordinator Brooke Hodge explained the acquisition: 'Toys, as interpretations of the world around us, give children the scope to learn and to fantasize about their surroundings'. But they are meaningful not just for children: 'They also provide evidence of the social and economic life of their period and, from wooden building blocks to steel construction sets, reflect distinct stylistic predilections. Especially interesting is how closely toy manufacturers followed and incorporated technological changes in their products. New industrial and building techniques used to create innovative building types were often used in the manufacture and assembly systems of the toys themselves' (1990:5). In conclusion, Hodge emphasizes the connections with other parts of the collection: 'The toy collection [...] opens the door to discussions of architectural ideas, to an understanding of certain theoretical and technological principles, to an appreciation of the built environment, and, finally, to the complexity of the CCA's collections and the architectural world in general' (1990:8).

The CCA collection consists largely of doll's houses and construction toys.[7] Board games are a rarity at the CCA, and after the acquisition of Brosterman's collection the museum did not continue to actively or systematically search for other games.[8] No known collection of architecture games of comparable size

6 See: Canadian Centre for Architecture (ed.) (1990, 1991, 1992, 1993, 1995, 1997 & 2000) and Coupland 2005.

7 Doll's houses and construction toys also feature in the collections of toy or technology museums, though not specifically on account of their architectural qualities or their relevance to architecture history or theory. Some examples are the National Collection of Childhood at the V&A Museum of Childhood in London (in the future: Young V&A), the private collection and the online museum of Jörg Bohn (www.puppenhausmuseum.de, last consulted on 3 July 2022), the Toy Museum in Nuremberg, and the games collection of the German Museum in Munich. In the last of these, the presentation *Technical Toys—A 200-Year History of Construction Sets* has since 1984 formed part of the permanent exhibition, with a fairly traditional presentation of construction toys arranged according to material (wood, stone, metal, plastic). Games can also be found in the collections of larger municipal museums, usually connected in terms of contents to the city where they were created. The Wien Museum organized a special exhibition on the subject in 2012 entitled *Games and the City: Luck, Winnings and Leisure* (Strouhal, Zollinger & Felderer (eds) 2012).

8 The Toy Museum in Nuremberg contains around 30,000 board and card games. The collection of the Strong National Museum of Play in Rochester (NY) houses almost 3,000 board games, which are exhaustively documented in the online search system.

08

and scale exists for the period since the 1990s.[9] There have, however, been some exhibitions. Some of them focused on a specific genre such as doll's houses, or games that originated from the Bauhaus—they are mentioned in the following chapters. In addition, some architecture museums and galleries have organized exhibitions about the intersections of games and their disciplinary field. For example, the National Building Museum in Washington has since 2012 presented *Play Work Build* →07, where 'visitors begin to see the connections between play, design, and the work of building professionals like architects and engineers'.[10] Most spectacular of all are the hands-on spaces where visitors can play with David Rockwell's *Imagination Playground* (2010): big blue blocks, cylinders, ramps and tubes of waterproof foam rubber that can be endlessly combined. Dozens of historical architecture games from the collection are exhibited as well, the majority of them in display cabinets in a rather traditional fashion.[11] Oversized building modules also featured in *Let's Play* at the Danish Architecture Center in 2016. The exhibition focused on movement in the city, and the construction toys were an instrument for exploring the phenomenon. Play in the city was also one of the themes of *Architects at Play* →08, held in 2019 at the International Centre for the City, Architecture and Landscape in Brussels and two years later at Garagem Sul in Lisbon, about 'themes as varied as childhood and education, urban planning, public space, history, architecture, art and creativity'. It presented places where 'childhood playgrounds and those of architects, artists and designers meet', on the basis of the idea that '[e]ach one of us is a playful architect'.[12] In a totally different way, People's Architecture Office (PAO) explored the relationships between architecture and play in the 2019 exhibition *Social Design: Learning at Play* →09 at the Design Society in Shenzhen. The office used its own projects to illustrate 'how design, with a playful attitude, can have real social impact'.[13] Visitors could

9 The National Building Museum in Washington contains a comparable and even larger collection, covering the period up to the 1990s, but it has published little and made very few exhibitions about it. The collection was amassed over thirty years by George Wetzel; it contains over 2,300 games from the 1860s up to the 1990s and was acquired by the museum in 2006.

10 Cited from: https://www.nbm.org/exhibition/play-work-build (last consulted on 3 July 2022).

11 The same combination of playable construction toys and exhibited historical items—albeit on a more modest scale—was featured in the exhibitions *Fabien Vienne. Point. Ligne. Surface. Volume* in 2016 and *Architectures en boîte* ('Architectures in a Box') in 2021, both at the Cité de l'Architecture et du Patrimoine (City of Architecture and Heritage) in Paris.

12 Cited from: https://www.ccb.pt/en/evento/arquitetura-jogo/2021-09-28 (last consulted on 3 July 2022).

13 People's Architecture Office mainly uses four game concepts as design instruments: '"Trial & Error" is about learning through failure; "Tinkering" is working with what is readily available; "Catalyzing" promotes social interaction and "Involving" allows people to participate in and with design'. Cited from: http://www.peoples-architecture.com/pao/en/project-detail/35 (last consulted on 3 July 2022).

PLUGIN HOUSE

experience for themselves the PAO methodology through all sorts of interactive models and form an impression of 'the city as an innovative learning environment'. For PAO, that ambitious aim is nothing less than '[a]n urban landscape stimulating a cohesive society full of playfully creative citizens and learners, perpetually inventing new prospects for their communities, for themselves, and for each of us'.

GAME STUDIES IN ARCHITECTURE

This book does not cover all possible manifestations of architecture and urban design in analogue and digital games. Rather, it limits its scope to games that deal substantively and explicitly with the built environment. In that sense, *Serious Fun* follows on from *Bricks & Balloons* and *Spots in Shots*, with their focus on comic strips and films that centre on architecture: '*Spots in Shots* [...] is not about [...] how architecture is deployed to tell stories. Instead, this book takes the reverse approach. It examines how film can tell stories about architecture and urban design' (van der Hoorn 2018:12). In the same way, *Serious Fun* explores what various types of games can contribute to communicating about and creating architecture and urban design.

An architecture game is both architecture and game. In this book, it is always approached from both perspectives: How does the game work technically? Is it dynamic? Can it be played repeatedly and in different ways? Are players given scope for their own interpretations, solutions and improvisations? But also: On what view of architecture is the game based? Does it convey relevant content? Does it encourage participants to reflect? Is it surprising and innovative?

Architects are not game developers. It is only logical, therefore, that their game applications and observations often pay no attention to game theory. This book is an attempt to bring the two disciplines closer together and to enrich game applications in the design disciplines with approaches taken from game theory. A manual such as *Characteristics of Games* (Elias, Garfield & Gutschera 2012) is very useful in gaining a better understanding of board games. The three authors are not only academics but also passionate players and game developers. They consciously employ a wide definition: card games and board games feature in their book alongside video games and sport. For them, the only aspect in which video games clearly differ from the others is that 'they are almost all deliberately designed' (2012:4), in contrast to classical games that have evolved over years gradually, naturally and much more unconsciously. Contemporary card games and board games are usually variations on, breakaways from or combinations of tried and tested formats. The three assert that 'new' games often illustrate the problems that can occur, while classics offer a reservoir of possible solutions—'not because ancient people were geniuses, but because the classic games that survive today have undergone a long process of evolution and of weeding out' (2012:4). That does not alter the fact that older and newer games consist of comparable aspects, and their book presents a clear overview of them: number of players, interactivity, rewards, luck and skill, hidden information, ending conditions, etc. These characteristics help to chart issues that are important in every game, such as: Can players optimize their own result only or can they also influence the performances of others? Can somebody in danger of losing still catch up? Alternatively, can that person determine which of the remaining players will win? Are the most important rules of thumb easy to grasp and can you rise from beginner to advanced or expert player? Does competition dominate, or entertainment? Do you play with or against one another? How are the game dynamics safeguarded when players in a cooperative game join forces and the only opponent is the game itself?

Another useful source is the text 'Behind Games: Playful Mindsets and Transformative Practices' (2014), in which Jaakko Stenros explains the differences

11

between games (tangible objects), play (socially regulated game activity) and (intuitive, spontaneous) playfulness: 'At the core of play and games is the mindset of *playfulness*. [...] As [...] it becomes socially framed, *play* emerges, and as these shared forms are codified, we call them *games*' (2014:201). The intuitive playfulness that Johan Huizinga wrote about in *Homo Ludens* (1938) is characterized by intrinsic motivation: the player plays 'for the sake of the game', without external factors prompting him to do. If a game is meant to achieve a specific goal (knowledge transfer, participation, simulation, etc.), that impulse no longer comes just from within. It is true that unrestrained playfulness is the breeding ground from which well-structured play variants and materials emerge, but as soon as the spontaneous, unpredictable and untameable is shaped in a mould, some of those qualities are inevitably lost (2014:207). There is therefore something contradictory about game development: '[I]n a way games are technologies for prompting, fostering, and harnessing playfulness, yet they are often born out of playfulness even if over time that connection may have been lost' (2014:204).

The 'central paradox of gamification' (2014:203) does not necessarily have to be a problem, though according to Stenros too many developers and researchers are obsessed by the games themselves. They lose sight of the game activity and incorrectly generalize the mindset of players: '[T]he emphasis is usually on game products as systemic artifacts' (2014:201) and playfulness is idealized as 'universally positive, liberating, fun, and character building' (2014:205). But playfulness as a human mindset is whimsical and erratic; it is not easy to force it into the compartments of a game. Sometimes it can lead to destructive and disrespectful 'bad play', in which rules are broken or ignored: 'Playfulness can be creative, emancipating, and liberating, but it is also unexpected, disruptive, and destructive' (2014:207). That ambivalent and uncontrolled quality is not necessarily harmful; inherent in it is a lot of creativity. According to Stenros, it should be grasped and more fully embraced. Those who admit that dimension are ultimately rewarded with more layered and richer games. Those who consistently suppress it as an undesirable side effect and totally restrict the breaking or redefining of the rules of play are left with games in which the entertaining and gratifying aspects of playfulness are sorely lacking: 'Griefing, trolling, and bullying are not unfortunate side effects of playfulness, they are part of its core. Constructing a totalitarian system that completely eliminates them also eliminates playfulness in general' (2014:217).

The same volume of essays includes the chapter 'Dissecting Playfulness for Practical Design' (2014), in which Jussi Holopainen and May Stain offer practical instructions for safeguarding playfulness within a regulated game structure. One way of doing that is by giving realistic play motifs the form of refined caricatures, because humour and identification enhance the involvement of players while maintaining their freedom of interpretation and movement. 'Protective frames' can also support playfulness: safety nets that guarantee a stress-free game experience; for example, '[s]ocial protective frames [that] shield people from embarrassment, awkwardness, and loss of face' (2014:428) or subtle hints that remind us that a game is not 'real' and that all steps are reversible. They give a sense of safety within which players are prepared to improvise, experiment, take risks and take on challenges (2014:434).

This book draws on insights from game theory to interpret architecture games more accurately and ultimately to improve them. It devotes as much attention to the structure and appearance of the games—objects or software—as it does to the game activity and mindset of the participants. How strongly is that activity guided, limited, manipulated? Which games offer scope for creativity and improvisation? What unexpected expressions of playfulness present themselves? Do they undermine the game or the underlying ideas? How constructive is the result? How much playfulness do you need to relinquish if a game is devised for a specific application?

MESSAGES BEHIND ALGORITHMS: DISSECTING VIDEO GAMES

Analogue and digital games appear side by side in this book. But the astonishing realism of present-day digital game environments and the refined artificial intelligence behind simulations have given video games a character all of their own. In particular, it is not always clear at first sight what a digital game permits. The choices and messages of developers are much less visible than they are in analogue games, because they are largely concealed within the programming, and many people are unable to decipher that language. Digital city building games in particular seem to allow a lot of latitude—they are also called 'sandbox games'—but in reality developers put an important stamp on the way in which virtual cities take shape and urban development is often technocratically directed from above according to rigid zones and grids.

The built environment is often very present in video games, even in those that do not concern architecture or urban design. For even when all attention is focused on directing sports cars or guns, a video game always needs a decor, and that is often an urban setting. Therefore, '[e]ven before game studies was a recognized research field, space has been a recurring, core topic of debate on the new cultural form of videogames' (Aarseth & Günzel 2019:7). That virtual space distinguishes itself from space in other media: '[W]here in most narrative media like written text or film narrative works primarily as a sequence of events in time, one of the unique features of games is the player's free movement through space' (Domsch 2019:103). That is why it always enjoys a special status in video games: '[D]ue to the dynamic nature of simulations, space was acknowledged as a constitutive factor of designing and playing games; their sine-qua-non' (Aarseth & Günzel 2019:7).

Not only authors but also artists have explored the nature of virtual spaces, for example by 'translating' them to the analogue world. Even if they do not explore city building games but mainly bestselling shooter games, their reflective works are valuable for the questions they raise about virtual spaces.

Translating Virtual Cities into the Here and Now: Artists on Video Games

Researcher, artist and game developer Lindsay Grace has spent years studying the ways in which video games influence or at least frame our behaviour: 'How do games affect the way we problem solve, socialize, or even view the world? [...] Do games encourage us to ignore consequence and wait for second chances at the same problems? Are we forgetting how to play with each other, because playing against each other is more fun?'[14] He often poses his questions in the form of mini-games in exhibitions; he calls that critical play: 'As Critical Cartography changes the way we perceive the world, Critical Gameplay seeks to offer alternate perspectives on the way we play'. In particular, he has studied the way we perceive the spatial surroundings in video games: often hastily and superficially, concentrated on the shooting or racing rewarded by the game. His work *Wait* (2005) →10, 'A game about slowing down', is the opposite of that: It starts in a steppe-like landscape of swaying grasses, bare rocks and scarce vegetation. Gradually, forest sounds come nearer, trees become visible, birds flutter into the picture and flowers start to blossom. The less you do, the more points you get. If you move towards the forest, you see it disappear. But if you hang around a butterfly, flower or other small detail, you are rewarded. If it takes too long, the surroundings still start to become vague, as a sign that it is time to move somewhere else, balancing carefully between movement, observation and reflection, like a digital life philosophy.

Aram Bartholl is another artist who frequently examines digital environments. *Dust* (2011) →11 is a preliminary study for a life-sized model that he wanted to make of the popular map of the same name from *Counter Strike*, one of the most played online shooter games around 2000.[15] Passionate gamers spend whole days and weeks in those virtual environments, which Bartholl sees as an integral aspect of our cultural heritage today: 'How many people in the world have seen the real Time Square, the Kaaba in Mecca or the Tiananmen Square with their own eyes?', he suggestively asks.[16] While '[m]illions of gamers experienced the same worlds in computer games. They all remember very well the spaces that [...] they have "lived" in for a significant amount of time in their lives'. For Bartholl, virtual and real environments are extensions of each other and '[a] computer game map like "de_dust" appears to be more real than many other places in the world such as artificially constructed places like supermarkets, airports or cities like Dubai'.

Gareth Damian Martin illustrates that aptly in *The Continuous City* (2018) →12, another example of 'materialized virtuality' and an attempt 'to transform the screenshot into a critical tool'.[17] The artist, game developer and writer regularly noted a 'cognitive gap' between 'people who are very interested in game architecture but don't play games' and 'people who play games a lot and experience that architecture in a very meaningful way, but don't necessarily communicate that to others'.[18] He wanted to give the former group in particular an impression of virtual environments. He projected enlarged versions of the screens of game consoles on a wall and photographed with an analogue camera the architecture and urban space in various video games, from the *Metroid Prime* (2002) of his youth to *Kane & Lynch: Dead Men* (2007), *Dishonored* (2012), *Grand Theft Auto V* (2013), *Yakuza 0* (2015), *Dark Souls III* (2016) and *Mirror's Edge Catalyst* (2016).

14 Cited from: https://www.criticalgameplay.com (last consulted on 3 July 2022).
15 Interview with Aram Bartholl on 13 September 2021.
16 Cited from: https://arambartholl.com/old/dust-rhizome-eng.html (last consulted on 3 July 2022).
17 Cited from: https://www.gamescenes.org/digital-print (last consulted on 3 July 2022).
18 Interview with Gareth Damian Martin on 16 September 2021.

27

28

The photo series shows places where nobody has ever set foot but which are deeply significant to passionate gamers—not as 'distant, sanitized, digital spaces' but as 'very human spaces that exist in people's minds and memories'. The virtual architecture is loosened from its original context and transported into the here and now: The outdated camera, the sensitive 35mm film and the chemical development have given the images the distinctive graininess and imprecision of analogue photography. Strengthened by the enlarged projection, 'non-existent details, additional noise and undetermined visual information' come into being, though they do not feature in the games. For Martin that is very similar to the way we experience digital cities and spaces: What we perceive blends with memories of real places and with experiences from other virtual environments. Our brain combines all of that into an imaginary *Continuous City*.[19]

Yuk-Yiu Ip explores through film the perception and meaning of virtual spaces that Bartholl tries to capture in his *Dust* model and Martin in his photography. *Another Day of Depression in Kowloon* (2012) →13 is an example of 'machinima' (derived from 'machine' and 'cinema'): The film was completely shot in the first-person shooter game *Call of Duty: Black Ops* (2010), in real-time game mode with in-game sounds. Only the user interface and weapons are hidden from view, in a special version of the game hacked by Ip. In this calmed-down state, traces of social life become much more noticeable: planted roofs, graffiti, utensils, photos, lettering, aquariums, etc. The setting is Kowloon Walled City, a very densely populated, almost anarchic part of Hong Kong that was demolished in 1994. Residents from other districts—Ip among them—were afraid to enter it. In his film Ip uses *Call of Duty* to gain access to that vanished, mythical piece of cultural heritage from his native city. He carries out fieldwork in that virtual world, critically studies the simplified impressions of the American game developers and, at the same time, pays homage to their work, the beauty and poetry of the virtual city where he spends hours almost every day.[20]

Ip deliberately avoids showing any human figures in his film—he just suggests their presence through the traces they leave behind. Other artists specifically research what happens to the residents of virtual cities. Alan Butler, for example, explores poverty and homelessness in the urban infrastructure of *Grand Theft Auto V (GTA)* with his in-game photo series *Down and Out in Los Santos* (since 2015) →14. For Butler, the difference between architecture and 'non'-architecture disappears in video games, because the entire environment and all objects and characters are artificial, created in computer-aided design (CAD): 'It's all CAD. And in *GTA*, you can't enter most of the buildings. They are less real and less "architecture" than a burger on the ground, which you can kick, or shoot, or walk around. A building in a videogame is usually a barrier made out of a jpeg'. Butler moves through the streets of the *GTA* city of Los Santos (an allusion to Los Angeles) as a social reporter, with the virtual smartphone of his avatar in his hand. He meets various groups, from traumatized war veterans to drug addicts and psychiatric patients, as well as Occupy Wall Street supporters. They come together, chat, beg, share drinks and cigarettes... The photographer remains on alert all the time because they are programmed to respond to his presence: They get scared and walk away, or become aggressive and attack his avatar; they can even kill him—provided he

19 Martin drew inspiration from Italo Calvino's *Invisible Cities* (1972), in which every city is a memory or potential version of Venice: 'In reality they are different digital artefacts but in our minds they become different versions of each other, or they describe a kind of connected space of potential places'. In his periodical *Heterotopias*, Martin writes about his first photographic experiments with *Metroid Prime*: 'Turning my camera to it, my grandfather's camera, the one I was learning to use back in 2002—loaded with the same black-and-white films I coveted as a teenager—is just another logical step. Its light leaks, soft lens, and the dreamlike haze it layers over its subjects, become tools for this particular kind of architectural hauntology. Of course, there is nothing authentic here, and the spectre of age the film gives the game's spaces is a false one. And yet, I have often found the screenshots of remasters or emulations of old games lack the layers of memory, meaning, and reference that are accrued over time. Perhaps this is a way of representing that. What follows then is an attempt to capture not just *Metroid Prime*'s spaces, but their ghosts, their ambiguities, and ultimately the unsolvable secrets that haunt me still' (2017:26).

20 Interview with Yuk-Yiu Ip on 5 July 2021. *Another Day of Depression in Kowloon* (2012) is the first part of a trilogy filmed in *Call of Duty: Black Ops*, which continues with *The Plastic Garden* (2013) and *Clouds Fall* (2014).

does not draw his own weapon. The game 'objectifies these individuals and reduces them down to aesthetics rather than beings in the flow of reality': they are flat characters without a biography. Butler is concerned not only about that aestheticizing representation but also about the society depicted here so realistically: 'The very fact that there are these homeless populations is more of an indictment of our reality than any sort of narrative in the game. It's a tragedy that in order for the videogame to be real, it has to include this human misery'.[21]

Butler's project is quoted in the performance *Everyday Daylight* (2021) by the artist collective Total Refusal, in which they tour through Los Santos as avatars and stop in places that appear in the work of other artists about *GTA*. They talk about various possibilities to use art projects as a way 'to intervene into contemporary video games, break their logic and thereby deconstruct the mechanisms of hyperreality'.[22] Total Refusal's first project of that kind was *Operation Jane Walk* (2018) →15, a performance whose essence is shown in a short film of the same name. The setting is the Manhattan of the third-person shooter game *Tom Clancy's The Division* (2016). The city is hit by an epidemic; abandoned cars are everywhere, and anonymous enemies can start shooting out of the blue at any time. Four people fully dressed in fight gear move through his sombre landscape, machine guns at the ready. The first avatar embodies the artist duo that guides three adventurous tourists around the virtual city. They pass architectural icons of modernism and capitalism, and discuss their cultural and historical background in the real world. The film title recalls a jaywalk—setting foot on or crossing a street in an unauthorized and reckless manner—but also the city activist Jane Jacobs, author of *The Death and Life of Great American Cities* (1961), who was quick to criticize car-centred urban development. Ironically enough, the huge SUVs have come to a halt in *The Division*, but that does not make the situation any less dystopian.

Inspiring Innovations

It is clear from the foregoing just how reliant an exploration of architecture games is on contributions from various disciplines, from architecture theory and history to cultural sciences, game studies and art, as well as the gaming industry. From time to time architecture and urban design can even benefit from innovations that originally had little to do with that field. One example is *A Blind Legend* (2015) →16, a video game without images in which you play the role of a blind knight who is guided by his sighted daughter. Wearing headphones, you follow her instructions by clicking the mouse or touching the screen. Bit by bit you learn to move faster and to turn around, and you ultimately even have the courage to engage in a sword fight with the enemy. The game makes use of sophisticated 3D binaural audio technology, which reproduces extremely realistic spatial experiences. People with and without a visual impairment share the same adventure in *A Blind Legend*. For blind and partially sighted people it is possibly their first encounter with video games, while those who can see are catapulted into an unknown world where they have to survive without any point of visual orientation. Even if the substance of the game has nothing to do with architecture, it offers a completely new spatial perception and experience, which can be of great relevance to designers who are usually very focused on the visual aspects of spaces. No wonder that the game developer DOWiNO, thanks to *A Blind Legend*, was commissioned to develop simulations of daily life in the living and working environments of people with a visual impairment, to be used in educating care workers and the designers of adapted homes.[23]

21 Interview with Alan Butler on 13 September 2021.
22 Cited from: https://totalrefusal.com/home/everyday-daylight (last consulted on 3 July 2022).
23 Interview with Pierre-Alain Gagne on 4 November 2021. The start of Chapter 3 contains more about *Sensivise* (2020).

31

15

STRUCTURE: FROM THE CLASSICS TO DESIGN PRACTICE

This book was written with two main objectives in mind: on the one hand to better understand how existing games function and what choices and ideologies they embody; and on the other to pinpoint what makes them suitable for design practice and how future games could do that more successfully. That exploration starts by dissecting classical games: doll's houses, construction toys and city building games in analogue and digital form. They are the focus of the first three chapters according to a recurring pattern: The first pages offer an historical overview, followed by a presentation and discussion of present-day examples. The latter always presupposes two approaches: playing and reflecting. You cannot learn about a game without diving into it yourself and trying it out, since that is the only way to experience playfulness. Yet a certain distance is required to analyse a game from the outside. In that regard, interviews with developers were invaluable in finding out more about their intentions and considerations, the difficulties encountered and changes made, as well as the distribution of their work and the reception it got. In addition, each of the first three chapters devotes attention to the work of artists who have critically analysed and reinterpreted the classical genres. Their surprisingly sharp eye, which sometimes pays little heed to prevailing conventions, often makes for interesting points of view alongside more sober analyses. Each of the first three chapters ends with a discussion about how some designers have used those classical genres in their work. Chapter 4 deals exclusively with games that have emerged from design practice and/or were specifically developed for it. Some elements from classic

A BLIND LEGEND

games lend themselves extremely well for that purpose—which is why it makes sense to first become more familiar with them.

The first chapter looks at doll's houses. They have a long history and are similar to models, frequently deployed instruments in architecture. They are the stage for all sorts of narratives and role-playing, but their structure and appearance are usually static and unchanging, which also makes them rather deterministic: Most doll's houses are faithful representations of dominant forms of and ideas about housing. Reinterpretations by artists illustrate which departures from the classical concept can reintroduce a dose of playfulness and how a doll's house can be an excellent vehicle for expressing a critical message.

Building blocks and construction toys are the focus of Chapter 2. They are much freer than doll's houses. Players can reconstruct or copy real or fictive architecture, but mostly they create their own buildings. Creativity and fantasy come to the fore: there are no rules and the models are almost always suggested without obligations. Even so, few construction toys can genuinely be called timeless and universal. Like doll's houses, most of them reflect architectural history faithfully in the way the makers incorporate new materials, forms and styles of building into their designs. Just by determining what modules or components look like and how they can be combined, they exert great influence on the game. Construction toys are often quite idyllic—and that becomes immediately clear if they contain buildings or styles that are almost always excluded, such as factories or barracks. Like with doll's houses, some artists have deliberately deployed the visual language of construction toys to articulate criticism of aspects of the built environment.

The city building games in Chapter 3 distinguish themselves from the first two genres through their rules and competitive character. Players develop an urban environment step by step—sometimes as equal though competing colleagues, sometimes in various roles with diverse skills, and sometimes by joining forces in a cooperative game concept. In so doing, they have to consider the interests, motivations and considerations of various parties involved: designers, investors, decision-makers, residents or users. One interesting aspect is always: what does the game reward? Do you win by building higher and higher? Or can you score on the basis of sustainability or satisfaction of residents? Do you have to beat the other players or can the city flourish only if players work together? Through such rules and scoring mechanisms, the maker is able to convey a certain message and value system. But players also retain a degree of freedom and can determine their own strategy. There are usually a number of ways of making progress in the game—a combination of luck (partly) and tactics (mainly).

Chapter 4 examines games that are used to tackle real issues. Often customized, such games are usually subject to rules, and the game developer plays an important role as moderator. Applied games help to visualize matters, thereby making them easier to grasp. Most people find them motivating, and humorous episodes can add some lightness to heavy discussions. A well-chosen division of roles invites players to work together and put themselves in the shoes of others, thereby promoting mutual understanding. The consequences of various options can be played through and considered with the help of simulation and scenario games. Above all, these games are aimed at fostering participation and communication, and often at democratizing complex themes. Usually, nobody emerges as winner in the sense of 'author of the highest score', but there are definitely benefits for the community involved.

BEYOND THE PITCHED ROOF ?

Breaking through the Walls of the Traditional Doll's House

Doll's houses are familiar, age-old architectural toys. They reduce existing and imaginary houses to a scale that everybody can grasp and engage with. They are powerful, widely used representations and have much in common with other frequently made miniatures: models. There could be no more appropriate way to start this book than to walk through their doors.

Doll's houses are of all ages and places. Whether Victorian mansions, modernist lofts or suburban villas, they are all manifestations of a simple concept that will continue to weather the test of time. Those changing appearances suggest diversity and development, yet the underlying ideas are fairly rigid. Often, a doll's house is little more than a miniature version of a family home with a pitched roof, with the front façade removed. That allows you to peer into the interior, consisting of a kitchen, living room, parents' room and children's bedroom, sometimes with the bonus of an attic or pool. The house, often at a scale of 1:12, is finished before you start to play with it and has few moveable elements, if any. Very occasionally, it comes as separate pieces, but once screwed or glued together nobody will take it apart again. Players can furnish, supplement or adorn the spaces with objects, but the basic structure remains unchanged. The house forms a decor for dreaming and imagining stories, usually with dolls.

Doll's houses are cultural heritage. Down the ages they have always faithfully reflected the lifestyles and living aspirations of their time; they embody an important piece of social history.[1] What happens if we extend that line to the present? What does the contemporary doll's house look like? What does it say about the way we now live? Has it evolved in tandem with types of housing in the 'real' world in terms of family compositions, styles, preoccupations? How do you play with it? What sort of interaction is possible? Can designers deploy it in their work? But first of all, what do we know about doll's houses up until the end of the twentieth century? What did their makers have in mind? How did people play with them?

A LONG HISTORY: DOLL'S HOUSES BEFORE TOYS

As simplified miniature buildings, doll's houses resemble models in many respects: both are made to lend our imaginations a helping hand. Yet they differ from each other in some respects. 'The main one is durability,' says architect, doll's house designer and tutor Tim Boyle: 'Models are very fragile; they're just for looking at. Dollhouses have to be strong enough that kids can play with them.'[2] That has not always been the case, however, because the makers of the very first doll's houses were not trying to create toys. So what were they aiming at?

01

Displaying and Educating

At least three hundred years before doll's houses ended up as mass-produced objects on the shelves of toy shops, they had been made to order for the elite, especially in Germany, England and the Netherlands. The best-known examples of these one-off products are now held as showpieces in major museums. The V&A Museum of Childhood possesses one of the world's finest collections and published a catalogue entitled *Dolls' Houses from the V&A Museum of Childhood* (2015).[3] This extensively illustrated journey through time starts with a *Nuremberg House* →01 from 1673. Doll's houses the size of wardrobes had been crafted in this Bavarian town since the early seventeenth century: precise

1 In *Toy Buildings, 1880–1980*, Patty Cooper and Dian Zillner write: 'Like other toy buildings, dollhouses were designed as a reflection of the real-life architecture of their times. Admittedly, commercially produced dollhouses were more caricatures than copies, but this serves to emphasize those elements considered most essential to their designers and young owners' (1999:18).

2 Interview with Tim Boyle on 27 October 2020.

3 The website of the Museum of Childhood is a gold mine of information. For extensive documentation about the doll's houses in the collection, see: https://collections.vam.ac.uk (last consulted on 16 February 2022).

imitations of stately residences with luxurious interiors, fitted and furnished with riches by the very best craftsmen.[4] Toys they certainly are not, but rather cabinets of curiosities and works of art. If anything, Dutch specimens surpassed their German counterparts in opulence, enabling the wives of wealthy merchants to impress their entourage.[5] German doll's houses not only inspired awe but also served a didactic purpose: educating children by initiating them into their future lives as adults. Girls in particular could not be manoeuvred young enough into their predestined roles as housewives and mothers, and miniature houses proved a useful tool in that regard.[6]

Until the eighteenth century, children were largely viewed as unfinished adults, who had to be shaped to fit the mould of their bigger alter egos. It was not until the Enlightenment that childhood came to be seen as a separate phase of life: children had to be protected, entertained and prepared for future life. There was a growing awareness of the educational function of toys. In the nineteenth century, the private domain became increasingly separated from public space. Middle-class children in particular were no longer to be found in the workplace, but at school or at home. Toys made their appearance in the home, and with them the representation of an idealized, protected world scaled for children. Doll's houses and construction toys with clear step-by-step plans were very suitable for such reassuring representations. In 1995 the Canadian Centre for Architecture presented examples of them in the exhibition *Dream Houses, Toy Homes*, devoted to various types of miniature houses (doll's houses as well as building blocks and construction kits). In the catalogue of the same name, Alice Friedman writes about a model from around 1900 that 'this toy calls attention to the separateness of the single-family dwelling, emphasizing the safety and comfort of the domestic sphere: ample windows, lace curtains, and small-scale ornament encourage the model-builder to peer into the romanticized world of the home' (1995:10).

The early, wonderfully detailed showpieces made way for simpler toy versions. Leonie von Wilckens describes that in *The Dolls' House: An Illustrated History* (1980), her cultural-historical survey of mostly German and, to a lesser extent, Dutch doll's houses. Nineteenth-century specimens and their successors were no longer as crammed and complete as earlier houses: some elements were emphasized and detailed realistically—von Wilckens notes the highlight of a tap with running water—while others were omitted. That was necessary, for while adults might be able to recognize a multitude of details, younger people need more space in order to identify with a house. Their fantasy can only unfold if enough emptiness or vagueness remains.

More playful, interactive elements were already a feature of English doll's houses, irrespective of whether or not they were intended as toys. The more recent *Queen Mary's Dolls' House* of 1924 is full of them. And even so, this was certainly not intended for children's hands: it was designed by the architect Sir Edwin Lutyens for the wife of King George V when she had already passed fifty. From the outset, it was intended as an exhibition item, a '*showcase* [...] of British art and culture of the time' (Jacobs 2017:18), fitted with technical innovations

4 For a detailed and lavishly illustrated cultural-historical analysis of early German doll's houses, see *The Dolls' House: An Illustrated History* (von Wilckens 1980). And for their Dutch equivalents, see *Het Hollandse Pronkpoppenhuis: Interieur en huishouden in de 17de en 18de eeuw* (Pijzel-Dommisse 2000).

5 This recalls the dioramas that Gerrit Schouten made in the early nineteenth century in Suriname: scenes of plantations, cities and camps in the former Dutch colony, which plantation owners and other wealthy individuals took to the Netherlands to show their guests. See: Medendorp 2008 and: https://www.rijksmuseum.nl/en/rijksstudio/artists/gerrit-schouten (last consulted on 16 February 2022).

6 Very few girls could read and write in the seventeenth and eighteenth centuries, so a miniature house was useful for instructing them about the proper running of a household. However, that educational function was less direct than often assumed in professional literature, according to James Bryan in 'Material Culture in Miniature: Nuremberg Kitchens as Inspirational Toys in the Long Nineteenth Century' (2018:222). For why would mothers not teach their daughters to cook in their own kitchen? Or, from the nineteenth century on, send them to one of the many domestic science schools set up at the time? Besides, according to Bryan, the toy kitchens differ from the 'real' kitchens in all sorts of ways. He convincingly explains why the Nuremberg miniatures were not purely instructional material: 'Instead, they were meant to generate wonder and amusement, thereby inspiring in girls an anticipation of and desire for their expected roles as household managers' (2018:229).

02

compared to which many real houses in Britain paled by comparison: hot and cold running water, electricity, functioning lifts... Ko Jacobs writes about it with admiration in the exhibition catalogue *1:12. Verbeeldingskracht in zorgarchitectuur* ('1:12. Imaginative Power in Care Architecture'), but expresses his surprise at the architectural style that, in stark contrast to that of a contemporary like the Rietveld-Schröder House in Utrecht, 'stands completely in a classical and classicistic tradition'. As though time had stood still: 'The innovations in modern architecture of the first decades of the twentieth century are absent here' (2017:21–22). That is perhaps not so surprising in the case of a royal example, but doll's houses are often rooted in conservatism: they confirm existing hierarchies and patterns, especially gender relations.[7] In that respect they clearly differ from models, which look to the future rather than the past. Jacobs expresses that perfectly: 'Models obviously differ greatly from one another, just as the building projects they represent are more traditional or pioneering. But every model is a projection of a future. That future tense contrasts with that of the doll's house. There a moment in time is "frozen" and thus incorporated into history' (2017:35–6).

Between Dreaming and Accepting

From the late nineteenth century onwards, doll's houses gradually became more affordable for the less affluent. They were manufactured by German and English family companies and sold at markets, and later in shops and through mail-order firms. Industrial mass production started to take off mid-way through the twentieth century in England and the United States, with more and more plastic toys from major brands that knew how to advertise their wares. In his article 'Dimensions of the Mass-Produced Dollhouse: Fisher-Price versus Playmobil', Mark Morris analyses two of these doll's houses. The Fisher Price models of the 1960s looked very different to their preindustrial predecessors: lightweight yet robust (because they were made for children), simple, with abstract pieces of furniture. They came printed with images of floors, wall coverings, an open hearth and some items of furniture, suggesting an imaginary world that extended

7 In de catalogue *Dream Houses, Toy Homes*, which accompanied the exhibition of the same name at the Canadian Centre for Architecture, Alice Friedman warns against the limiting effect of doll's houses (and some construction toys): 'Toys shape the world of children, guiding girls and boys toward various activities in the family and society, and outlining a system of values with which to make sense of the world around them. This is particularly true of model houses and building toys which focus on the home, gender roles, and family life. These toys often have an explicit educational purpose: not simply to teach dexterity and design skills through play, but to mould the behaviour, aspirations, and desires of future citizens and consumers' (1995:7).

03

beyond the walls: 'The "world" represented by the lithographic decals is more detailed and evocative than the simplified figures or plastic furniture. [...] When one plays with the Play Family House →02, one is really playing with two houses: a tangible house and an image-based (or imaginary) house' (2014:63–64). That switching between 'what is' and 'what could be' crops up frequently in theoretical literature on the nature of playing.[8]

Concepts for toys constantly balance between dreaming and accepting. Some toy developers confirm stereotypical role patterns, for example by emphasizing ad nauseam the differences between boys and girls. A good example is a pair of *Mega Bloks* sets, which Friedman (1995:22) discusses in the CCA catalogue: the *Lion's Kingdom* castle →03 and the *Build and Decorate Dream Home* →04, both from 1993–1994. *Mega Bloks* function according to the same principle as the world-famous *Lego* blocks, but these two sets contain many large, ready-made walls with hinges that can be connected together in one go to form a decor: they are more doll's houses than construction toys. In terms of structure, the castle and dream house are almost identical: a big rear wall flanked by two moveable side walls of two or three levels, into which some ten rooms fit. Apart from that shared basis, however, they are two totally different worlds. The grey-brown castle has a gate, portcullis and drawbridge, and the stronghold is defended with horses, shields and weapons. It's more a place of combat than a place to live. In the pink 'girl's version' the house itself is much less important than the interior. It invites the user to rearrange and reposition the furniture and decoration over and over.

04

The focus on domesticity is also a feature of *The Sims*, the best-known digital doll's house, the first version of which appeared in 2000. Maaike Lauwaert wrote a fascinating analysis of the earliest editions in *The Place of Play: Toys and Digital Cultures* (2009). Like in analogue versions, everything happens within the four walls of the home: unimaginative, comfortable single-family houses in

8 Brian Sutton-Smith writes in 'Does Play Prepare the Future?' (1994:130) that some theoreticians regard games as a preparation for the future, while others see it as an adaptation to the present (and past). Sutton-Smith views the former as optimistic, imaginative, focused on children and progress, and the latter as more pessimistic, more focused on confirming adult patterns in everyday reality.

05

06

American suburbs, inhabited by the well-to-do middle class with a fondness for luxury goods. The outside world never enters this space; 'the dollhouse symbolizes and reinforces domestication: the move to the inside, the interior and the private' (2009:88). When the digital dolls head off to work, you cannot follow them. You can, however, have them purchase furniture, clothing, toys, electronic items and gadgets to boost their happiness, or direct them into virtual tableaux vivants and photograph them there. Almost everything revolves around consuming and parading a socio-economic status that appears to lie just beyond the reach of most players in their real lives. The behaviour of their figures reflects a lifestyle that they themselves aspire to and that the toy developers promote.[9] Even with unexpected moves, players have little opportunity to deviate from those intentions without hacking the game. Lauwaert expresses it aptly: you cannot turn *The Sims* into an 'eco-minded, bike-riding community' (2009:92). The degree of control goes beyond that of traditional doll's houses because the figures are also programmed to do things 'themselves'.[10]

Nonetheless, there have always been toy makers who, with their doll's houses, emphatically engage with developments and turning points in architecture and social history. Some examples feature in the catalogue from the V&A Museum of Childhood, among them an *Ultra Modern Dolls' House* →05 from 1937, and the *Whiteladies House* from 1935 (2015:96–103, 137). The first is a product from the English firm Tri-ang Toys, which included numerous Tudor-style cottages and houses in its range yet also always had an eye for innovation. That found expression in a series of modernist white doll's houses with sleek, geometrical forms and green frames. The second, the *Whiteladies House* →06, is a unique copy. It was designed by amateur artist Moray Thomas (pseudonym of Marie Thomas) to raise funds for a charity. Thomas deliberately gave the house, the furnishings and the dolls a unique style and atmosphere that exude a carefree youthfulness and modernity.

07

Commercial and artistic models continued to exist alongside each other during the second half of the twentieth century. New toy concepts and housing forms appeared, among them open doll's houses that you could play with from all sides. One of the best-known examples is the *Open-Sided Dolls House* →07 by Roger Limbrick, which won the main prize in the James Galt Toy Competition in 1962. Another innovation was *Jennys Home Dolls' House* →08, from the second half of the 1960s: a plastic modular system of separate rooms measuring 28 × 20 × 14 cm, which could be bought as a set or individually (2015:138–139).[11] Once again, Tri-ang Toys reflected contemporary housing situations: placed next to one another, the modules formed bungalow-like ensembles, but you could also stack them to form residential towers. East German toy manufacturers also produced a relatively large number of high-rise toys at the time, in reference to the modular structures that were home to millions of citizens of the GDR. A good example of them is the *Plattenbau Hochhaus* made by the Vereinigte Erzgebirgische Spielwarenwerke Olbernhau in 1966, which is twice as tall as it is wide.[12]

9 See also: Jenkins 2007 and Flanagan 2007.

10 *The Sims* is one of the few video games that appeals to both boys and girls, though Lauwaert points out that they play it in different modes: you cannot build while you are shopping and socializing, so it is as though you have a 'boys' version and a 'girls' version within the same game.

11 The *'Ultra Modern' House* (1937), the *Open-Sided Dolls House* (1962) and the *Jennys Home Dolls' House* (1960s) are mentioned only briefly in the V&A catalogue, but they are extensively documented on the V&A website. See for example: https://collections.vam.ac.uk/item/O88603/ultra-modern-dolls-house-dolls-house-lines-bros-ltd (last consulted on 16 February 2022).

12 For a cultural-historical analysis of GDR doll's houses, see *Traumwelten der fünfziger Jahre: Puppenwelt und Wirklichkeit* (Metzger & Tremmel-Endres, 1996). These doll's houses also play a key role in the documentary *Eigenheim* (2012) by Anja Dornieden and Juan David González Monroy (OJOBOCA). See: http://ojoboca.com/eigenheim (last consulted on 16 February 2022). In 16 minutes of close-up shots you walk through the miniature world of East Germany in the 1960s and 1970s. The modern amenities and functional interiors that residents were eagerly looking forward to when they relocated from historical buildings, the cheerful pastel shades, the plastic flowers: the doll's houses are filled with them. We also hear snippets of interviews: memories of people who once played with such houses, the thoughts of collectors who recently acquired one…

08

09

SOLAR PANEL ON PITCHED ROOF: CONTEMPORARY UPDATES

A history of the doll's house, even a brief one, illustrates how various periods of architectural and social history left their traces in these miniature worlds: in appearance and interior, in the structure and play opportunities. What happens if we extend that line to the present? What does the doll's house of the twentieth century look like?

Modern Displays

While showpiece doll's houses have been in the minority for quite some time, they have not totally disappeared from the public or private domains. For example, architect Siebe Tettero in 2008 created a snow-white, classical doll's house measuring seven by nine metres →09 for a retrospective of the fashion designers Viktor & Rolf held at the Barbican Art Gallery.[13] The imposing structure was essentially subservient to its priceless contents: a grand cabinet for the work of the celebrated duo, presented as haute couture for hand-made porcelain dolls. A few years later, in 2014, the Stedelijk Museum in Amsterdam also displayed an oversized doll's house: the *Dutch Design (Doll) House* →10 in the exhibition *Supermodels*, based on an idea by Gilian Schrofer. The sixty rooms were filled with miniature furniture by the crème de la crème of Dutch designers since the

10 →46–47

13 See the Barbican exhibition archive: https://www.barbican.org.uk/whats-on/2008/event/the-house-of-viktor-rolf (last consulted on 16 February 2022). The exhibition also travelled to the Centraal Museum: https://www.centraalmuseum.nl/en/exhibitions/the-house-of-viktor-rolf (last consulted on 16 February 2022). See also: *The House of Viktor & Rolf* (Evans & Frankel 2008).

11

12

start of the twentieth century. Here, too, the presentation centred on the contents, while the appearance of the house itself was of lesser importance. Yet by referencing the age-old tradition of showpiece doll's houses, it furnished the canon of Dutch design with a venerable setting.[14]

Although such old-style doll's houses are more the exception than the rule today, keen collectors are still prepared to spend large sums acquiring decorative miniature houses. Houses not to play with but essentially to marvel at and showcase their valuable contents (furniture, dolls). An ambitious example of the type is the *Spiral Dollhouse* →11, which a private individual in 2014 commissioned from the office Architecture BRIO, as a gift for his life partner, an ardent collector of Barbie dolls. The architects gave the excessively slinky mannequins a suitably stretched house with a vertical scale of 1:6 and a horizontal scale of 1:13. With their sleek, contemporary wooden design, they emphatically distanced themselves from the familiar kitschy Barbie glamour.[15] The house is at the service of its occupants, yet it had to be both attractive and playable, because the designers were not told for whom it was intended and therefore assumed it was for a child. The same was true for Linda Stenberg when she launched the *Arne Jacobsen Dollhouse* →12 in 2009 under the brand name Minimii: a faithful copy in miniature of Jacobsen's house in Charlottenlund of 1929. The walls are held in position by invisible magnets, enabling children to open and play with it from all sides. But it is mainly adults who want to acquire it, often as a showcase for the modernist furniture that Stenberg also produces and that ultimately generates most of her turnover.[16]

Modernist is Already Quite Modern

Stenberg started Minimii because within the available range of doll's houses she saw nothing but 'old Victorian styled dollhouses furnished like [her] grandmother's house with terrible old brown chairs'.[17] That was also the motivation for other designers. Amy Whitworth, who came up with the *Qubis House* (2012) a short time later, was completely unable to identify with the old-fashioned world she encountered at doll's house fairs for aficionados, where time appeared to have stood still: 'It's a big market with exquisite, absolutely amazing replicas of traditional pieces of furniture in different historical styles: Edwardian, Victorian… Some of these little chairs and tables would cost thousands: beautifully done and painstakingly put together…'[18] Architect and toy designer Wolfgang Sirch puts it even more emphatically: a lot of toys are 'olde-worlde; as though designed for the Flintstones'.[19] Since the rise of Asian imports and online commerce have made the range so uniform, there is scarcely any room for 'exotics that do not conform'.

Disillusioned by the existing market supply, all these makers sought alternatives. Sirch and his companion Christoph Bitzer designed in 2004 the *Villa Sibis* →13 and in 2012 the *Maison Rive Gauche*, two sleek, simple houses made of high-quality material. *Villa Sibis* has a base measuring 114 × 62 cm, supporting a house measuring 73 × 33 × 25 cm and a swimming pool, both in the form of an

14 See the Stedelijk Museum exhibition archive: https://www.stedelijk.nl/en/exhibitions/supermodels-100-years-of-dutch-design-and-iconic-architecture (last consulted on 16 February 2022). An earlier, smaller version of the *Dutch Design (Doll) House* (with 35 of the 60 rooms) was on display at the Salone del Mobile in Milan in early 2014.

15 See: Marwaha 2014. The stereotypes of Barbie, Ken, their lifestyle and home are widespread and persistent. They are zealously driven by Mattel, the Barbie company that constantly releases new products. It is also interesting to note that a miniature house can, conversely, be enlarged; for example, Malibu boasts a full-scale Barbie house, which could be rented for a few nights in October 2019: https://news.airbnb.com/barbie-opens-the-doors-to-her-iconic-malibu-dreamhouse-on-airbnb (last consulted on 16 February 2022). On the other hand, there are always designers and artists who deliberately turn the Barbie clichés upside down. An example of that is the brutalist *Barbie Dreamhouse* that Roksanda Ilincic and SHOWstudio designed in 2013, a 'base with a modern and contemporary feel'. It was never built, but the presentation film of the virtual 3D model gives a good impression of it: https://www.youtube.com/watch?v=SrPyQi6piP4 (last consulted on 16 February 2022).

16 To meet that urge to collect, Stenberg devised in 2011 the much smaller *MiiBox*: a halved Arne Jacobsen house, clearly recognizable by its typical façade, behind which lie six small rooms for displaying miniature furniture. You can play with it, but *Miibox* is largely intended to hang on the wall.

17 Interview with Linda Stenberg on 9 March 2021.

18 Interview with Amy Whitworth on 27 November 2020.

19 Interview with Wolfgang Sirch on 3 November 2020.

Royal Auping
Royal Auping
Royal Auping
Makkink & Bey
Royal Ahrend
Studio Stallinga
Liberty Global

LEOXX
Royal Auping
LEOXX
Royal Auping
LEOXX
Royal Auping

13

14

open wooden module with transparent sliding panels on both sides.[20] There are many similarities with the *Modular House* →14 by Mini Archi from 2013: they are roughly the same size, consist of simple wooden frames with sliding partitions, and at first glance they look like modernist villas with a pool. But Ana Maia and Laurent Maes, the founders of Mini Archi, want to fill in as little as possible for people playing with the *Modular House*, preferring instead 'to sharpen children's aesthetic sense'.[21] The full and half modules, panels and blocks that appear when you open the biggest box can be positioned freely on top of or next to one another. The villa with swimming pool is just one of the countless options. The pair envisaged a gender-neutral, sustainable, modular house that you can play with again and again in different ways.[22]

When asked about their sources of inspiration, many contemporary makers refer to the first half of the twentieth century: the Bauhaus, the Barcelona pavilion by Ludwig Mies van der Rohe (1929), the post-war Case Study Houses… Stenberg also went back 80 years in time with her *Arne Jacobsen Dollhouse*. Were there no recent architects in Denmark around 2009 considered eligible? To her, Bjarke Ingels seemed like a suitable candidate, but the collaboration with the Arne Jacobsen estate just happened to be established more smoothly. Yet didn't she want to avoid children playing with an interior that was just as old as their grandparents? That was something she could partly solve: to be sure, the exterior had to be a faithful copy, but the Jacobsen estate gave permission to replace the tiny 1920s interior spaces with more generous rooms that reflected contemporary standards. Despite those adjustments, the *Arne Jacobsen Dollhouse* confirms the impression that 'modern' still means 'modernist' in the Land of Doll's Houses. Flat roofs, columns instead of walls, large expanses of glass, abstract furniture, and no ornaments or decorations: that package seems to be enough to do away with the pitched roof.

15

Tim Boyle, architect and designer of, among others, the *Emerson Dollhouse* (2010) →15 for Brinca Dada, confirms this.[23] His houses are more complex in terms of infrastructure—they have electricity for example—but in terms of design he drew inspiration from the architects of the Case Study Houses, an experimental, modernist housing programme in the Los Angeles area, just after World War II.[24] Boyle's doll's houses are intended as toys, but their realistic appearance had to appeal to adults in particular as potential buyers. He responded to their ecological awareness with sustainable materials, solar panels and LED lights, and to their dreams with the modernist look. Because in his surroundings, modern architecture is rare and therefore: 'You don't have to do very modern and everyone is already like: "Wow! Look at that! It's so modern!"'

Liliane Limpens also recognized that you needed little to create a discernible, contemporary appearance. In 1999 she came up with the *PoppenVilla* →16, 'the Bentley among doll's houses'. What sets it apart, above all, are its dimensions: 130 cm tall, 120 cm wide and 62 cm deep. Several children can play with it at the same time, with 30-cm-tall dolls or soft toys. Limpens wanted to make a sustainable design house out of high-quality materials: clear-varnished birch wood and stainless steel. Her motto was: 'Papa and mama have a granite kitchen working top, stainless steel taps, double washbasins, a design bed… Thus so should the

20 In hindsight, *Villa Sibis* turned out to be somewhat voluminous, which is why the base was omitted in the *Maison Rive Gauche*; the dimensions remained roughly the same. In the second house, two columns hold the floor and ceiling in place; the players determine the position of the glazed corner walls.

21 Cited from: https://www.miniarchi.com/en/brand (last consulted on 16 February 2022).

22 Interview with Ana Maia and Laurent Maes on 27 March 2016.

23 The *Emerson Dollhouse* won in 2010 an Eco-Choice Award and in 2012 a Creative Play of the Year Award. Boyle also designed the *Bennett Dollhouse* for Brinca Dada in 2010, and the following year the *Edward Dollhouse* (a cheaper version of the *Emerson*, in other colours and without electronics) and the *Dylan House* (inspired by the designs of Paul Rudolph and Tadao Ando). The price varied from 200 to 600 dollars. Brinca Dada was disbanded in 2015.

24 For example, the form of the *Emerson Dollhouse* (2010) is derived from the Kaufmann Desert House (1946) by Richard Neutra and the materials have been taken from A. Quincy Jones, who designed a villa for film star Gary Cooper and his wife in 1954.

children and their dolls.'[25] Such details do of course come at a price that, despite the miniature size, is beyond the reach of many people: over 1700 euros without furniture. It also features a ramp, a recent feature to make the *PoppenVilla* supposedly 'gender neutral'. Limpens advises every new customer to immediately place a car on it, because: 'Then the little boys know: "It's also for us."'[26] Will this substantially help to solve gender problems? Whatever the case, the house is immensely popular: thousands of hospitals, crèches and primary schools in various countries have ordered one over the past two decades. It looks modern, is a niche product with a good marketing concept and has scarcely any competitors. Yet the innovative aspects are not architectural: this is an upper-middle-class family home with a pitched roof, which suggests a classical family unit comprising two parents and two children.[27]

The success of the *PoppenVilla* has not been matched by all manufacturers: Sirch, Minimii and Mini Archi have reason to be satisfied if they sell fifty houses in a year. So what does the *PoppenVilla* have that they lack? It is certified for sale in the EU and US, because the toy market is strictly regulated and official testing agencies apply high standards. Smaller producers of doll's houses that cost 300–500 euros can scarcely afford the necessary quality, safety and environmental certificates. Moreover, the required sturdiness places demands on materials and construction, which in turn do not always chime with elegance. And that is precisely what Sirch, Minimii and Mini Archi value so highly: they reach many more customers through museum shops, design shops and concept stores

25 Cited from: https://poppenvilla.nl/LilianeLimpensVisieMissie.htm (last consulted on 16 February 2022; see the heading 'Gelijkwaardigheid'.

26 Interview with Liliane Limpens on 2 October 2019.

27 The washbasins, mirror, rails and worktop make the bathroom and kitchen instantly recognizable. The other rooms are almost automatically designated as living room, parents' room, children's room and study. Limpens calls the seventh room (on the ground floor) a 'recreation room': it could be a horse stable, bike shed, garage, sports or music room. In that respect, the slightly smaller *PoppenVilla Light* is more abstract, with three indoor spaces and one outdoor space that are not further defined.

than they do through toy shops. Alain De Rauw, international sales director of PlanToys, knows all about it.[28] He also says resolutely: 'We're more fashion article than toy.'[29] PlanToys certainly does come up with didactically well-considered concepts and certified products, but a traditional toy shop that does not follow trends is not the place to sell them: 'too stuffy, too old-fashioned, too little eye for opportunity'. But, then, how and where? The six doll's houses currently marketed by PlanToys illustrate the complexity of answering that question.

Social Media: The Contemporary Showcase

In 1990 PlanToys launched the very first doll's house that came as a kit: *My First Dollhouse* →17, assembled with ten screws and playable from all sides. That, combined with the sustainable material, was highly innovative for its time. *My First Dollhouse* was (and still is) a resounding success; that is why De Rauw refers to it as the *'Classic' Dollhouse*. It was followed almost thirty years later by the *Slide N Go Dollhouse* (2018) →18, which could be taken everywhere, and the *Contemporary Dollhouse* (2020 →19, a hip version with curved corners. All are made of sustainable rubber wood, not very big (less than 50 cm wide and high), open and relatively abstract, in natural shades and neutral colours. The pitched roof suffices to read it as nothing but a house, and the spaces are not defined further. The *Slide N Go* is not a bestseller but performs reasonably well; of greater concern is the *Creative Play House* (2004) →20, although that, according to De Rauw, is one of their most remarkable products: 'The more children who see that house, the better and more beautiful the architectural structures we will see within twenty years'. So why are the sales figures so disappointing? Perhaps the lifestyle stores that are interested in PlanToys products expected more fashionable colours; they are under consideration in a newer version. But the chief reason: 'The *Creative Play House* is too difficult: You can build it in a hundred different ways'. And that richness is precisely the problem: 'You have to explain more. Simple toys sell more easily.'[30]

However, De Rauw doesn't throw in the towel that quickly, fortunately, as demonstrated by the *Victorian Dollhouse* (2003) →21: a striking three-storey house, much bigger than all others (over 70 cm tall and 60 cm wide), with windows and doors that open and close. It's also more expensive: about 350 euros (compared to 150–250 for all others), but that does not explain why it has sold so poorly for so long. So poorly in fact that in 2016 De Rauw reluctantly decided, with pain in his heart, to drop it from the collection. Yet a month later he changed his mind at the very last minute. Two female bloggers from Denmark had discovered the house and, from one day to the next, it went viral. Annual sales in Belgium rose from 1 to 76; in Germany they went from 3 to over 500. And the success continues. 'The style and quality are excellent; the *play value* is fantastic.' People turn it into something very personal: they paint it, spend a lot of time on additional illumination, wallpaper, furnishings… 'It's a must-have for all bloggers, vloggers, everybody with style. The impact of social media is gigantic.'[31] The biggest hits on Instagram are perhaps the twenty-first-century equivalents of the showpiece doll's houses: For this is where people display abundance, taste and originality in an attempt to become part of the elite.

28 PlanToys was set up in 1981 by Vitool Viraponsavan, architect and co-founder of PlanArchitect, one of Thailand's most successful design offices. The 'child product company' distinguishes itself by a deeply rooted sense of ecological and social sustainability. The assortment consists of hundreds of wooden toys, including six doll's houses, for babies and especially young children.

29 Interview with Alain De Rauw on 30 October 2020.

30 That is also confirmed by the makers of the *Modular House*: not everybody embraces an open concept. According to designer Laurent Maes, adults in particular experience a sort of writer's block when faced with virginal white or natural wooden units. Hence the idea of holding workshops. Players receive supervision while furnishing one of the rooms, selecting (and depicting) a setting for the house, and even devising a new module. Responses are invariably enthusiastic (but sales remain sluggish).

31 It is even better if you can secure a celebrity for your product. The *Victorian Dollhouse* entered the limelight without such backing, but Tim Boyle knows what a difference it can make. His *Emerson House* enjoyed huge popularity among celebrated New York actors and editors in chief of fashion magazines, reaching more than four million readers within the first year. It was lauded by film star Julianne Moore on social media, appeared in rapper Nelly's video clip *Just a Dream* (2010) and won numerous prizes.

17–21

22

Eye-Catchers with Body

Commercially successful or not, some doll's houses leave a lasting impression because of the ideas they convey; a case in point is the *Green Dollhouse* (2009) from PlanToys. What the *Creative Play House* subtly indicated with discrete solar panels on the rear side of the green roof is impossible to miss in the later model: contemporary living is inextricably linked to energy questions. The *Green Dollhouse* →22 is all about ecological awareness: it has solar panels, a wind turbine with transformer, separate waste collection units, a vegetation-covered wall, a rain barrel, a vegetable garden and adjustable solar shading. It is along the lines of the *Wonky Fruit & Vegetables* from PlanToys, the curved wooden toy cucumbers, carrots, apples, pears and tomatoes full of imperfections that proudly promote the shapes of authentic products of nature. If children become familiar with them in a playful manner, PlanToys hopes, perhaps it can help in some way to reduce food waste. The same applies to the hands-on elements of the *Green Dollhouse*: integrating environmental awareness into toys at an early age might go some way to making it a matter of course later in life.

The educational *PowerHouse* →23 that Rainer Köthe developed in 2010 for Kosmos focuses on the same theme, but it is aimed at children aged 10 and older.[32] It is a single-family home made of polystyrene, with a sun lounge, over 20 cm tall and just under 30 cm wide. A hundred different experiments in and around the house teach children in a playful way how to live more ecologically. The first tests show which materials are suitable for heat and sound insulation. Then there are experiments with sunlight: dark colours and glass admit more heat than light colours and insulated walls do. A hothouse is created in the attic during the summer because heat penetrates the house through all openings. How quickly does it cool down again if you open all the windows? And what happens if the door to the sun lounge is left open? A number of assignments then illustrate how you can regulate the indoor temperature with a few simple interventions: How do you avoid direct sunlight in the summer? How does a heat accumulator work? Can you power a light with the solar panel on the *PowerHouse*?

32 *PowerHouse* won the ToyAward in the category Ecology and Environmental Awareness at Nuremberg Toy Fair in 2010.

23

Köthe's product is not recognized as a doll's house and its appearance is a joke—no architect was involved in the project—and yet, isn't this kit of experiments the ultimate contemporary doll's house? What other example better embodies the essential challenges facing housing in the twenty-first century?

The *PowerHouse* was originally not intended as a house: it was first and foremost designed as a package of educational experiments about future-oriented, sustainable energy. For Köthe, the single-family home served as a suitable vehicle to address specific questions.[33] That is also what child psychologist Anne Kooijman does in a totally different context: She developed the *3 Huisjesspel* ('3-Home Game') (2011) →24 as an aid for conversations with children caught up in divorce situations. Each of the three houses has its own style, recognizable on the exterior walls (natural stone, red wood or white stucco), but their cardboard components are also often mixed up together during construction. The children themselves are allowed to give them names—in view of their situation they often choose 'dad's house', 'mom's house' and 'child's house', but 'school', 'grandparents' house' or 'sports club' are equally valid labels. Playing with the houses, and possibly with freely chosen dolls or animals, can unlock stories and their underlying significance.[34]

The *3 Huisjesspel* and the *PowerHouse* give a possible shape to the doll's house of the twenty-first century in two very different ways (and without consciously aiming for that). They do that more through 'living' than through architecture, but of course you cannot completely separate the two. For the concept of *PowerHouse*, it made sense to shed the architecture of excess baggage, but a single-family house is not the most ecological type of building (and polystyrene

33 Interview with Rainer Köthe on 17 September 2020.

34 *3 Huisjesspel* also features an extension set, *Het dak eraf* ('The Roof Removed', 2011), which helps in identifying and listing positive and negative feelings and atmospheres related to each of the places. This is achieved with 40 cards containing statements that the child inserts into or between the houses. For example: 'They do listen to me here'; 'They don't have much time for me here'; 'They keep their promises here' or 'There's lots of complaining here'.

24

25

not a particularly eco-friendly material to represent it). The appearance of *3 Huisjesspel* also raises questions. Two graphic designers came up with all sorts of motifs for the walls to stimulate associations and conversations: a clock, bunkbed, drum kit, blackboard… but their style is sometimes very distinctive, even Kooijman thinks. What often passes for 'mom's house', for example, is really 'very feminine' and 'children are then pushed too much into thinking that "A mother lives in a Laura Ashley house"'.[35] All the same, architecture is more of a container than a genuine essence in the toys by Köthe and Kooijman; what happens inside is of greater importance.

In two other examples, the *Kaleidoscope House* (2001) →25 and the *Qubis House* (2012), the architecture is deliberately aligned with contemporary living. The *Kaleidoscope House* was made by artist Laurie Simmons and architect Peter Wheelwright.[36] A limited number were produced, and they quickly became collector's items handled by the most prestigious auction houses.[37] Simmons is a well-known name in the art world, and she asked designer friends to provide miniature versions of their creations.[38] That resulted in fashionable furniture ensembles for each of the rooms and two art sets for the walls: the type of things that collectors are fond of. Yet despite that, the house was actually intended for children to play with; the architecture had to reflect their experiences as millennials. Simmons and Wheelwright used the examples of their own households and those of family friends: trendy, urban, emancipated, double-income households.[39] The house became a kaleidoscope on account of both the flexible floor plan with sliding partitions in primary and complementary colours, and the colourful families that could feel at home there. Except for Barbie and Ken, which Wheelwright wanted to avoid at all costs: 'The fixed sociality and domestic practices of the Barbie dolls, with their coy relationships to publicity and privacy (not to mention their political-correctness benignly concealing an assimilationist conservatism), would require quite an adjustment in the transparent, flexible and minimal open plan of this dollhouse' (Wheelwright 2000:123). So what did he put in its place? Admittedly, here again: 'One of the subtle ironies about the Kaleidoscope House is that it was not really "modern" when it was designed in 2000.'[40] Wheelwright found inspiration in the Rietveld-Schröder House (1923–24), De Stijl, and to a lesser extent Philip Johnson's Glass House (1948–49) and Mies van der Rohe's Farnsworth House (1949–51).[41] Despite those historical references, the *Kaleidoscope House* is nonetheless a well-considered reflection on housing today. The 'Home Working' extension kit never materialized unfortunately, but as early as the turn of the century Wheelwright did envisage a house with Wi-Fi and electronic security, a place where young and old are connected to school and work through their own laptop. Irrespective of whether this is home to a single-parent or patchwork family, or whether the parents are gay or straight, they combine work and private life in a creative way and share the duty of care fairly. Simmons and Wheelwright make short shrift of binary gender categories, for example by giving the kitchen a totally different look than in the traditional doll's house: no longer the

35 Interview with Anne Kooijman on 4 February 2020.

36 The *Kaleidoscope House* was initiated by former gallerist Larry Mangel, the founder of Bozart. From 1996 on, the American company supported artists in creating high-quality toys, from design all the way to distribution.

37 The original price was 250 dollars, but in 2015 a set of three was valued by Christies at 5,000–7,000 pounds sterling, and in 2019 a *Kaleidoscope House* sold at Phillips for 1,375 dollars.

38 Dakota Jackson and Karim Rashid designed dining room furniture, there were living room accessories by Jasper Morrison, Karim Rashid, Ron Arad and Keiser/Newman, artworks by Peter Halley, Laurie Simmons, her husband Carroll Dunham, Cindy Sherman and Mel Kendrick… and even the outdoor furniture for the terrace of the swimming pool extension were by Michael Graves and Gandia Blasco.

39 Simmons and Wheelwright underlined the personal aspect of their design even further by making the dolls look like themselves and their own children: Simmons's daughter Grace and Wheelwright's son Matt in the first set, and their other children as well as friends and pets in extension sets.

40 Cited from the documentation about the *Kaleidoscope House* in the collection of the V&A Museum of Childhood: https://collections.vam.ac.uk/item/O74396/kaleidoscope-house-dolls-house-simmons-laurie (last consulted on 16 February 2022).

41 Karen Stock and Katherine Wheeler explain why the play of colours in the *Kaleidoscope House* and the integration of large expanses of glass in the architecture are a direct reference to the work of the modernists (2018:200–204).

26

58

domain of the woman, but completely open and centrally positioned, so that 'whoever prepares the meals is not relegated to a separate room away from the family and is central to the "story" of the house' (Stock & Wheeler 2018:205).

The *Qubis House* →26 by Amy Whitworth is aimed at a comparable target group: 'affluent, urban, creative families', this time from London rather than New York.[42] It is not a representation of contemporary living in a trendy metropolitan neighbourhood but more a response to it. If you live in a compact home without a designated playroom, toys quickly find their way into the living room. Whitworth is convinced that if you want to turn such a shared space into an 'imaginative environment', then an eye-catcher like a doll's house must at the very least be 'aesthetically pleasing'.[43] The *Qubis House* had to be able to serve as a coffee table and appeal to multiple generations. It became an elegant, S-shaped birch frame, 45 cm in height, with two levels. For adults it acts as 'a conversation piece'; it only becomes a doll's house when you turn it into one. You can do that with sliding, coloured acrylic sheets and flexible partitions, possibly complemented with abstract oak furniture. Whitworth does not specify whether or how someone lives there—you can just as well turn it into a car park, school or disco. But she secretly imagines the ideal customer: residents of the Barbican Estate, 'conscious of style, conscious of habit'; parents who do not impose any restrictions on their children but who don't want to be ashamed of an ugly doll's house when their adult friends call around. The *Qubis House* embodies an ideal conception of housing by itself becoming part of that ideal: 'Living without any clutter, with just minimalist, beautiful pieces and materials.' With sustainability as the cherry on the cake. After all, since the *Qubis House* has so many faces, appeals to both young and old, and blends in harmoniously, it never ages.

THE PITCHED ROOF ON ITS LAST LEGS: DOLL'S HOUSES AS CRITICAL ART

A number of architects and toy developers have sought to bring the traditional doll's house up to date or to criticize it, but, with a few exceptions, they have been tentative adjustments. Artists set to work more radically. They give the traditional concept of the doll's house an unexpected twist or turn it completely upside down to convey a critical message.[44] Children are also often skilled at side-stepping prescribed patterns: their ultra-thin Barbies in pink plastic play settings quickly find themselves embroiled in bloody massacres, and hacked Sims suddenly experience the wildest adventures in shady scenarios. But that often happens behind closed doors. Artists make the subversive possibilities of play public.

42 With her *Qubis House* prototype, Whitworth won in 2012 the BOOST Design Competition organized by the Southbank Centre and *The Observer*, who helped to market the product. In terms of distribution and sales, it is comparable with the *Modular House*, *Arne Jacobsen House* and the doll's houses of Sirch: It costs 500 pounds and reaches most customers through museum shops and design stores, with over three hundred sold since 2012.

43 The V&A Museum of Childhood writes in the object description: 'The last quarter of the twentieth century saw children increasingly sharing adult space, and making claims on living rooms with toys and games. In twenty-first century Britain, middle class homes are smaller and increasingly open-plan, with fewer separated play rooms or nurseries.' Cited from: https://collections.vam.ac.uk/item/O1300006/qubis-haus-dolls-house-amy-whitworth (last consulted on 16 February 2022).

44 Like showpiece and toy doll's houses, artistic doll's houses have existed for some time. Two important examples are the *Stettheimer Dollhouse* (1916–35) and the doll's house by Miriam Schapiro and Sherry Brody from 1972. The first was made by Carrie Walter Stettheimer, the eldest of three wealthy, art-loving sisters who ran a celebrated salon in Manhattan. The doll's house contains miniature works by the then international avant-garde who were regular visitors to the home of the Stettheimers. It certainly is a showpiece, but it embodies in particular the position and attitude of three modern, free-thinking ladies: 'The dollhouse works in tandem with the salon to achieve a complete revisioning of domesticity, transforming the private space of the home into a realm for creative expression and feminist subversion' (Olsen 2017). The work that Schapiro and Brody developed half a century later goes even further: 'Through parody and exaggeration, the six rooms […] critique the roles that white, middle-class women in mid-twentieth-century America were expected to perform.' As part of the feminist installation/performance *Womanhouse*, it is 'a subversion of the "toy" dollhouse as a place for the normalization of gender roles' (Balducci 2006:20–21). For a discussion of other subversive doll's houses and art projects with miniature houses, see the chapter 'Scaled Down' in *Playing at Home: The House in Contemporary Art* (2013) by Gill Perry.

60

Dramas in the World of Make-Believe

Artists Van Sowerwine, Jon Haddock and Sabine Bloch completely undermine charming and soothing illusions: their doll's houses provide a stage for physical and psychological violence.[45] Van Sowerwine's house is a child-size timber hut that requires that adults stoop to enter. A closet contains a few games and books and a cuddly monkey; you can drink tea from the mini-kitchen at a small table. It is home to a doll wearing a blue pinafore dress over a white jumper, with a ponytail and huge eyes. You can see her in an animation on a screen, as if she is seated opposite you at the table.[46] The installation title reveals what she expects of you: *Play with Me* (2002)→27. She walks to the kitchen counter, fills the teapot and looks at you expectantly: 'Cup of tea?' The pot in her hand and the cups on the table light up; she waits until you decide with the computer mouse how the story will unfold. But if you click on the pot, something surprising happens: she lifts it up, seeks eye contact again, deliberately lets it fall, kneels down, picks up the fragments and... rubs them deeply into her eyes. Shocked, you try to click back, but no matter what you choose, matters don't improve: she pulls down the bookshelf, tears up her drawing, pours cleaning liquid into her cup, drinks it and falls back in her chair. And in each of the six scenarios, her penetrating gaze incriminates you: after all, you made that choice. Why, actually? Did you expect her to draw princesses and drink tea while chatting to friends? Well, no; reality has caught up with you. Game over.[47]

Jon Haddock's *Isometric Screenshots* (2000)→28 is another work that you do not leave unscathed. His version of *The Sims* is not a place of carefree consumption but of world tragedies. Haddock had high expectations for *The Sims*, but was bitterly disappointed that the game remained so other-worldly. That inspired him to examine video games and other 'escapist mediums' without mercy, 'perversely and deliberately trying to ruin the escapist quality of each one of them'.[48] His screenshots are completely in the isometric, pixelated style of the first version of the computer game, but they show extremely dramatic events, such as the 1968 murder of Martin Luther King, nine-year-old Kim Phúc running from a napalm bomb during the Vietnam War in 1972, or the killers of Columbine High School (1999) caught on security cameras just before their suicide.[49] As Haddock became better at creating the screenshots, he began to take more liberties in the montage. In the case of Kim Phúc, for example, he changed the camera angle from in front of to behind the children to emphasize the soldiers, who are often overlooked in the original photo. A top-down perspective such as in *The Sims* gives players the feeling that they can control a situation, but 'that comfort is double-sided', because the dominant position also makes them accountable for their deeds. Haddock wanted to shake visitors awake and make them responsible: 'Look, this is our fault—this is *your* fault.'

29 →62–63

The unexpected moves of Van Sowerwine and Haddock are forms of 'critical play', of which Mary Flanagan writes: '[P]layers specifically enact "forbidden" or secret scenes, unfortunate scenarios, or other unanticipated conclusions often in opposition to an acceptable or expected adult-play script. [...] This critical kind of play reverses traditional expectations regarding care-giving behaviors and allows players to rethink the conventions involved in these social roles' (2009:33). *MärchenHaft* (2005–2006)→29, *AllEinig* (2013) and *ProThesen* (2017) by Sabine Bloch are full of this. In *MärchenHaft*[50] the photo artist shows doll's houses from the 1950s and 1960s, fitted with original items of furniture. Except they are home

45 The unexpected presence of physical and psychological distress in charming miniature interiors recalls the *Nutshell Studies of Unexplained Death* by Frances Glessner Lee from the 1930s and 1940s. The forensic doctor helped police investigators to solve murders by minutely reconstructing real crime scenes in dioramas. See: Botz 2004, Miller 2005 and Goldfarb 2020.

46 The animation was made by Isobel Knowles, with whom Van Sowerwine often collaborates.

47 Interview with Van Sowerwine on 19 October 2020.

48 Interview with Jon Haddock on 22 September 2021.

49 Three of the twenty *Isometric Screenshots* are taken from classic films, though for Haddock that does not make them any less traumatizing. For example, for him the key scene of *The Sound of Music* symbolizes 'that we ignore the rise of fascism, sitting in the field and playing the guitar, just letting it happen'.

50 The title is a play of words in German: Märchen = fairy tale; Haft = imprisonment; märchenhaft = fabulous.

Feinkost

64

to some pretty strange figures: not dolls, but 'real' people. In the kitchen of the house with the red roof, for example, a paparazzo takes pictures of a woman picking her nose above a tray.[51] In the bedroom, another woman sits on the double bed with a shackle around her leg, while somebody dips their head into the toilet bowl in the bathroom. Upstairs, a pianist and cellist play music impassively while a vindictive girl points a pistol at a miniature replica of the doll's house. In the sitting room two ladies use up a box of tissues. Are they dying of laughter or crying their eyes out? The cleaner with disproportionately large ears doesn't miss a word of their conversation and shares everything with her chortling friends next door. But how funny is all this really? What do these bittersweet scenes tell us? Bloch's montages look colourful and witty at first sight, but as soon as you 'pull back the first curtain' it all gets a bitter taste.[52] The shelves of the delicatessen are lined with social criticism: new vaginas, 'horny penises', orange peel, nostrils and 'extra arrogant brain matter'. In front of the door a husband is waiting until the grocer at the counter lists the desired dimensions, a doctor wearing a butcher's apron arrives from upstairs, while in the attic a Barbie doll spreads her legs. If you have the courage to dig further, you will discover stomach-turning horrors and endless tragedies. The photographer proves to be a masterful transformation artist who plays every single role herself—sometimes caricatured figures, sometimes herself and often looking back at dramatic episodes in her own life. For example, in the miniature doll's house that she fires at as a young girl: a child bends over the toilet vomiting, two others wander decapitated around the house, and downstairs somebody is being abused and impregnated. Is there any solace to be found? If you want to escape this insane world, the wallpaper points to a room with the same motif in another house, and from there to another: there is no escape from this tangle.

Sowerwine, Haddock and Bloch show us that doll's houses suggest a fake reality with their idyllic scenes. Their occupants invade those illusionary worlds and fill them with blood and tears. Other artists let uninhabited doll's houses tell a story 'themselves'. Lucy May Schofield, for example, whose message is comparable to that of Bloch: Not all living spaces provide protection; in fact, some do just the opposite. The focus of her installation, *Reflect Forward* (2008) →30, is a pink, almost empty doll's house of the classical kind: red pitched roof, with room for two parents and two children. For Schofield, born into a family of 'madness, chaos and movement', such a house is a remote spectacle: a 'prefabricated, inherited structure imposed on children', a 'make believe world'.[53] That is why she placed it in perspective with a series of separate rooms, 'surreal vignettes' filled with 'disconcerting couplings of objects': one for each of the places where she stayed regularly in her youth. For instance, the closed timber shed with a knife and rabbits symbolizes her mother's house, 'where you always had the feeling that you could get into trouble very easily, because she had a violent partner and his energy was very dominant'. When she was with her father her stepmother took control, and she and her sister Lucy were no better off with their grandmother. Schofield's installation is like a personal, poetic and engaged version of *3 Huisjesspel*.[54] It features no dolls, but objects that refer to concrete individuals and constellations. As with Sowerwine and Bloch, emphasis is not put on architecture, but on the unpleasant atmosphere and experiences associated with a place. In that regard they differ from the following examples, in which the architecture itself is subverted.

51 When Bloch completely blows up the portrayal of 'the' traditional housewife, it recalls Laurie Simmons's collection *In and around the House* (2003): 'Once Simmons inserts the housewife doll, [...] the illusion of reality is hopelessly broken, creating an emotional resonance and even pathos in the scene. The housewife appears hysterical in a number of images depicting the kitchen. She stands on her head, lies on the floor, sits in the sink, and seems generally ill equipped to perform her domestic duties. The bathroom scenes exhibit the most dramatic lighting. As the doll stands next to the tub, she appears caught in a film noir type scene suggesting a narrative that cannot be deciphered' (Stock & Wheeler 2018:197).

52 Interview with Sabine Bloch on 22 October 2020.

53 The first quote is taken from an interview with Lucy May Schofield on 20 October 2020. The second is cited from: http://www.lucymayschofield.com/museumofchildhood (last consulted on 16 February 2022).

54 *Reflect Forward* arose during a residency at the V&A Museum of Childhood in 2007. In 2009 the updated and extended version, *All I Ever Wanted, All I Ever Needed*, was on show at the Frank Gallery in Whitstable.

32

Together in the Same Rickety Boat

In Yinka Shonibare's *Untitled (Dollhouse)* of 2002 →31, the interplay of architecture and interior supports direct social criticism.[55] The house is a miniature version of the Victorian townhouse in London's East End where the artist himself lives. The glum, self-satisfied style contrasts with the colourful, extrovert wallpaper and the furniture covering of Vlisco batik. Vlisco is a company in the Dutch town of Helmond that imitates Indonesian batik and exports it on a large scale to West Africa. The fabric symbolizes the complexity of (post-)colonialism, globalization and the creation of multicultural identities: themes that Shonibare, with English and Nigerian heritage, has much affinity with. That is also echoed by the reproduction of his work *Diary of a Victorian Dandy: 14.00 hours* (1998) on the wall of the doll's house: a photo with himself as a dandy in a Victorian salon, surrounded by white 'admiring gentlemen and fawning servants'.[56]

Shonibare uses the architecture of his doll's house as a cultural reference to convey a critical message. Other artists attack the doll's house as a material object, independently of its specific cultural or political connotations. They ask questions concerning qualities that appear unchangeable. For example, a doll's house is always freestanding, without neighbours and forever 'young': never subjected to patina or decay. It 'speak[s] of separateness and privacy' (Perry 2013:86). But what if that were not the case? In 2017, Rachel Whiteread made *Place (Village)* →32 for the V&A Museum of Childhood, a settlement of 150 doll's houses.[57] They stand on a hill of crates; it is night time and lights are on everywhere. Inside, the buildings are empty, which means that '[t]hese empty homes have lost their domestic contents and gendered associations' (2013:84). Whiteread's simple concept leaves it up to observers to fill in what replaces them. Many visitors see in the place an abandoned, uncanny ghost town, but cheerful parties and stimulating conversations could just as well be taking place beneath each light. And if you leave the domestic for what it is and look solely at the buildings, you see a medley of living ideals packed tightly together. That layout has an alienating effect, because it does not align with the intentions of the individual makers: '[T]his closeness suggests a compression which most of its symbolic homes were built to deny' (2013:86). Whiteread pushes the individual doll's house into the community and deprives it of its unique status. Will it hold its ground amidst all those competing versions of the same species? Is such a form of living tenable or desirable if everybody aspires to the same?

55 The doll's house by Yinka Shonibare was created as part of the Peter Norton Family Christmas Project. Norton is a collector of modern art and supporter of charity initiatives. Since 1988 he has asked an artist every year to make a Christmas edition as a gift for his colleagues and friends. The remaining specimens of Shonibare's doll's house were on sale for some time in the museum shop at the MoMA in New York.

56 See the eight-page project brochure, which is described in detail at: http://new.diaspora-artists.net/display_item.php?id=1128&table=artefacts (last consulted on 16 February 2022). In 2018, *Untitled (Dollhouse)* was on show in *Unrecorded: Reimagining Artist Identities in Africa*, an exhibition at the University of Michigan Museum of Art: https://umma.umich.edu/exhibitions/2018/unrecorded-reimagining-artist-identities-in-africa (last consulted on 16 February 2022). There it acquired added significance within a debate about how work by artists with an African background is labelled.

57 Slightly smaller precursors of them were on show at the Museo Madre in Naples in 2007: https://www.madrenapoli.it/en/exhibition/rachel-whiteread (last consulted on 16 February 2022) (see also: Codognato 2007) and at the Hayward Gallery in 2008 (see: Rugoff 2008).

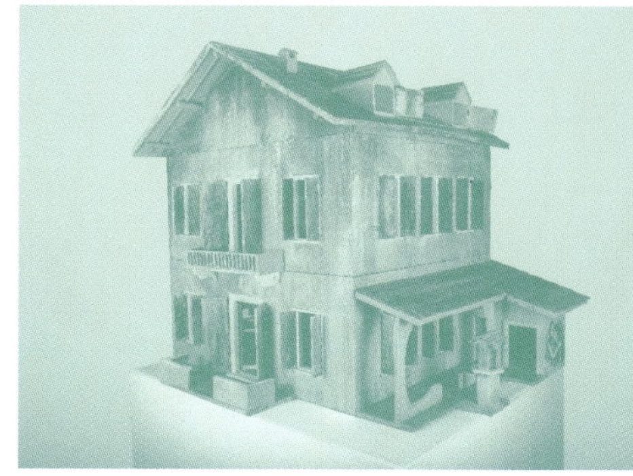

33 →70–71

Wrinkles and Cracks

Alice Pasquini, Do Ho Suh and Heather Benning even go so far as to strip the doll's house of its eternal youth. History leaves behind deep grooves—in the case of Pasquini under the very title: *The Unchanging World* (2018) →33. Windows hang askew in their frames, the glass is broken, the wallpaper has absorbed moisture, the parquet floor has come loose and tiles are missing in the kitchen. Floors are covered with children's toys, broken pottery and upturned furniture. Every visitor can think up their own story, and as far as Pasquini is concerned, it doesn't have to be all that dramatic: for her, a doll's house is a transitional object that guides its owner into adulthood.[58] In the process, that object gradually loses its topicality, but it does continue to exist—and moreover, it is precisely in that abandoned state that, for Pasquini, it acquires a remarkable beauty. This is quite unique: the natural ageing of architecture, its dilapidation and decay, seldom occurs in toys.[59]

Self-development is also the focus in Do Ho Suh's *Fallen Star 1/5* (2008–2011) →34, a highly detailed miniature house about 3.5 metres tall, wide and deep, cut in half and folded open: the home of the artist in Providence (Rhode Island) at a scale of 1:5. A smaller house has burst through the roof like a meteorite and caused damage on a number of floors.[60] The visitor is right on top of things; after all, when it comes to a doll's house you can peer inside unashamedly. You are not presented with a smooth success story: the work embodies the friction between Suh's Korean background and his self-chosen life as an artist in America. The little house from his youth has taken him by airspace to his new destination, where a parachute has softened the landing: not a full-on collision but turbulent all the same. Even without any knowledge of that autobiographical background, *Fallen Star 1/5* provokes reflection. It can just as easily evoke associations with war or natural disaster; whatever the case, it destabilizes the foundations of a secure and stable home.[61]

The Dollhouse (2007) →35 by Heather Benning does the same: a modest farmstead on the Canadian prairie, from which the residents have suddenly fled. The pastel-tinted interior, books and magazines indicate a moment around 1968; a handbook *How to Sell by Telephone* suggests they were desperately looking for a source of income. The weathered exterior walls reveal how nature has since attempted to reconquer the place. All of this at full scale, in a doll's house at a scale of 1:1, which was on view from 2007 to 2013 along the side of the motorway in the hamlet of Redvers. You had to circle around it curiously to discover that the north façade of the farmer's house had been replaced by Plexiglas. Apart from that, it hardly differed from the many other abandoned farmsteads in the depopulated countryside of Saskatchewan. For Benning, *The Dollhouse* represents the history of the whole community: 'I created a contemporary art project *in* the rural, *for* rural people and *about* rural people and their stories. It is a conversation about the end of the family farm.' When the decay had continued after some years, Benning let the house go up in flames. She asked director Chad Galloway to film the event; the title was once again *The Dollhouse* (2014), but it is an autonomous work that takes the viewer into the burning house, until the last beams collapse in thick smoke.[62] And still, in the final shots the house stands undisturbed in the snow-covered landscape, its interior illuminated colourfully. What is dream and what is reality? Has ruthless capitalism destroyed the authentic life in the countryside? Or is that idyll perhaps an illusion? 'In the prairies we have this romanticizing of the farm: "Let's go back to the country and have a little organic farm with

58 Interview with Alice Pasquini on 28 October 2020.

59 Pasquini's work is reminiscent of Robert Gober's *Half Stone House* (1979–80) and *Burnt House* (1979–80), two abandoned, desolate, dilapidated doll's houses. For an overview of Gober's work, see: Temkin (ed.) 2014.

60 *Fallen Star 1/5* is well captured in a short film by Chris Burke on Vimeo: https://vimeo.com/48092714 (last consulted on 16 February 2022).

61 See also Gill Perry's discussion of *Fallen Star 1/5* in his chapter on 'Broken Homes' in *Playing at Home: The House in Contemporary Art* (2013).

62 See: https://vimeo.com/108923600 (last consulted on 16 February 2022).

34

a few cows and a chicken, and life will be fantastic. But there is a reason why all these places are abandoned: It just wasn't sustainable.'[63] The doll's house lent itself perfectly for highlighting that ambivalence; Benning's work became a subtle and layered form of architectural criticism.

THE DOLL'S HOUSE AS TRAINING FOR DESIGNERS

Doll's houses generally reflect architectural and social history, albeit with some delay. They give an indication of prevailing ideas and ideals, comparable with other forms of popular culture such as advertising, magazines and video clips. That impression is often a distorted snapshot: the doll's house stands in its own right, in a world where everything is fine and nothing ages. Toy developers and architects who attempt to come up with contemporary versions surprise us only sporadically; innovations are rare even among competition entries.[64] Those in search of radical rethinks are better off consulting artists: they do not shirk from rigorous changes of direction and give their doll's houses dimensions that are consistently banished from the classical models. That generates a palette of powerful, stimulating works: rich material for communicating about architecture and the way it is used and experienced. Can designers take anything from that into

63 Interview with Heather Benning on 24 November 2020.

64 There have been at least three competitions in which architects have been invited to design a contemporary doll's house. *Architectural Design* took the initiative in 1983. All results were presented with texts and photographs in special issue 46, entitled *Dolls' Houses* (Papadakis 1983). In 2013 the property developer Cathedral Group organized a charity exhibition, for which 20 architects designed doll's houses that were then auctioned. A catalogue was not compiled, but complete lists do exist: https://www.theguardian.com/artanddesign/gallery/2013/oct/08/dolls-houses-architecture-zaha-hadid (last consulted on 16 February 2022). In 2017 the exhibition *1:12. Verbeeldingskracht in zorgarchitectuur* went on display at various venues in the Netherlands. Eighteen architects designed doll's houses that children with and without physical disabilities could play with. A catalogue of the same name was also published by ArtEZ Press (Brand & Vos 2017).

35

36

their practice? And does that then remain a matter of conjuring with representations or do doll's houses have other potential?

Whatever the case, it was more than enough for architect and tutor Dirk Somers to devote two master studios to the subject in 2014 and 2015 at Delft University of Technology and Ghent University.[65] As an architect who deals with models on a daily basis, he offers a remarkable observation: a doll's house is actually *not* a representation. It 'relies on the real world, but is not a reproduction of that world. Primarily, the dolls' house represents itself' (Somers 2015:51). It can refer to comparable buildings, but unlike a model it is usually not a miniature copy of an existing or future house: '[T]he dolls' house is, first and foremost, itself' (2015:51). That gives the designer of a doll's house unprecedented freedom, because: 'The building at full scale exists in the imagination only' (Somers in van Gerrewey 2016:8). It is not subject to all sorts of regulations and conditions: 'An analysis of the site, orientation, urban context, design brief, energy performance regulations, drawing conventions, computer programmes—all that is absent' (2016:8). That is why the doll's house is, for Somers, an excellent didactic tool. After all, prospective architects rarely enjoy an opportunity to really build; they almost always have to resort to simulations of actual practice, and often 'those images threaten to become more important than the architecture or the design itself' (2016:8). When they design a doll's house, the design and its representation fuse into one and the same object: 'Cardboard is cardboard and balsa wood is balsa wood. Students become their own contractors' (2015:51). Somers goes even further: 'You probably cannot get any closer to building practice in an educational context' (2016:8).

The students of Somers made realistic structures, concentrating on 'the visual language, the tectonics, the architectural unity of material, structure

65 In 2015 a selection from both groups was exhibited at deSingel in Antwerp: https://www.vai.be/nieuws/het-poppenhuis-als-architectuur (last consulted on 16 February 2022). See also: van Gerrewey 2016 and Frenken, Mandias & Schreurs (eds) 2015.

and spatial experience', or in other words 'the tangible and visible qualities that make the object successful' (2016:8). One question was given particular consideration: the relationship between inside and outside. Because this is vitally important to a doll's house: recognizing domesticity tempts you to stare inside unashamedly, like a voyeur. But that appeal needs to be carefully measured, because 'the dolls' house lives by grace of the tension between explicit intimacy and blatant exhibitionism' (2015:51). To make the house too open or closed is to get it wrong. Somers suggests that this is why doll's houses are perhaps resistant to contemporary styles of architecture. First, because the transition between inside and outside is now much more fluid than it was in historical buildings, which eliminates some of the tension that is so challenging. Second, because looking into an undefined space, you automatically search for an indication of scale. You find that to some extent in door openings or, even better, risers on stairs, since there is little variation in their height; they are fairly accurate measures. But sometimes you can search in vain for orientation in sleek, modern architecture: 'A scale model of Mies van der Rohe's Farnsworth House or Johnson's Glass House', Somers laughs, 'can therefore easily be mistaken for a coffee table.'[66]

Finally, the doll's house is the container for a collection, even if the house remains empty: '[T]he miniature house is a collection of rooms that differ in character more than in size' (2015:51). The viewer can extract a narrative from that wealth of atmospheres and experiences. Somers posits that this could also benefit experienced designers in their practice: 'The objective overview and analytical gaze allow for the discovery, in the stacking of rooms and the juxtaposition of atmospheres, of new starting points from which to design' (Somers, Verschaffel & van den Driessche 2019:192).

A unique example in which all of this comes together is the *Luisterhuis* →36 ('Listening House') by architect Machiel Spaan and composer Rozalie Hirs.[67] For a charity exhibition in 2017 they were invited to design a doll's house that children with and without disabilities could play with. They came up with a house-shaped wooden sculpture with seven rooms to explore with your ears. Each room is defined by a verb: flowing (bathroom), crackling (open fireplace in the living room), whistling (kitchen), playing ping-pong (attic), snoring (bedroom), ringing (hall) and splashing (scullery). Hirs used real sounds to compose *musique concrète* (concrete music) that reflects the function of each room: In the kitchen the water bubbles, the kettle whistles, the tea pours into the cups. In the anteroom a dog is yapping and shaking itself off while someone runs up the stairs. You can count bleating sheep in the bedroom. If you approach one of the hollows with your ear, the music starts. If a number of visitors do that at the same time, the house fills with life on all sides. All of this closely reflects reality, because in a real house there is interaction between use and sound: you hear the tap upstairs, the doorbell downstairs, someone flushing the toilet as the clock strikes five... The music makes the space many times bigger than the modest 50 × 50 × 70 cm of the tangible architecture; the visual experience is totally subservient to the acoustic. That goes deep, because sounds are emotional anchors and every visitor creates their own personal narrative by connecting sounds and associating them with meanings. At the same time, it is also a game: 'You do it for pleasure, and while doing it you discover something, you learn something.' No two visitors perceive the *Luisterhuis* in the same way: 'The sculpture invites you to shape your own spatial listening experience.' As such, this innovative doll's house is also a game of discovery. More astonishing games of this kind are discussed in later chapters.

66 Interview with Dirk Somers on 27 April 2021.

67 The exhibition *1:12. Verbeeldingskracht in zorgarchitectuur* was organized by Peter Masselink and was on show in 2017 and 2018 at the Brabants Kenniscentrum Kunst en Cultuur (now Kunstloc Brabant) in Tilburg, SCHUNCK in Heerlen, Dutch Design Week in Eindhoven, Arcam Amsterdam and the Public Transport and Toy Museum in Doetinchem. The project is extensively documented in Brand & Vos 2017.

THE BLOCK AS TRANSFORMATION ARTIST

The Versatility of Building Systems

Is the *Creative Play House* from PlanToys a doll's house or a construction toy? The company presents it as a doll's house, but is that an accurate description if it consists of 28 individual slabs and columns? A doll's house generally comes ready-made; even if nobody plays with it, everybody recognizes it as a place to live. The *Creative Play House*, however, first has to be assembled. You must decide how you want to position the components on top of and beside one another, and you can adapt it as often as you want.[1] As long as you do nothing, the pieces could be anything. A construction toy not only scales down reality but also splits it into fragments. Taken individually, they do not form recognizable entities, but a myriad of endless possibilities: '[B]uilding blocks are most powerful and compelling in their unbuilt form, when they are not images of things, but ideas' (Brosterman 1991:8). Players not only feast their eyes but also want to roll up their sleeves immediately.

Like doll's houses, construction toys have existed for centuries, in all shapes and sizes. You can replicate buildings with them or design your own structures, from a single tower or villa to an entire city or region. For who isn't familiar with the traditional wooden blocks and the romantic villages with red pitched roofs arranged around a church, a school and possibly a fire station for some excitement and, to top it all off, a station to discover the wide world? Such an idyllic scene appears to be of all times and places, yet each era has generated its own variations. Starting in the early twentieth century, pastoral green settings faced stiff competition from ambitious skyscrapers. And as soon as connections between components improved the stability of structures, the competition to build the tallest tower really took off. Besides stone and wood, metal made its appearance and, in the 1940s, plastic, which grew to become the most common material on the toy market. A very late arrival around the turn of the millennium was the digital world. While *Lego* dominates much of the analogue market, in the world of video games it is difficult to ignore its digital counterpart, *Minecraft*.

A feature of construction toys is that their makers often harbour didactic ambitions. Ever since the first half of the nineteenth century they have been viewed as pedagogically useful tools: playing with blocks, slabs and columns makes you more determined, smarter and happier.[2] How do contemporary makers see their role? Can they add anything with their products to the rich legacy of their predecessors? How can makers influence the behaviour of players and, at the same time, emphasize their creativity and fantasy? Construction toys do not come with rules but, at the very most, with models, and they are in principle informal. But the maker does determine the material, the shape, the size and the appearance of the components. Sometimes they are abstract, such as the unchanging wooden *Kapla* planks measuring 11.7 × 2.34 × 0.78 cm; sometimes they faithfully reflect a particular style of architecture or region. Whatever the case, the components tell their own story—even if the makers promote a toy without rules. That is also interesting to architects. Some of them use construction toys as tools in a design process, while others use them to stand out with a striking form of expression.

BECOMING A 'BETTER PERSON' WHILE PLAYING

Children have always stacked things on top of one another, but the first specially made construction toys date from the early nineteenth century. Carpenters used leftover pieces of wood to make blocks or houses—each one

1 In 1924 Ludwig Hirschfeld-Mack had already devised a *Pädagogische Puppenstube* according to the same principle. Eight columns with slots and indentations could be positioned along the edge of a base plate. Between them was space for wooden plates of various sizes and colours. Players could determine whether these were walls, tables, bookshelves, overhangs or something else. Though never commercialized, this doll's house does belong to the 'canon' of toys that originated at the Bauhaus. See: Luyken 2004:37, Hollein & Luyken (eds) 2004: 148–149 and Grisebach 2019.

2 '[T]he "object lesson" [...], which holds that active engagement with material things unlocks an individual's higher faculties and allows sensory information to be transformed into concrete knowledge, has become a foundational tenet for childhood development and education for learners of all ages' (Fanning & Mir 2014:39).

unavoidably slightly bigger or smaller than the next, making their stacking quite a challenge. Moving the stack was out of the question, for the structure would collapse immediately. By the middle of the nineteenth century, industrial production meant that the shapes and sizes became more uniform, and towards the end of the century edges or ridges prevented components from sliding out of position all the time. It still wasn't possible to transport a structure without repercussions, but stacking had become more precise. Over the course of the twentieth century, connecting pieces appeared so that components could be held together in all directions (Hodge 1990:5–6).[3] Maaike Lauwaert sees this as a transition 'from building to designing toys', or rather, a second generation of construction toys that came to exist alongside the first: 'To put it bluntly, construction toys have changed from wooden and stone generic building blocks to designing toys of diverse materials, with different shapes and, crucially, with an interlocking mechanism' (Lauwaert 2009:46–47). The appearance of these new toys was accompanied by an unshakeable belief in technological progress and in the ability to shape society: 'Second-generation construction toys epitomized a culture's belief and optimism that indeed, thanks to new technologies and materials, everything seemed possible' (2009:47).[4]

Big Questions on a Small Scale

The architect and sculptor Norman Brosterman collected more than three hundred architecture games, which he sold in 1990 to the Canadian Centre for Architecture (CCA). In the years that followed, the CCA devoted a number of exhibitions and catalogues to the relationship between architecture and construction toys. The second, *Potential Architecture* (1991), is an inspiring voyage of discovery through the eyes of Brosterman, who outlines the history of construction toys in vivacious and occasionally humorous fashion and, in the process, corrects a few errors,[5] offers some perfect descriptions of the aesthetic qualities of toys[6] and, using pertinent examples, illustrates how their genesis is interwoven with technological, economic and cultural backgrounds.[7] For example, entrepreneur Whitney S. Reed in 1884 devised an ingenious *Church and Sunday School* →01. The blocks were emblazoned with the Ten Commandments, quotes from the New Testament, and images of Gothic windows. The toy was customized for children from the Protestant community who could not partake in any form of entertainment on the Lord's Day. But the instructions featured completely free structures as a subtle invitation to take all that with a pinch of salt (Brosterman 1991:12). Such a socially desirable adaptive capacity was also demonstrated by the *Anchor Blocks*, when the German company was severely hit in World War I by delivery problems,

01

3 A number of very early construction systems are still produced, among them the world-famous *Anchor Blocks* by Otto and Gustav Lilienthal, the first four sets of which came on the market in 1884: https://anker-bausteine.de (last consulted on 17 February 2022) and the *Lincoln Logs* devised in 1916 by John Lloyd Wright (son of Frank Lloyd Wright): https://www.basicfun.com/lincoln-logs.html (last consulted on 17 February 2022). For an extensive review of these construction systems, see: Vale 2013:24–37, 77–88 and Zinguer 2015:52–95.

4 Unfortunately, technology, innovation and progress were increasingly seen as the exclusive domain of boys and men: 'Typically, these second-generation construction sets would show a boy at play, often with a father or grandfather hovering over the scene. Mothers, if depicted, would look on the scene benevolently from an easy chair. Sisters, when present in these building tableaux, would be helping their brothers' (Lauwaert 2009:48–49).

5 For example, *Lego*'s founder Ole Kirk Christiansen is often seen as the inventor, in 1949, of the hollow plastic blocks with round studs, while from 1923 on, Louis Cousin from Belgium held a patent for such blocks under the name *Batima*, which were made from compressed and coloured cardboard, with linseed oil as binding agent. The accompanying building instructions were of exceptional quality: 'Seldom was such a comprehensive set of models issued with a building toy, and seldom were these models so graceful, convincing, and architecturally plausible' (Brosterman & Lewis 1991:24). A number of examples can be downloaded from the site of the Museum of Old Techniques in Grimbergen: https://www.mot.be/resource/Organization/batima?lang=nl (last consulted on 17 February 2022). More than twenty years after Cousin, child psychologist Hilary Page came up with the *Kiddicraft Self-Locking Building Bricks* (1947), which Christiansen used, adjusted and improved to create *Lego*. In doing so, he paid little heed to copyright.

6 Brosterman, for example, compares with infectious enthusiasm two construction sets with minimalist connections: the *Crandall Blocks* patented in 1867 and the *Batima* blocks of 1923. 'While Batima was a slave to gravity, on the level of mud-brick architecture, the Crandall Blocks permitted light tensile structures, springing upward or outward, and the security of its tongue-and-groove joints made it possible to transport a finished piece without disaster' (Brosterman 1991:10).

7 See also: Canadian Centre for Architecture (ed.) 1990, 1993 & 1997.

02

export restrictions and declining sales. The manufacturer made a virtue of necessity and launched—successfully—new sets to construct realistic miniature bunkers. When their popularity became somewhat embarrassing after the war—especially for exports—the manufacturer again came up with a solution: extension kits transformed the bunkers in no time into innocent medieval castles and churches (Brosterman & Lewis 1991:30).

Religion, international politics and economics all left their mark on construction toys. That is illustrated once more by Stanlo →02, a direct spin-off of the financial difficulties encountered by Stanley Works, a company that made hinges and locks, during the depression of 1933. Stanlo switched to toy production using the same material and machines.[8] The result was a fascinating combination of coloured metal sheets and hinges, accompanied by powerful illustrations of industrial infrastructure—but the heaviest construction toy ever... Unsuccessful it may have been, but it was nonetheless a good indication of what were already becoming the three pillars of (American) toy production: 'the exploitation of industrial processes, the often unscrupulous marketing, but also the playful and wonderfully unrestricted imagination of many of the designers' (Brosterman & Lewis 1991:22). One toy that fits surprising well on this list is the Cleveland Wrecking Game of 1977. It was released by the toy manufacturer Pressman, but the instructions are signed by the chairman of the local demolition company, who urges players to swing a wrecking ball towards a brick tower with boarded-up windows, under the motto that '[c]learing old buildings to make way for new American cities and towns with new schools, offices and homes, eliminates urban blight and makes our cities better places in which to live'.

Construction toys are much more diverse than doll's houses, which makes it difficult to define them unambiguously. They are in any case composed of modules: three-dimensional components of fixed dimensions and proportions, to be combined together in various ways. Some allow for endless variations, but in all cases construction is not limited to one predetermined pattern. The components can subsequently be pulled apart again and reused. Authors do not always agree about whether a construction toy also should be constructional. If a set consists of ready-made houses, is it still classified as a construction toy? No, says Peter Lingens, curator of a major retrospective exhibition at the Staatliche Museen in Kassel in 1999: a minimum of technical and constructional actions must be possible (Lingens 1999:17).[9] The CCA is not as strict in that regard, and it closes the *Potential Architecture* exhibition with *Urbania* (1935), a collection of wooden blocks with paper wrappers that depict a nineteenth-century town.[10] That toy emphasizes 'planning a town, rather than designing a building' (Brosterman & Lewis 1991:35). For the CCA, what is essential is the intrinsic connections between the components—not so much whether each of the buildings is also composed of a number of parts: 'Together, they illustrate how children learn to invent relationships between space, structure, and building forms, and hence better to understand the world around them' (Olsberg 1991:5).

8 The current Stanley Works cleverly weave that episode as a sort of genesis myth into the history of the company, which 'was able to save the livelihoods of its factory workers while feeding the imaginations of the next generation of engineers and builders'. Cited from: https://www.stanleyblackanddecker.com/who-we-are/our-history/responsibility/stanlo-making-world-piece-piece (last consulted on 17 February 2022).

9 The catalogue *Baukästen: Technisches Spielzeug vom Biedermeier bis zur Jahrtausendwende* (1999) offers an extensive overview of German, Swiss and Austrian construction toys of the nineteenth and twentieth centuries. In the introduction (1999:18–19), Peter Lingens presents a classification based on the connections between the parts. In the case of '0- connection toys', the pieces are stacked or combined, but not attached to one another. With '1- connection toys' the pieces stay connected without the use of additional pieces, such as small studs. '2- connection toys' have special parts to attach other pieces, for example tiny rods to screw into openings. With '3- connecting toys' the connection always consists of two parts, for example a bolt and nut. The same book also contains a fascinating contribution from Karl Debik about his personal quest for construction toys from the former DDR, and a chapter in which Lingens sheds light on construction toys made of plastic.

10 *Urbania* is the first in a series of nine, about various types of city. The others include a port city, a 'colonial', and an 'American' city (1991:35).

03

04

Building to Learn

The educational qualities of construction toys quickly attracted attention. Educationalist Friedrich Fröbel was one of the first to recognize the potential. In 1836 he set up the first kindergarten in the German town of Bad Blankenburg, where children were not only cared for but also taught. He devised teaching material to discover the world in a playful way: the world-famous *Fröbel Gifts and Occupations*, which are produced and used to this day. Four of the ten *Gifts* consist of building blocks—by placing these together and then separating them again, children learn to understand the relationship between a whole and its parts, and they become familiar with shapes, proportions and symmetry. In other *Gifts*, volumes are split up further into planes, and from there into lines and eventually points. In the ten *Occupations*, those different dimensions are completed in reverse order (from point to volume) in manual skill assignments with available paper or clay.[11] Fröbel's body of work marks a turning point: '[N]ever had a toy been thought out so precisely, nor the pedagogy of play been formulated with such great clarity' (Zinguer 2015:38). A big advantage is also the timeless simplicity of material, form and elaboration, which is why Fröbel's games are still a source of inspiration for many toy developers today. But Fröbel also had strict ideas about their use and '[i]n this respect they represent the end of an era' (Shubert 1993:17). Because modernism meant that construction toys became much freer in the 1920s and 1930s: 'The most significant aspect of modern toys is their extraordinary flexibility; they allow children maximum freedom to explore ideal designs based on their own creative instincts, unfettered by preordained outcomes or established rules' (1993:17–18).

Technology, economics and politics were not the only factors to influence toy innovations in the twentieth century; artists and architects also played an active role, and they, too, sought to 'educate' young and old. Their toys didn't always make it into the market, but they do form an important piece of cultural history.[12] Very early, the Viennese architect Josef Hoffmann, for example, made *Fabrik* (1920) →03, a collection of building blocks whose shades of grey, repetitive patterns and large dimensions clearly represent industrial buildings, blast-furnaces and skyscrapers: architecture that was appearing increasingly frequently in the built environment of that time but rarely in toys.[13] The following year, architect Hermann Finsterlin designed his *Stilspiel* ('Style Game') (1921) →04, a direct illustration of his vision of how monuments are created. He saw the sphere and the cube as two poles from which all other forms are derived: cones, pyramids, bell- or onion-shaped objects and so on. The *Stilspiel* had to clarify that world monuments (temple, pagoda, pyramid, mosque, cathedral…) were composed of those basic components, and it had to invite players to take those miniatures apart and combine the pieces in different ways. This motley collection would offer a good impression of the architecture of the future.[14] Perhaps the most expensive and most enchanting of modernist construction toys appeared the following year: *Dandanah* (1922) →05, by Bruto Taut and Blanche Mahlberg.[15] Probably the only glass construction toy ever made, it consists of sixty glass blocks in five different shapes and colours, with six sheets of illustrated models. Manfred Speidel (2006:7) presents it as a magnificent and unique work, and also proof

05

11 An important difference between the *Gifts* and *Occupations* is that the *Gifts* do not change if somebody plays with them—they 'survive' the game—while the material in *Occupations* (paper, wool, clay, etc.) is used to realize something (Bordes 2010:26). The work of Fröbel has been extensively documented from various perspectives (pedagogy, architecture, cultural history, etc.). See in particular: Brosterman 1997 and Zinguer 2015:18–51.

12 '[I]n the first decades of the 20th century, […] many architects sought to create pedagogical toys and experimented with quality materials, "good" form and appropriate content' (Yagou 2013:47). Toys by artists and architects from that period have been the subject of a number of exhibitions and publications. See for example: Millar Fisher 2018 and Hensel, Eikmeyer & Kraus (eds) (2019) on the toys of the Bauhaus, and the catalogues: Canadian Centre for Architecture (ed.) (1993), Hollein & Luyken (eds) 2004 and Stals (ed.) 2010.

13 See: Luyken 2004:32–33 and Zinguer 2015:4.

14 See: Döhl 1988 & 2000 and Luyken 2004:33–34.

15 In 2003 the Vitra Museum released a remake of 500 copies. The price was 550 euros and the German retail chain Manufactum provided the distribution, but ceased to do so in 2009 (Yagou 2013:48).

that glass is totally unsuitable for a construction toy: too expensive, too fragile, and hence too dangerous if a piece is chipped off—and especially far too smooth: even the six designs supplied are difficult to construct with them, if at all.[16] But as a concept it is absorbing and versatile, and it is inextricably linked to Taut's architectural ideals and his fascination for glass and light. A century after its creation, it remains elusive, provocative and impressive: 'Situated at the intersection of several discourses, the *Dandanah* presents itself as an icon of the complexities and contradictions of Modernism' (Yagou 2013:55).[17]

'Responsible' toys acquired greater significance after World War II: '[G]ood toys were positioned in opposition to what many saw as the needless novelty, realism, or chaotic and violent associations of cheaper mass-market toys' (Fanning 2018:92).[18] The makers of *Lego*, the undisputed bestseller among construction toys, also had explicit educational intentions. They succeeded spectacularly in bringing them into the commercial toy industry—in a 'questionable' material, plastic, it is worth noting, often associated with 'artificiality, superficiality and fakeness': 'While the prescriptive notion of the "good" or "real" toy typically described objects made in wood, emphasizing tradition and refined craftsmanship, LEGO consciously situated the plastic bricks in this discourse' (2018:92).[19] From then on the company combined 'creativity and imagination as an explicit corporate code' (2018:94) with a profit model that encouraged the purchase of more and more sets. That provided the basis for unmatched global success.

If the impact of construction toys on the creativity and identity of young users in particular is so big, can you then detect their influence in the later designs of some architects? Various authors have considered this question, among them Brenda and Robert Vale: '[D]oes the type of construction toy affect the inclinations and capabilities of the child who uses it?' (2013:189). This is of course difficult to trace (and prove) in retrospect, but the Vales investigated what type of architecture is easiest to realize using fourteen of the best-known construction toys. A small selection from the rich collection: The famous *Anchor Blocks*, which have been marketed for over a century, 'have just sufficient realism to be recognized as German' and 'are part of creating "Germanity" or *Heimat* and its exportation to the rest of the world' (2013:37). In the England of the 1930s 'it was the red plastic hipped roofs in the Bayko box that guided the Bayko builder towards the construction of interwar suburban Britain on the carpet' (2013:99), while the Minibrix from the same era prompted 'small models of ordinary buildings': '[A] wall of dyed rubber Minibrix looks like a wall of brickwork somewhere (anywhere) in Britain, though perhaps on a wet day' (2013:126, 111). Players can employ the sets in all sorts of ways, but sometimes the right pieces are simply missing: in the case of Bayko, for example, there is nothing long enough for a skyscraper. For that purpose, the *Girder and Panel Sets* from the second half of the 1950s are more appropriate: they were intended to 'build the way real modern buildings are built' and in particular to imitate the structure of modern high-rise as faithfully as possible (2013:154).

The influence of construction toys on the creative development of children is also a familiar theme for Douglas Coupland. The artist, author and toy

16 In 2013 Artemis Yagou spent months immersing herself in Dandanah. In *Preprint*, the series of publications for scientific research from the German Museum in Munich, she noted that the images on the sheets of illustrated models and the sketches for the patent mainly helped to present the toy more attractively, but paid no attention to friction and gravity. In the text that accompanies the patent, Blanche Mahlberg suggested that a future extension kit with metal connections might be able to hold everything together, but for Yagou, '[t]his is an indirect admission of the non-feasibility or impracticality of the proposed structures and, in fact, undermines the whole concept and the value of the patent itself' (2013:20).

17 'Was the *Dandanah* Taut's way to shape young generations? A manifesto not in words but in glass? A promotional object for Taut's architectural theories and practice? The architect's utopia materialized on a small scale? Being unavoidably small, was it an admission of failure, an acceptance of the end of grand schemes and of utopian, visionary projects? Was it all of the above and more?' (Yagou 2013:55).

18 After World War II, certain toys were still created as a continuation of the modernist tradition. For Howard Shubert, Arthur Carrara's *Magnet Master* (1947) and Charles Eames' *The Little Toy* (1952) are even 'the culmination of modern architectural toys' (1993:26).

19 Plastic brought great improvements to the quality of connections, paving the way for more ambitious designs. With Lego it was also increasingly valued as a 'cheap, easy to clean, colorful and (generally speaking) durable' material (Lauwaert 2009:52).

06 →84–85

collector incorporated his personal vision into an installation for the CCA in 2005. Besides *Lego*, he was always a big fan of *Super City*→06, a plastic construction toy by Ideal Toys from 1967–1968 and '[t]he best building kit ever made'.[20] In his view, *Lego* and *Super City* had '[a] profound effect [...] on how I see the world, on the objects I make and the words I write. Basically, I see the world in terms of bricks and nubs and modules and crisp clean lines' (2005:66, 7). Construction toys also had a gigantic impact on society as a whole, argues Coupland: '[A]fter 50 years of intense kit usage, the binary sensibility that defines them has now overtaken the world—not just the built world but also the electronic metaworlds like the internet where we spend so much of our lives' (2005:64). To honour *Super City*, which had existed for just two years, the artist gave his installation at the CCA the same name.[21] It was a futuristic city measuring 3.65 × 3.65 m, made of *Super City*, *Lego* and other construction toys, or interpretations of them. With the exception of a few *Super City* components, everything was snow white, which for Coupland was the ultimate colour of the *Lego* world: 'perfect and crisp and anti-death. Lego was the future. White. Clean. Plastic.'[22] Clearly recognizable are the former Twin Towers and the Canadian National Tower in Toronto, as well as iconic American highways and water towers and all sorts of imaginary structures. The mixture of fiction and non-fiction was an invitation to visitors to assess the influence of construction toys on their personal perception and experience.[23]

Lego has now been in the hands of children for over seventy years, and the Vales extend the line into the present with *Lego*'s 'Green City'. They do not mention more recent construction toys though—they only note a 'dumbing down' (2013:190), as if contemporary toy manufacturers increasingly take users by the hand. Previously, all you received was a list of components and a picture of the final product, but today every *Lego* set comes with a book that shows every detail of every step of the process. Does that observation really apply to the construction toys of today? What do those toys look like and what 'can they do'?

IN SEARCH OF LATITUDE AMONG THE CLASSICS: CONTEMPORARY INNOVATIONS

Many contemporary doll's houses are created out of frustration with the existing range, but that is much less the case with the makers of construction toys. They do not necessarily distance themselves from existing toys but mostly try to combine the advantages of various concepts in one new version. More so than the makers of doll's houses, they harbour didactic ambitions. A case in point is the young designer James Paulius, who asked: Which set of building blocks would you want to give future generations? In 2013 he set out to answer that question for the product design company Areaware.[24] He explored the history of wooden toys in search of characteristics of the 'Universal Toy' that merit a modern

20 According to Coupland, *Super City* is 'the first purely modernist building kit. Anything made from Super City looked like a Craig Elwood or a Richard Neutra or a Wallace K. Harrison or a set from *2001: A Space Odyssey*. [...] It was drop-dead sexy. Even the directions were modernistic and programmatic. Instead of bridges or gas stations, Super City supplied suggestions for research centres and science parks' (2005:66).

21 Super City was on display at the CCA in Montreal from 9 June to 20 November 2005: https://www.cca.qc.ca/en/events/2740/super-city (last consulted on 17 February 2022).

22 Quotation from Coupland in the CCA press file, on the occasion of the opening on 9 June 2005.

23 The installation by Coupland is remarkably multifaceted and well-considered, but some artists have also made installations out of *Lego* and other construction toys. One of them is Olafur Eliasson's *The Collectivity Project* for the Triennale in Tirana in 2005, and later in Oslo (2006), Copenhagen (2008) and New York City (2015): https://olafureliasson.net/archive/artwork/WEK100711/the-collectivity-project (last consulted on 17 February 2022). In Tirana, Eliasson invited the public to build their city of the future in public space using three tonnes of white *Lego* blocks. In New York City, he invited leading architecture firms such as BIG, Diller Scofidio + Renfro and OMA New York to make one of their designs out of *Lego*. Visitors could then extend or alter those buildings or integrate them into their own structures.

24 Paulius, then a student at the School of Design at Rochester Institute of Technology (RIT), was one of the participants in the third edition of the Metaproject, an annual collaboration since 2011 between RIT and a partner from the product industry, which commercializes some projects. See: https://www.rit.edu/metaproject (last consulted on 17 February 2022). The Metaproject from 2013 was a collaboration between RIT and Areaware, a New York producer of 'functional and uplifting objects, designed with integrity'.

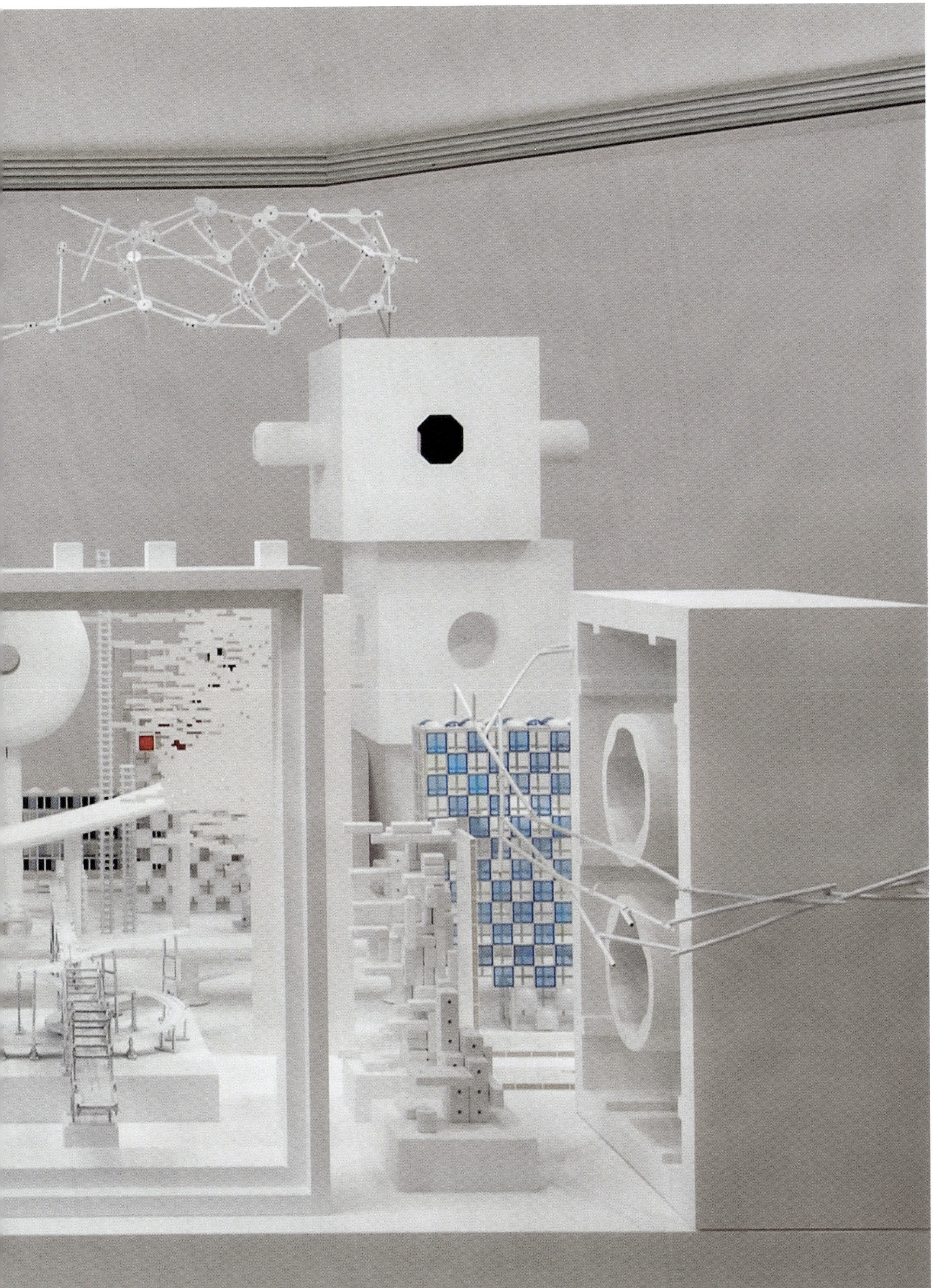

07→88–89

interpretation. That resulted in *Blockitecture*→07, a well-built modular system with a unique stacking mechanism: 'Hexagonal blocks nest together in various formations, allowing them to counterbalance each other and create unique cantilevers found in modern and contemporary architecture'. [25] Most blocks can be placed on top of other blocks thanks to an indentation on their bottom side. That can be done in various positions, but they tumble down if no successive block counterbalances the leverage effect. Paulius challenges players to experiment with gravity and sees that as a form of 'empowerment': 'Blockitecture encourages the idea that the environment we live in is something we can create for ourselves'. It is made of sustainable wood and has a simple and sleek appearance in refined colours. The hexagonal blocks from the 'Habitat' basic set can be combined with floor pieces for areas of greenery or water, which underline the impression of a future-oriented 'green' city.[26] Apart from that, Paulius's search for a 'Universal Toy' confirms that a construction toy still cannot be created without a good basic module. Later extension sets that were not designed by Paulius show that you should not tinker with a strong module. The 'Deco' sets in particular are full of unnecessary frills: gaudy colours, ridiculous roofs and, especially, windows that interrupt the carefully sophisticated continuous lines between the original modules.[27]

Integrate with Everything

The question of extension kits arises with many construction toys. For the makers (and manufacturers) they constitute an efficient revenue model, and for players sometimes an incentive to ignore building instructions and come up with their own structures using a motley collection of pieces. But the more special such kits look, the more they curb creativity. *Lego* is forever releasing new models with striking components and is often criticized for that over-zealous commercialization, which is so far removed from the original concept of blocks. Architect and toy developer Dane Scarborough was so fed up with it that he set off in another direction: his *Überstix* (2004) encourages players to cherish existing pieces (including *Lego*!) and put them to new uses. The toy is compatible with every other construction toy in the metric and imperial system, and also with 'things that every kid has access to: straws, popsicle sticks, water bottles, paperclips, cups...'[28] *Überstix* is so flexible that many pieces can even be made with a 300-dollar 3D printer. Scarborough also encourages that to reduce storage and transport and to make the toy accessible to more children.[29] He seeks sustainability in both an ecological and social sense, because: 'When kids grow up playing with a construction toy of some kind, they develop spatial skills, the ability to move things around and visualize things from different angles and perspectives'. *Überstix* adds another challenge to that: 'Depending on the parts that you integrate, you have to modify the design to accommodate them. So it teaches kids about problem solving and engineering'.

25 Interview with James Paulius on 12 November 2021.

26 James Paulius devised 'Parkland' and 'Desert Garden' to introduce more greenery into *Blockitecture*. For the basic 'Habitat' set and the later 'Garden City' with its pavilions and roof gardens, he drew inspiration from Moshe Safdie's Habitat 67 apartment complex in Montreal and Safdie's publications *For Everyone a Garden* (1974) and *The City after the Automobile: An Architect's Vision* (1998).

27 The zigzag structures in the 'Brutalism' set and the arches and the curved roof of the 'Factory' also limit the compatibility of components and weaken the well-thought-out abstract concept of Paulius. And, anyway, to what extent does a factory belong in the green city he envisages?

28 Interview with Dane Scarborough on 20 October 2021. *Überstix*'s compatibility also keeps the production relatively cheap compared to construction toys with 'tension' or 'compression' connections, where the slightest variation in dimensions means they no longer fit together, and then the structure is in danger of collapsing. The required precision makes production expensive. That problem does not occur with *Überstix* components with a 'living spring', because space is exactly what is needed in order to be compatible with other construction systems.

29 In the past there have also been construction kits where players first had to make the components themselves or were encouraged to add to existing components with their own creations. The oldest known example of them is *Döcö*, from the Berlin firm Döhle, from around 1920. It consisted mostly of metal strips that had to be cut to size and perforated. 'The child was freed of the tyranny of standardized parts—and in exchange accepted the toil of making his own!' (Brosterman & Lewis 1991:34). More than a decade later the American company Northwestern Products released the bricklayer's set *Konkrete Bild-m-up* (1933). You could only start to build after first creating concrete blocks. The brickwork could start sooner with *Bild-a-Brik* (1952) by Peter Gruhn for the Creative Toy Company: the blocks came ready-made with this toy. That toy concept is still available today under the name *Teifoc Creative Building Kit*.

41
UBERSTIX ARE DESIGNED TO BE MODIFIED. YOU CAN USE NAIL CLIPPERS AND AN EMERY BOARD TO CREATE NEW PARTS FOR STRUCTURAL AND AESTHETIC PURPOSES.

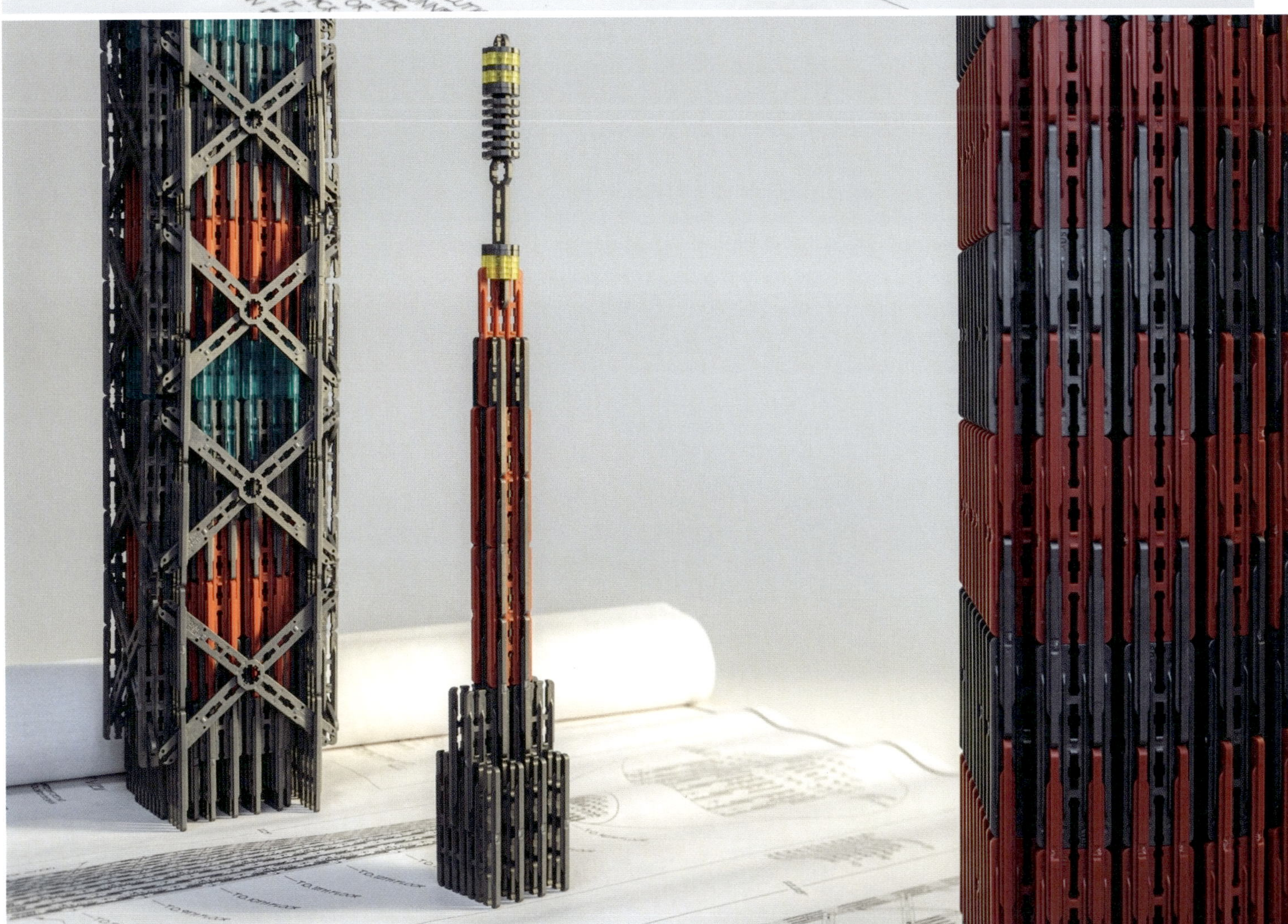

09

Scarborough's educational ambitions also become clear in the building instructions for *ÜberArc* (2008) →08, the architecture line from *Überstix*. Its pieces are the same, yet the primary focus is no longer on compatibility with other toys. The plans are reminiscent of construction drawings by architects, except at a scale of 1:1. Not every intermediate stage is depicted, but the important steps are illustrated in a crystal-clear way with front and side elevations and isometrics that you can place the pieces on directly to check the structure. The effect is spectacular: young players learn to decipher construction drawings more quickly than their parents can, and 'that is like a superpower that serves you well your whole life'.

Between Toy and Tool

Scarborough is, with *Überstix*, not the only toy developer that seeks out the space between tried and trusted construction systems. Others do that through material or in terms of scale, among them Damien Murtagh, the creator of *Arckit* (2015) →09. With this toy you can build in many different dimensions. A base plate measures 25 × 25 × 5 mm.[30] Floors and roofs have holes; walls and windows have studs.[31] You can determine the scale yourself. If you picture your dream house, then the basic scale of 1:50 might be obvious. But if you want to build a complete city, then 1:500 is more suitable. In that case, a wall plate does not represent the height of a window or a few rows of bricks, but a complete façade. And a block does not equal a brick but a whole building. You can also choose no scale at all; *Arckit* calls that the 'Dreamer Scale'. All components are compatible; only their colour sometimes indicates a function: sets for younger children are usually more colourful, while those for hobby architects and budding designers are often white-grey, and stickers can give them an even more realistic appearance, as a step towards a real construction project.

30 The standard size of 25 × 25 mm makes the conversion between the metric and imperial systems fairly straightforward. At a scale of 1:48 they correspond with 1.2 × 1.2 m; at a scale of 1:50 that is 4 × 4 ft. The minimal difference between them is scarcely visible and *Arckit* is very compatible with model-making materials at 1:50.

31 Roof plates and roofing materials fit into the square sockets in the centre. That is useful for floors, terraces and top layers. The basic principles of *Arckit* are explained here: https://www.arckit.com/pages/getting-started (last consulted on 17 February 2022).

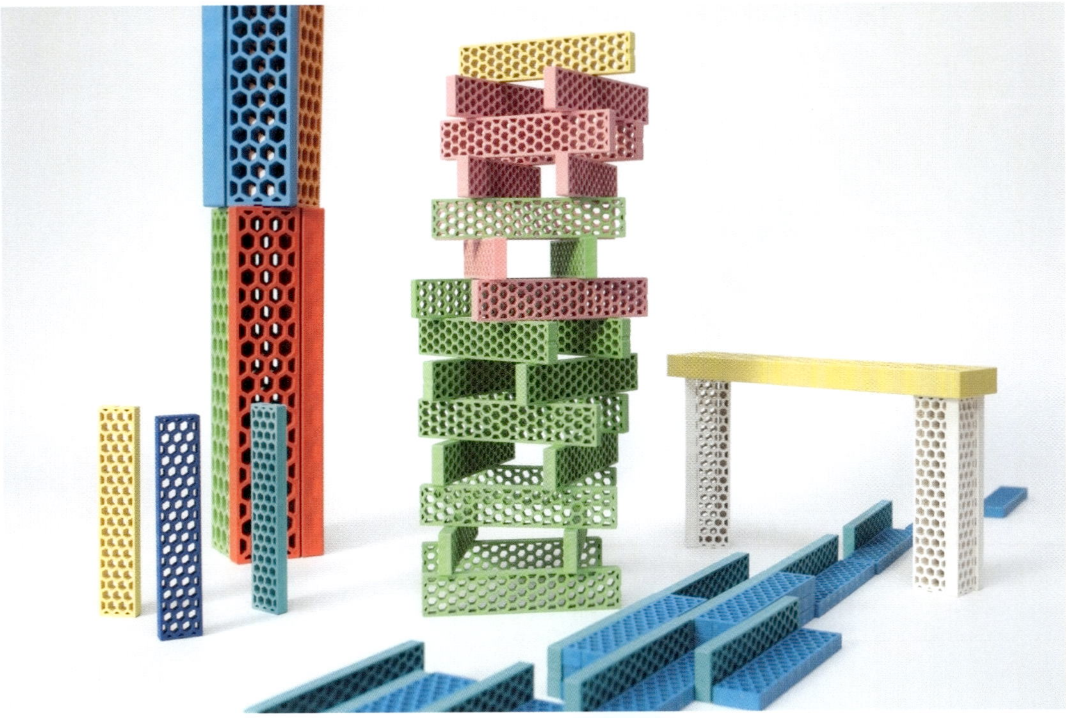

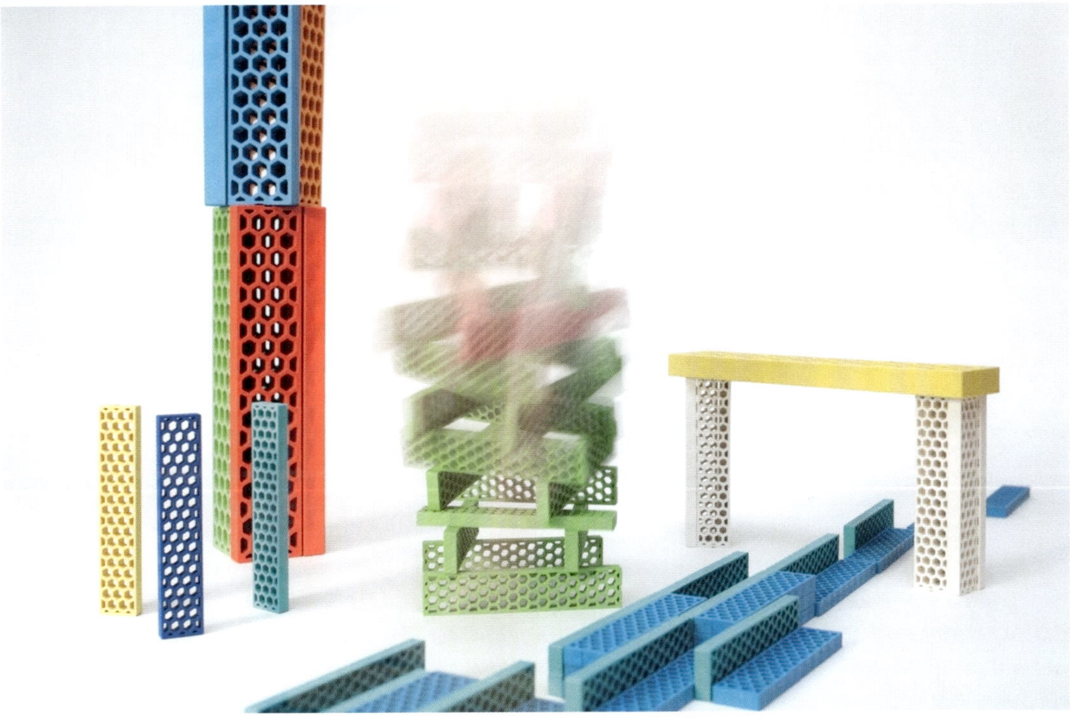

The flexible scale makes *Arckit* unique: hardly any other building system appeals to such a wide target group. It is halfway between a 'toy' and a 'tool'.[32] Now that it has existed for some time and the constructional aspects have crystalized, educational intentions 'beyond the components' are gaining in importance, for example through teaching kits for schools. *Arckit* not only stimulates creativity and collaboration but also provides a form of 'empowerment', and recent sets devote increasing attention to sustainability.[33] Moreover, *Arckit*, just like *Überstix* builds bridges to the digital realm. All components already exist in the 3D Warehouse of the drafting program SketchUp and for the professional design program Autodesk Revit. *Arckidigital*, the little digital brother of *Arckit*, is currently being expanded with *Arckit Infiniti 3D*, a web shop to order self-created *Arckit* components from the 3D printer.[34]

Better than Plastic, Cooler than Wood

Arckit prioritizes educational concepts, but sustainability has not yet influenced the choice of materials: only the ecological add-on sets are made of cardboard, while all other components are plastic. That is not the case with *Bioblo* (2014) →10, where material is the top priority. The makers proudly promote their building blocks thus: 'It's what's in it that makes us want it!' Entirely in line with contemporary preoccupations, the website describes in great detail what the blocks are made of: 55% natural raw materials, mostly woodchips from sustainable forestry, 42% recycled plastic, and 3% ecologically harmless colour pigments—a mixture called Lasal.[35] All components are '100% free of plasticizers, PVC, BPA and other harmful contents'. When the founders speak about *Bioblo*, the conversation usually concerns those components and the excellent balance between wood and plastic. For instance, it would be complicated and expensive to make the characteristic *Bioblo*-honeycomb structure from pure wood, but the Lasal granulates are suitable for all moulding machines and you can also use them to create complicated designs. Despite that process, the smell and feel of the blocks still recall wood; moreover, they are easy to wash and varnish is not needed, because the colour is processed into the material. In short, *Bioblo* is 'cooler than wood and better than plastic'.

Every era comes with new materials and varieties. *Bioblo* offers a possible answer to the question of what today's material is: in principle everything, as long as it is ecologically responsible.[36] A second answer could be: no material at all, because today almost everything is digital.

32 *Arckit* has its roots in Murtagh's own design practice. He tried to develop a modular construction system and needed models with flexible walls. After some attempts using magnets as connecting elements, he quickly switched to small protrusions for *Arckit*. Murtagh has a wide target group in mind, but he has also carefully considered limitations: '*Arckit* came out of an architect's mind, as a kind of working tool, but I see it not just for architects. It might not even be for architects proper, because there is so much use of the digital today—but it certainly is something for *inspiring* architects. It's for late teenagers and adults to enjoy as well, as well as self-builders. People see it in different lights'.

33 See for example: 'Greenscape Village' (5+ years), the 'Living Series' (7+ years) and 'Go Eco' (10+ years). The add-ons for sustainable building (wind turbines, solar panels, separated waste bins, bikes...) are all made of cardboard and are therefore separate from the construction itself. They are mostly intended to enhance the decor for short stories.

34 The page has already been prepared: https://www.arckit.com/pages/infiniti (last consulted on 17 February 2022).

35 Interview with Stefan Friedrich on 3 November 2021. Lasal is an invention of the Institute of Natural Materials Technology in Tulln an der Donau, which tries to replace plastics with natural materials. One of the three *Bioblo* founders is affiliated with that institute and came up with the idea of making toys out of Lasal. See also: https://bioblo.com/nl/pages/nachhaltigkeit (last consulted on 17 February 2022).

36 In 2015 *Bioblo* received the Green Product Award in the category 'Kids'. It is not the only initiative in that direction. *Pestas* building blocks also come with a detailed explanation of every ingredient: https://pestas.com/pages/produktinformation (last consulted on 17 February 2022). And in 2012 a Japanese company succeeded in making precise wooden reproductions of *Lego* and *Duplo* blocks: *Mokulock*. It is still a luxury product: one set of sixty blocks costs sixty euros. But they are excellent in terms of sustainability: they are made of trees that are only felled to provide other trees with space in which to grow and they contain absolutely no harmful substances. The producer offers an explanation of each of the six types of wood. The Japanese Bigleaf Magnolia combines 'dark green heartwood' with 'calm white sapwood'; birch surprises with its bright colour and soft forest scent; the surface of the Japanese Zelkova is 'hard and cool' but its scene is 'rich and sweet like an incense'. The German *FabBrix* blocks are slightly cheaper wooden *Lego* imitations, but without variations in colour. The German company Bena also produces *Lego*-like blocks, though not in compatible dimensions.

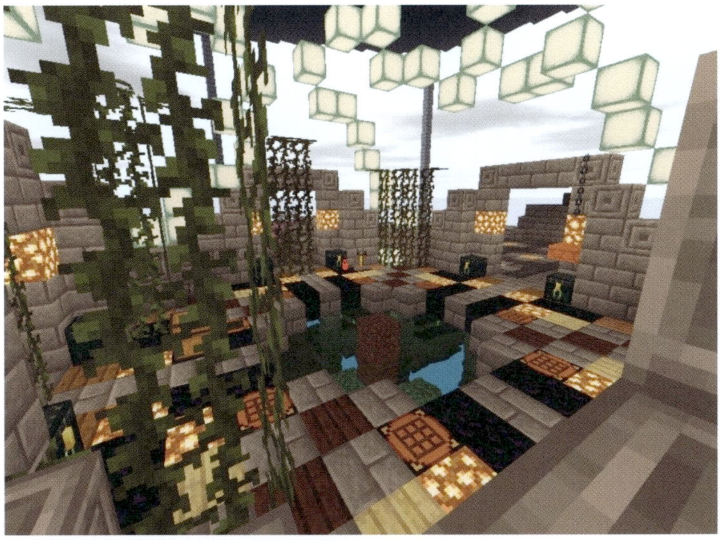

12

Blocks of Bytes

Terms such as 'building blocks' and 'construction toys' are rarely used for their digital counterparts: after all, you cannot hold bytes in your hand, and that makes quite a difference. But all other characteristics remain unchanged: the modular structure, the process of combining, demolishing and rearranging, the lack of rules and the open end, which stimulates creativity enormously. The term 'sandbox game' is commonly used in the digital world, and the best-known among them is *Minecraft* (2011) →11. For Colin Fanning and Rebecca Mir, it aligns almost seamlessly with its wooden and plastic predecessors.[37] Virtual wood is even one of the most important basic materials: players have to crush voxel trees[38] into planks in order to make sticks, doors and simple tools (2014:44). Fanning and Mir recognize in the makers of *Minecraft* the pedagogical passion of their predecessors, and they are convinced that: '*Minecraft*'s manifold play experiences, its ability to bridge generational gaps, and the increasingly widespread educational uses of the game [...] enable an intriguing reading of the game itself as a "good toy" that encourages creativity, rewards independent development, and evokes longstanding notions of productive play and its social benefits' (2014:40). Another fascinating similarity is that *Minecraft*, just like *Lego*, unites proven and 'responsible' game concepts with a medium that many educators mistrust: plastic for one, video gaming for the other: '*Minecraft* seems to counter contemporary anxieties censuring videogames as inherently antisocial or violent' (2014:53).[39]

Minecraft is the bestseller among the sandbox games, but definitely not the only one. Game developer Oskar Stålberg extends the digital possibilities even further with *Townscaper* (2020) →12. What distinguishes this game is that the blocks automatically become buildings. The grid that lends structure to the 'floor' is deliberately not orthogonal: it consists of quadrangles that are not squares, like a sheet of squared paper that has been stretched on various sides so that all lines are curved. Everything takes place on an endless water surface, on which

37 Almost twenty years before the appearance of *Minecraft*, Douglas Coupland wrote the epistolary novel *Microserfs* (1995), in which the leading characters develop *Oop!*: 'Object-oriented programming', or design software on the basis of blocks—a fictive *Minecraft* predecessor. Coupland later noted: 'Lego is very much like computers. Both are open-ended systems that do nothing on their own, but can become whatever it is you want to make them into. Both employ modules—bricks and beams in the case of Lego, and 1's and 0's in the case of computing. A Lego brick is either connected or it is not. A computer code uses either a one or a zero' (Coupland 2005:63).

38 A voxel is a three-dimensional pixel.

39 Fanning and Mir even suggest that *Lego* paved the way for *Minecraft*: 'LEGO's success has, in part, helped distribute the building block and construction toy conceit thoroughly in popular visual culture, setting an important precedent for *Minecraft*'s blending of new media and "old" toy concepts' (2014:49).

you click to position blocks. These never remain abstract, because the game immediately gives them a recognizable appearance. When you click once, an island appears. Click the adjacent space and the two boxes fuse to form a bigger island. If you continue along that line, you make a pier or a quay, to which the game automatically adds railings and steps. And if you click again on one of the same places, houses appear on the islands, which you can then extend in all directions: if you continue to click on the same spot, you get a tower as tall as you wish. The form of the roof changes as the building does. If you build an enclosure, the space in the middle automatically becomes a courtyard with trees and benches, with an occasional pigeon or seagull flying around. And if you connect various islands with one another, the lines become bridges and viaducts. You can determine the colour and level of detail for each block and alter the sunlight at any time—if it is night-time, lights appear inside all windows. And in case you miss something tangible, you can export your design as an OBJ file and make it appear out of the 3D printer with a few mouse clicks.

In *Townscraper*, everything revolves around creativity and fantasy: it is extremely easy to understand and players receive no assignments or feedback; they can simply do as they please without constraints. Only the style cannot be altered very much: that remains colourful and organic, unless you turn off the colours completely and make all façades of light-grey concrete. You will never come across desolate, dilapidated buildings or industrial ruins on disused sites: Everything looks neat and tidy here. If that gives you the creeps, then a better option would be *Cloud Gardens* (2020) →13 by Thomas van den Berg, a sandbox game of modern ruins set against a smog-like backdrop.[40] Such a landscape begins with heavy blocks of concrete, brickwork or rusty metal, which are left hanging in the mist. You can combine them with car wrecks, fragments of wall, containers, skeletons of towers and abandoned stations. Further embellishments include some broken fridges, dented suitcases, dumped computers and lost toys, and the picture of urban blight is complete. Oddly enough, it is neither ugly nor depressing; it exudes the same force of attraction as those places that inspire urban explorers to force their way through fences and barbed wire. Moreover, you can sow seeds for all sorts of plants, and the more rubbish lying around, the better they grow. While the dioramas created in *Cloud Gardens* have a somewhat timeless look, the growth of the plants, like the flexible blocks in *Townscaper*, is determined by algorithms that you could only dream about twenty years ago. The shells of buildings are overgrown with vegetation and flowers, and intertwined with that fearless nature, the remnants of bygone utopias form fascinating sculptures.

OUTLIERS IN THE WORLD OF CONSTRUCTION TOYS

What do we want to learn from the history of construction toys and how do we continue that development? Not only the maker of *Blockitecture*, but also the inventors of *Überstix*, *Arckit*, *Bioblo* and *Minecraft* have asked themselves that question. Their games build bridges between existing concepts and often add something contemporary to them: ecological awareness or an invitation into the digital realm, with 3D printing for example. The latter makes it possible not only to extend analogue construction toys with self-designed components, but also to 'carry over' creations from video games into the tangible world, as is the case with *Townscaper*. Hybrid games, with a foot in both worlds, also increasingly occur in other game genres.

40 You can play *Cloud Gardens* in two modes: 'campaign' or 'sandbox'. Van den Berg feared that the 'blank canvas' of a pure sandbox game would prove too 'intimidating' for some players. In the 'campaign mode' you learn all locations and options of the game through small assignments at over one hundred levels. This is an excellent stepping stone towards the sandbox, but you can also activate all options in the main menu and immediately enter the sandbox.

In terms of appearance, all these examples are relatively neutral—at least, they cannot be traced to any particular architectural style or type of building.[41] That is the case with other construction toys, however. The makers want to get their players not only to build but also to think. These are examples that fluctuate between games and art.

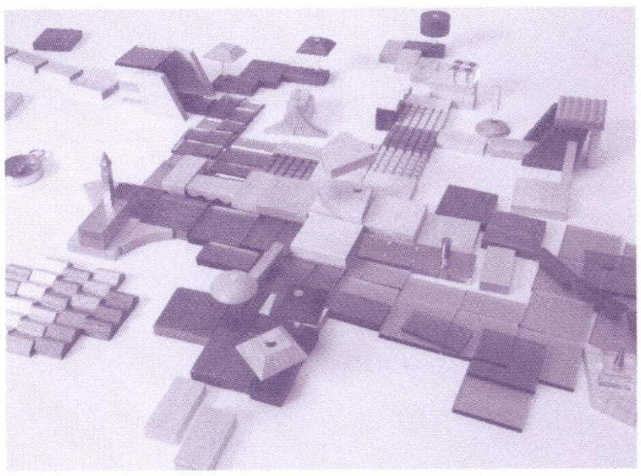

14→98–99

Against the Grain

At first glance, the *Capital Game* (1988) →14 by Maria Auböck, János Kárász and Axel Ott looks like a refined collector's item. The beautiful box contains almost two hundred blocks, plates, domes and pyramids in three different types of wood and acrylic, and the centre looks like a jewellery box. Contained inside it are five special pieces, one of which resembles a church and one an obelisk; the others are more abstract. The equally elegant instruction sheet is inviting: 'There are no rules. You play however you wish.' Or no: 'There are indeed rules. You determine them yourself.' Apart from that, just some general, informal ideas: you can use the three types of wood for housing, industry and leisure, the blue acrylic for water. The three other 'jewels' turn out to be an opera, airport and pagoda. Questions only arise on the second page: it contains the plans of eight cities: Sankt Pölten, Pompei, Paris, Szeged, Brasilia, Old Cracow, Bern and Peking. Why those? That only becomes clear when two of the three makers explain the genesis of the game. Sankt Pölten became the capital of the state of Lower Austria in 1986, but many people had difficulty getting used to that new status.[42] Three exhibitions in 1988 set out to change that, in part by showing how new capitals come into existence. Although also invited, the landscape architects Auböck and Kárász were initially somewhat sceptical: 'The new capital was such a pompous affair. Urban discussions were terribly solemn and cramped. Even though there was something remarkable and even humorous about suddenly establishing a new capital in the late twentieth century ...' So the two designers set about to 'go against the grain, open up the debate and propose an alternative model to rigid urban planning'. A game seemed like the right form for that: a sensory experience full of childlike curiosity and with a healthy helping of irony. The *Capital Game* became criticism packaged with a smile: Openly, by taking city planning away from the rigid urban designers and placing it in the hands of everybody at the games table in an exhibition setting. And more subtly, by placing Sankt Pölten between shining examples like Paris and Peking on the model sheet, by questioning the feasibility of urban design with Pompei and Brasilia, and by including Szeged, Kárász's provincial town of birth, in the line-up.[43]

Adorable Eyesores

If you come across the *Capital Game* by Auböck and Kárász outside the context of the original exhibition, you will not immediately recognize the critical message. In the more recent *Critical Blocks* (2012) →15, 16 by designer Maykel Roovers, there is no missing it. While the pieces resemble simple, recognizable buildings of natural wood from the toy shop, this is anything but an idyll. The set consists of a nuclear plant, a mega-farm and a huge block of flats, with motorways

41 *Bioblo* has flashy colours but that did not stop the makers from building a 2m60-tall Tower of Babel based on the 1563 painting by Pieter Bruegel the Elder. The *Bioblo* tower was on display in 2018 in a Pieter Bruegel retrospective at the Art History Museum in Vienna: https://bioblo.com/en/pages/inspiration (last consulted on 17 February 2022). *Arckit* clearly looks contemporary, but the abstract appearance leaves players relatively free in their designs. The website features models of the Taj Mahal (1648), Ludwig Mies van der Rohe's Farnsworth House (1951) and Tadao Ando's Church of the Light (1989). See: https://us.arckit.com/pages/architectural-buildings (last consulted on 17 February 2022).

42 In other words, Vienna and Lower Austria were separated. Auböck and Kárász explain that Lower Austria suffered from an inferiority complex since the state had been governed by Vienna for decades. For administrators and officials it was awkward: they were moving from offices in the imperial city centre into an as yet undefined new building. And the Viennese looked down derisively on their new small neighbour. (Interview with Maria Auböck and János Kárász on 20 October 2021.)

43 Around thirty copies of the toy were made. One of them is held in the collection of the CCA in Montreal. An enlarged version was also made for the exhibition, of which the CCA has ten blocks.

15

between them. You are immediately startled into reality. Is this a toy? Art? Model-making? Are the miniature colossuses innocent or indeed provocative?

Roovers wanted to investigate why his grandfather's model-making so thrilled him long ago. He completely failed to identify with recent sets: an 'idealistic, antiquated and romanticized image' of 'hilly landscapes, small artisanal companies, little farms, steam locomotives that puff past picturesque mountain villages'.[44] He went in search of the very opposite: buildings that embody socially sensitive subjects. His *Critical Blocks* also had to remain 'uncluttered, airy and accessible': he wanted contrasts, not provocations. That is why he left out superfluous details and his buildings became abstract icons of steamed beech wood, a very common material in toy blocks. With the surprising contrast between the innocent material and the 'harshness' of the buildings, Roovers wanted 'to shed light on the excessive nature of contemporary large scale architecture'. Japanese critics accused him of trivializing the nuclear disaster at Fukushima, but to him the *Critical Blocks* are value-free—they are primarily intended to make people think.[45]

16 →102–103

That is also what David Navarro and Martyna Sobecka want to provoke with *Blokoshka* (2016) →17 and *Panelki* (2019) →18. On his first visit to Poland, Navarro, a Spanish photographer and graphic designer, became fascinated by prefab blocks of flats in the former Eastern Bloc. After the disappearance of the Iron Curtain, these were at best ignored and often demolished or given a facelift with a cacophony of colour intended to counter 'the ugliness of grey'. But for Navarro the prefab blocks of flats were a discovery and a genuine piece of cultural heritage that deserved recognition. In 2012 he and Sobecka, united under the name Zupagrafika, began to release books and construction kits devoted to the controversial architecture.[46] *Blokoshka* and *Panelki* are two remarkable projects within that crop: no faithful reproductions of specific buildings but playful interpretations of *Plattenbauten* in general. The entertaining *Blokoshka* lies somewhere between a construction toy and the world-famous matryoshkas. The 'mother doll' is a Moskow *Plattenbau*, which contains an East Berlin specimen, which contains a

44 Artist Clemens Fürtler also dealt with this theme in his work *Turm zu Babel (Bildmaschine 08)* of 2018. Fürtler's tower consists of *Märklin* rails and houses, 'objects of petty bourgeois, lower middle class architecture and tackiness at a scale of 1:89, [...] all representing a "perfect world" and suburban romanticism, and embodying a contemporary variant of cultural standardisation'. Cited from: https://fuertler.jimdofree.com/turm-zu-babel-bildmaschine-08 (last consulted on 17 February 2022).

45 Roovers planned to commercialize *Critical Blocks* in a smaller size, but that has not happened to date.

46 The first was *Miasto Blok-How* (2012), about the architecture of the communist era in Poznán. Later construction kits covered not only prefab architecture in the former Eastern Bloc countries but also Brutalism in Paris or London, for example.

17

18

und Spielen |
Arwag Holding AG
BDN Fleissner & Partner
Bundesimmobiliengesellschaft m.b.H. Buwog Group
EGW Heimstätte Ges llschaft m.b.H. Eternit Österreich GmbH
Gesiba, Gemeinn. Siedlungs- & Bau AG Gewog – Neue Heimat
Grohe Ges.m.b.H.
iC Projektentwicklung
Immobilien Privatstiftung
Josko Fenster und Türen GmbH
Kallco Development GmbH
Kallinger Projekte GmbH
Mischek Bauträger Service GmbH
Neues Leben Gemeinn. Bau-, Wohn- und Siedlungsgen.
Österreichisches Siedlungswerk AG
Österreichische Volkswohnungswerk
Sozialbau AG
Strabag Real Estate GmbH
Vasko+Partner Ingenieure

Warsaw one, which contains a slightly smaller Prague version. The *Panelki* construction toy is part of a book of the same name about social housing in the former Eastern Bloc. At the back are 162 cut-out cardboard tiles, a floor plate and a roof: all to be used to imitate construction in prefab panels. The floor plate determines the form of the building and there is enough material for nine floors. Some tiles can only be used for corners or the bottom or top floor, but the rest can be combined in any way. The illustrations on the tiles are Navarro's interpretations of the WBS 70 prefabs from Berlin, the P-44 from Moscow, the W-70 from Warsaw, and the KT from Kiev. They are personalized with graffiti, lace curtains and colourful drapes, satellite dishes and air-conditioning units, as silent witnesses to the everyday life that some of these residential buildings accommodated for almost sixty years. The work of Zupagrafika does not amount to a political pamphlet; it is, instead, the understated observation of an outsider who assesses the merits of the prefab blocks of flats without judgement and shares his findings and wonderment. With *Panelki*, Navarro initiates a process of reconciliation with a past that still surrounds hundreds of millions of people every day.

Metropolitan Satires

Auböck and Kárász, Roovers and Zupagrafika have proposed eye-openers in the form of games, but they do not determine what their players are supposed to infer. The following two artworks are more explicit statements; they concern the darker sides of the metropolis. The first is only to look at (and listen to!), the second mainly to play with.

19 →106–107

Chris Burden's *Metropolis II* (2010) →19 booms into your ears. It is a room-sized kinetic sculpture of intertwined high-rises and motorways, along which over a thousand tiny cars race.[47] The buildings are made of *Lego*, *Erector*, *Meccano*, *Lincoln Logs*, *Haba* blocks and Charles Eames' *House of Cards*. Apart from the Eiffel Tower, none of them are existing designs. Instead, they are Burden's interpretations of metropolitan structures. They are more decor pieces than leading actors, because Burden's priority did not lie with the architecture itself, but with the noise disturbance and permanent stress in vast cities: 'I want to evoke the energy of a city, and the sound is a really important part of it. [...] It provides a tension, more than anything else'. Yet *Metropolis II* was not intended as a dystopia—nor even as a dismissal of car-oriented cities. On the contrary: 'The city of the future is that every car is going to be controlled [...] by Google, not by a driver. [...] My dream for the city of the future is that the cars go faster and be totally automated.'[48]

The architects Sandra Youkhana and Luke Caspar Pearson (You+Pea) are considerably less enthusiastic about the city in which they live and work. Their video game *London Developers Toolkit* (2015) →20 was prompted by incomprehension and frustration with the property market in London, of which they have made a complete satire. Comprising twenty-four different modules, it allows you to build three-part megalomaniac, phallic structures, caricatures of the tasteless skyscrapers erected by and for the superrich in global capitals, but then in a *Minecraft*-like voxel style. Some modules imitate existing buildings, others represent unbuilt projects, and others are purely fictive. The distinction is irrelevant, because dream and reality blend seamlessly in this insane world. Each tower is already gaudy enough, but 'the real horror comes from many of them together and how they don't

47 *Metropolis II* is 6.4 × 9.1 m in size, with a maximum height of 3 metres. Thirteen trains and five trolleys also run on miniature railways. The work is held by the Nicholas Berggruen Foundation and was loaned from 2012 to 2022 to Los Angeles County Museum of Art (LACMA), where it is on permanent exhibition. There are numerous good filmed documents of the functioning work, among them *Metropolis II (The Movie)* by Henry Joost and Ariel Schulman (2011): https://vimeo.com/87798784 (last consulted on 17 February 2022), and *Behind the Scenes of a Kinetic Sculpture: Metropolis II by Chris Burden* by Nandi Jordan (2019): https://vimeo.com/375197590 (last consulted on 17 February 2022). The maintenance and restoration team has written a thrilling report about the meticulous monitoring of the installation. See: Gilberg, Walker & Sandomeno (2018).

48 See: https://metropolismag.com/projects/chris-burden-recreates-mini-city-metropoli-ii (last consulted on 17 February 2022).

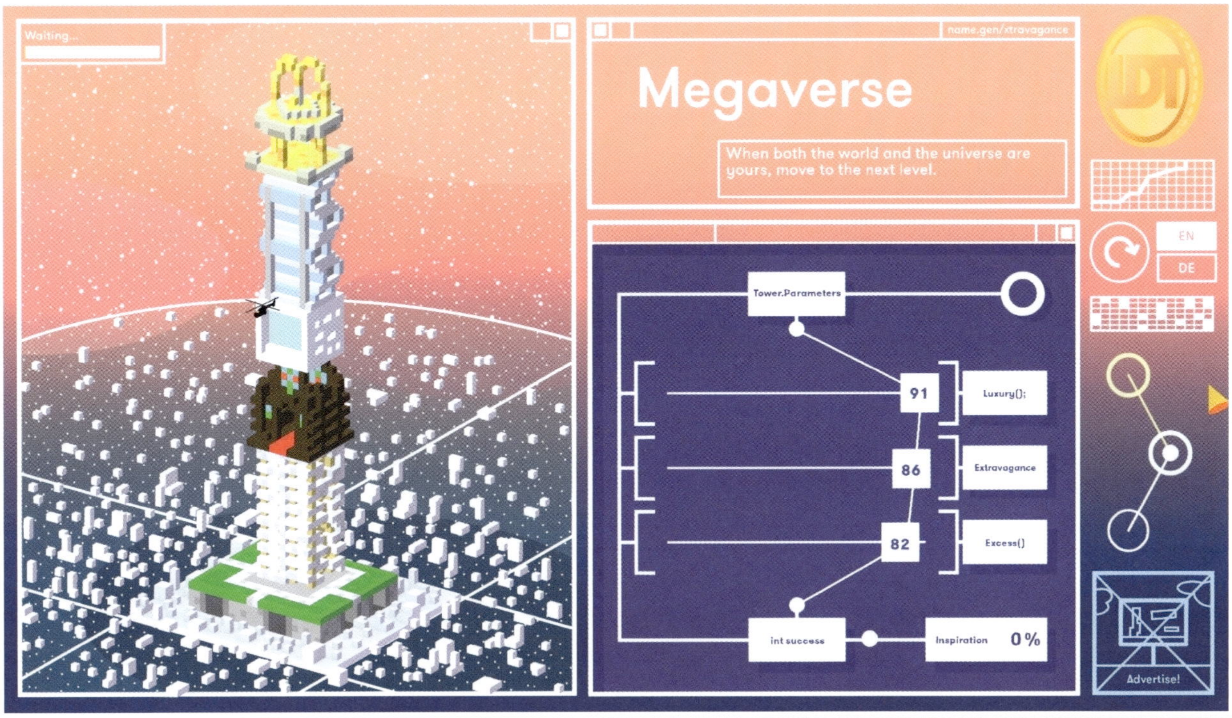
Waiting...
name.gen/xtravagance
Megaverse
When both the world and the universe are yours, move to the next level.
Tower.Parameters
91
Luxury();
86
Extravagance
82
Excess()
int success
Inspiration 0%
EN
DE
Advertise!

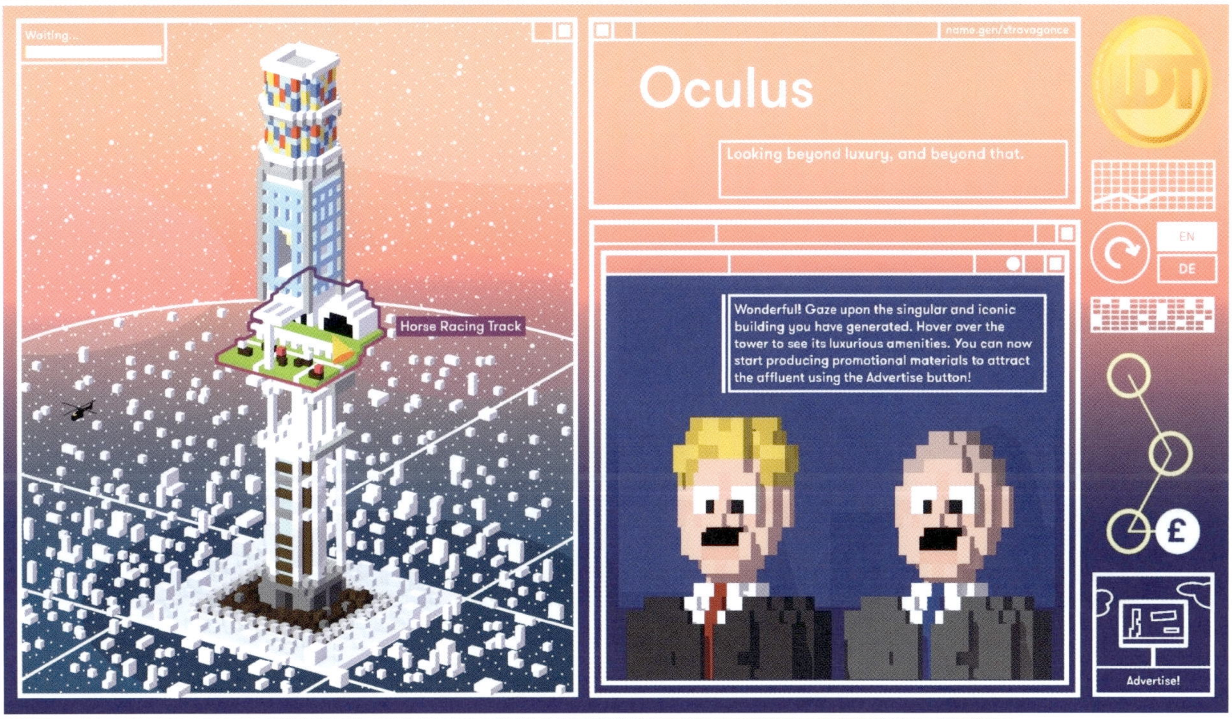
Waiting...
name.gen/xtravagance
Oculus
Looking beyond luxury, and beyond that.
Horse Racing Track
Wonderful! Gaze upon the singular and iconic building you have generated. Hover over the tower to see its luxurious amenities. You can now start producing promotional materials to attract the affluent using the Advertise button!
EN
DE
£
Advertise!

Oculus
Looking beyond luxury, and beyond that.
90% SOLD!
EN
DE
Atmosphere
Context
People
Effects
Render!

20

21

talk to one another at all'. The totems of big money not only change the skyline; they also affect the spirit of the city. But the *London Developers Toolkit* is more than a digital construction kit for luxury residential towers; the game also points up the complicity of some designers, whose slick plans and renderings continue to sustain the insanity. In the game you are one of them. If your proposal is approved for its 'luxury, extravagance and excess', you get to design a garish poster to promote your tower. As extras you can choose for 'Wealth Creators', 'Investment Sharks', 'Cold Brew Creatives' or 'Oligargh Chic' [sic], and the special effects vary from 'Money Rain' to '80s Thatcher Retro' or an unequivocal '90% Sold!'[49] Once finished, you can forward the poster to all sorts of social media or print it in postcard-size format. That is an important addition, according to You+Pea, because 'it blurs the line between a satirical game and a design tool; people are actually designing things using this game.' The designs themselves might be nonsense, but that extra step anchors the game in design practice and makes it less noncommittal.[50]

FROM TOY TO TOOL

Architects are often involved in the development of construction toys, and sometimes they look suspiciously like the toolkit they use for their designs. What can construction toys contribute to design practice?

One project exhibited all over the world that still attracts a lot of publicity is *Porous City* (2012) →21, by The Why Factory (think-tank and research wing of MVRDV) in collaboration with architecture office KRADS. It consists of 676 different white *Lego* towers measuring 68 × 68 × 400 mm at a scale of 1:1.000, which depict how a 'full' tower can gradually be made 'porous'.[51] How can you 'open' towers? The Why Factory presents 26 options in 26 steps: 'Some designs perform better in their facilitation of daylight, others in their provision of terraces. Some offer

49 For a teaser of the *London Developers Toolkit*, see: https://vimeo.com/247518431 (last consulted on 17 February 2022).

50 You+Pea are affiliated with the Bartlett School of Architecture, where they head the department of Videogame Urbanism. The *London Developers Toolkit* is just one of their projects in that area. A less satirical exhibition project was *Peep Pop City* (2018): https://www.youandpea.com/peep-pop-city. See also Pearson's personal website: https://www.alephograph.com (last consulted on 17 February 2022) and: Pearson 2019.

51 The project started as the *EuroHigh* design studio at the Faculty of Architecture at TU Delft in 2011–2012, which examined cultural aspects of high-rise development and 'the potential of porosity as a European approach to urban density'. See: https://thewhyfactory.com/project/porous-city and: https://www.mvrdv.nl/projects/179/porous-city-lego-towers (last consulted on 17 February 2022). It was first shown in the summer of 2012 in the exhibition *Opening the Tower* at TU Delft; it later travelled to various cities.

22

diversity and others continuity throughout the building. In fact, every design is driven by an intention' (Arpa, Maas & Ravon 2018:132). A second arrangement goes deeper into specific building typologies, such as 'The stair-maker', 'The cavity-maker' or 'The spiral-maker': sixteen towers of 50 × 50 × 250 cm at a scale of 1:100, with a fifty-fifty ratio between private and public space—a 'collection of recipes for porous towers' (2018:134).[52] The voxel structure of *Lego* lends itself excellently to research into porosity: the blocks form grids of 'closed' and 'open' pixels, or 'occupied' and 'empty' places in all possible ratios between private and public.[53] The abstract, binary arrangement makes the variations very easy to express in numbers, for example the balance between private and public, or their distribution within a tower.[54] But apart from that, the recognizability, accessibility and attractiveness of the world-famous blocks was also crucial for the spread of this project. In another style, such an abstract, fundamental study would not have attracted as much attention.

The power of *Lego* is also what appealed to Bjarke Ingels (BIG) when he presented a design for a multifunctional building in Copenhagen called *Lego Towers* (2006) →22, although he used no *Lego* at all for the design. The project began as a study of modular systems in architecture and an updating of functionalist principles.[55] Gradually, however, the dimensions of the most basic *Lego* block proved ideal for presenting the project at a scale of 1:500. An assistant translated the design into Lego Digital Designer, special software for *Lego* models. Within a few days a package of ready-to-use blocks arrived in the post, and by the end of the week the finished model was ready for presentation to the client.

52 What started as an experiment developed into a vision of the creation of architecture: 'Nearly organic, pixelated buildings can be imagined as living organisms, composing interconnected webs of prefabricated cells. [...] Buildings [...] become computational objects—an architecture driven by data and emerging from a set of spatial, social and environmental rules' (Arpa, Maas & Ravon 2018:78).

53 In the project description the towers are also described as 'three dimensional Nolli Maps of non-existent cities'. Cited from: https://thewhyfactory.com/output/opening-the-tower (last consulted on 17 February 2022). Nolli Maps are named after the architect Giambattista Nolli (1701–1756), who also coloured, on his city plans, the public space that was located within buildings. That generated a totally different pattern than on customary plans, which roughly distinguish between 'inside' and 'outside', or 'built' and 'unbuilt'.

54 The 676 towers were arranged in a 26-x-26 square: 'along the x-axis according to the percentage of their mass within a given envelope (10%-200%)' and along the y-axis 'according to the size of their "open pixel" surface'.

55 See: https://big.dk/#projects-lego (last consulted on 17 February 2022).

110

23

The photos went viral, and ever since Bjarke Ingels has increasingly been seen as 'the' *Lego* architect—in 2017 he even built the Lego House in Billund, the Mecca of the plastic blocks.

While BIG deployed *Lego* for a smart marketing strategy, The Why Factory went so far as to use it as an instrument for fundamental research. Can *Lego* and other construction toys also serve as tools in the design process? Architect Carlos Mourão Pereira sought an answer after blindness prevented him from continuing to work with the usual design instruments. He pointed to the ocular-centric nature of design practice and the importance of 'spatial knowledge beyond vision' (Pereira, Heitor & Heylighen 2017). *Lego* proved unsuitable as an enduring and intensive tool: there was too much 'haptic discomfort', and the 8 mm between the studs complicated the translation to other scales. But Pereira saw plenty of potential in construction toys as an alternative to text, diagrams and technical drawings in 'user-centred design and co-design working meetings'. So did the founders of *Block by Block*→23, when in 2012 they took the first steps towards what would be the most widespread application of a construction toy in design practice, under the motto: '[P]eople without design or architectural skills need easy ways to use tools to effectively describe their ideas and desires to professionals' (Lahoud (ed.) 2021:9).

Block by Block is an initiative from *Minecraft* developer Mojang and UN-Habitat, the housing programme of the United Nations. *Minecraft* is deployed in special workshops to support participatory construction projects in public space.[56] After less than ten years, there have already been 30,000 participants in 134 projects in 87 cities.[57] What explains that success? Just as BIG and MVRDV profited from the aura of *Lego*, *Block by Block* can also piggy-back on the triumph of *Minecraft*. That acts as a powerful magnate, especially for young fans: *Minecraft* 'brings people to the table'.[58] But apart from that, the game is also very easy to learn: even somebody who has never heard of it before can grasp the basics within a few hours. Particularly in the 'Global South', that is essential 'as one way of breaking down the digital divide and the skills gap, thus facilitating a more equal dialogue between experts and non-experts' (Lahoud (ed.) 2021:10). Before every workshop, *Block by Block* staff make a *Minecraft* model of the site that the session will examine so that participants can get to work straight away and visualize their proposals as quickly as possible with the simple blocks: '*Minecraft* simplifies everything to large blocks, so it forces you to think about your concept rather than worrying about its representation'. A decisive factor is that the game revolves around a lot of cooperation. Various participants can work on a model at the same time and everybody has an avatar, so while you are working you see what others are doing. That creates a very different feeling than with professional design programs, where multiple users can also work on the same file but they do not appear on the screen. A *Minecraft* avatar is about 1.8 m tall, so you experience the virtual environment more or less at human scale in that skin. That also makes orientation for non-professionals a good deal more concrete and easier than it is in the top-down perspective of CAD software. For the further detailing of a design, *Minecraft* with its lumpish blocks of roughly 1 m^3 is perhaps too limited, but in any case an architect will have to elaborate and implement the workshop results.[59] That has been accomplished successfully many times thus far.

56 UN-Habitat organizes the *Block by Block* workshops and hosts them with local partners. Mojang/Microsoft mostly provides technical and financial support.

57 Recurring focal points in *Block by Block* workshops are: sustainability (especially in highly polluted regions with little greenery), equality and justice (in particular, the health and safety of girls and women), inclusivity (especially mobility and accessibility for people with disabilities) and the care of refugees.

58 Interview with James Delaney on 25 October 2021.

59 *Block by Block* would probably reach its limits quickly at the scale of a complete city. That has never been attempted, but neither does it have the right scale for it. The *Block by Block* methodology is, however, ideally suited for 'individual public spaces' at neighbourhood level, such as squares, markets or playgrounds. The architect who implements the results of a workshop must be present early in the process to get a good sense of the wishes and priorities of the community and to interpret them. Prior to that, *Block by Block* arranges permits, financing and support from local authorities, for nothing is worse than raising expectations if they cannot be fulfilled. Participants continue to be involved in the realization as well, and follow-up sessions are held. UN-Habitat has outlined all steps of the *Block by Block* methodology in great detail in a manual: Lahoud (ed.) 2021.

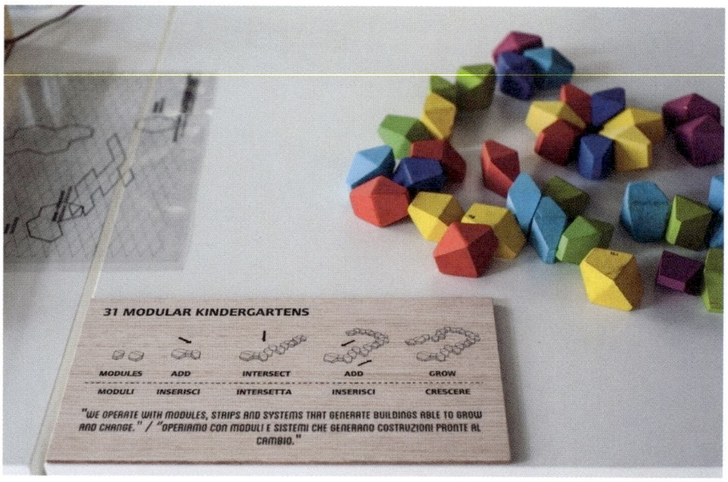

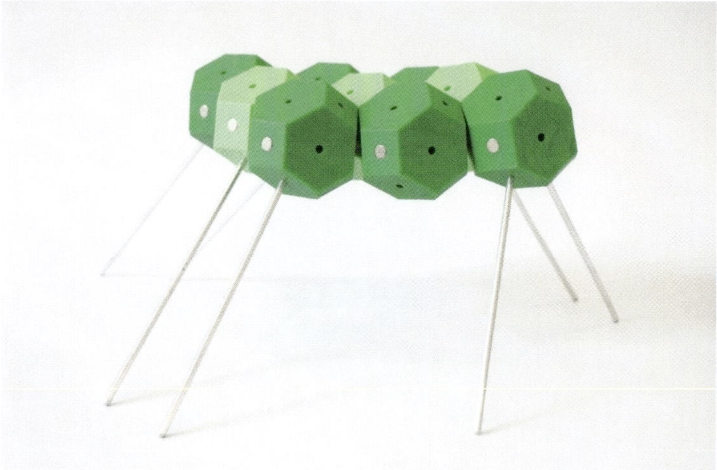

24

For example, *Block by Block* is the proud driving force behind Kosovo's first skate park in Pristina, multifunctional water-squares in the Kathmandu Valley, and vibrant meeting points with sports and games facilities in Lima.

Lego and *Minecraft* were not created for design practice but sometimes prove ideal. Are there also designers who come up with construction games of their own specially for their projects? Building blocks in all shapes and sizes are standard equipment at El Equipo Mazzanti, the office of Giancarlo Mazzanti in Bogotá, Colombia. They help in solving architectural problems, in explaining design principles and in involving users in projects. In 2017 Mazzanti made the exhibition *We Play, You Play* →24 for the Spazio FMG per l'Architettura in Milan, which perfectly illustrated how his architecture and games blend seamlessly with each other. That is because his projects are often composed of modules. They enable him to concentrate on the configuration, which he finds much more important than the styling: 'We think architecture is a matter practice; it has to connect, multiply, inspire rather than being images and meanings.'[60] And modular systems are sustainable, because they lend themselves excellently to later extensions. Sometimes Mazzanti himself is no longer even involved, but he does not regret that: he sees himself as somebody who provides 'the rules of the game' which people can then apply without supervision. The construction games help him to convey those rules. For him, the integration of games into his practice is a way of reviewing his role as a designer.[61]

Hans Venhuizen also defines himself as a planner largely through games, especially with *Parquette* (1991–2009) →25, which he has developed in stages. One

60 Interview with Giancarlo Mazzanti on 13 July 2021. See: https://www.spaziofmg.com/en/event/we-play-you-play-el-equipo-mazzanti (last consulted on 17 February 2022). The favourite module is the dodecahedron, which the office used for more than twenty schools and for the roof of the outdoor sports centre Forest of Hope in Soacha (Colombia). The toy version of that project consists of 16 modules of recycled polypropylene with tiny magnets on every surface and 30 connecting pieces (20 of polypropylene and 10 of metal). In the lead-up to a commercial version, Mazzanti made a prototype, one of the first specimens of which is held at the Centre Pompidou in Paris.

61 Mazzanti's work is reminiscent of that of the French architect Fabien Vienne (1925–2016) who, from the 1990s on, came up with one geometric construction toy after another. Vienne's toys were closely related to his architecture projects, but they only arose afterwards, at the end of his career, when he had already retired as an architect. See: Dousson 2020 and: https://www.citedelarchitecture.fr/fr/hors-les-murs/article/geometrie-par-le-jeu-les-inventions-de-fabien-vienne (last consulted on 17 February 2022).

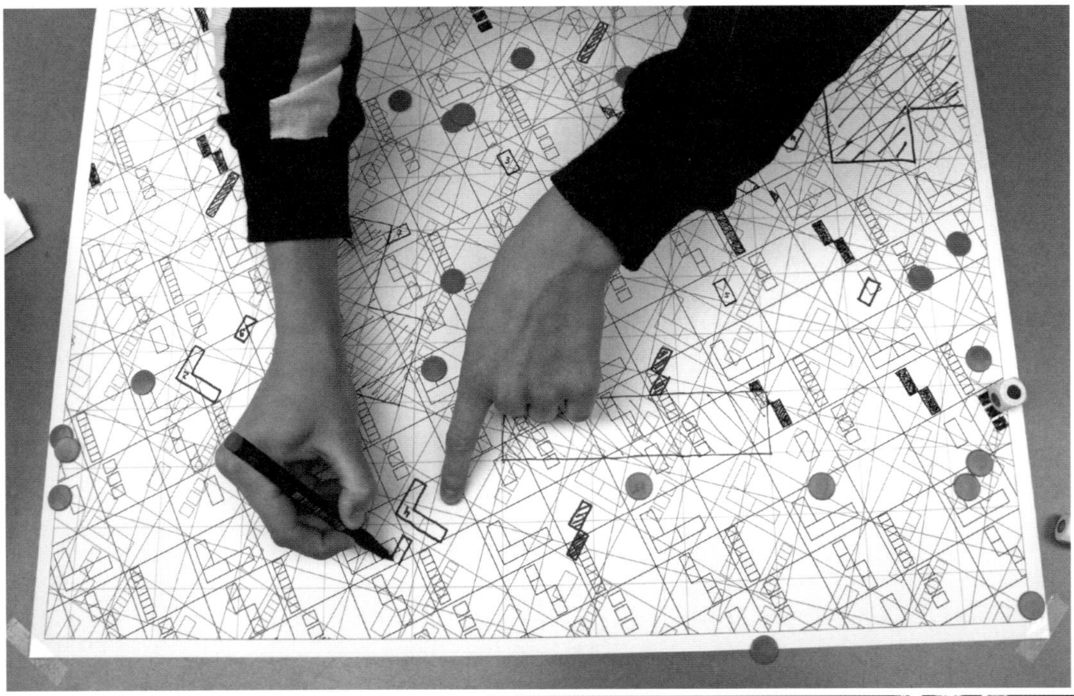

25

of the most remarkable episodes was the historical origin of the first *Parquette* playing field. It struck Venhuizen that the history and unique quality of a place were often ignored in planning processes. In some cases, such factors seem to be simply absent, for example in newly developed areas such as the Dutch IJsselmeer polders. But even if such an apparent tabula rasa proves alluring to some city developers, in reality it doesn't exist and it is certainly undesirable. With *Parquette*, Venhuizen criticizes this approach and promotes 'the positive side of conflict in urban-planning processes' (2010:120). Are history and social dynamism nowhere in evidence? Then we have to coax them out of the closet. The basis for Venhuizen's playing field is a simplified plan of a so-called ideal city in a 'low-context area': the type of situation that he often encountered in practice. Unconnected to any context, such a plan might seem ideal, but as soon as a number of parties become involved in it, their proposals will always differ from one another in some respect. And that is a good thing, too, because 'it is the very imperfection of the situation at hand that makes the design process that is now to commence special' (2010:120). Venhuizen therefore overlays a copy of the same plan on top of the first one, like the diagonal lines of a herringbone parquet. From that moment on, there are automatically conflicting interests: one party tries to realize the plan in this way, the next in that way—and nobody fully succeeds. The herringbone parquet is the basic principle of *Parquette*: it simulates time, chance and conflict, creating meaningful 'obstacles and limitations for an ideal plan devoid of context'.[62] The result is 'a chaos of fragments [...] of missed ideals—mixed up, kooky and damaged, but each in and of itself strong enough to survive' (2010:124, 120). To aggravate matters, Venhuizen then sawed the playing field in the first version of *Parquette* into strips and rearranged these modules into a new landscape.

Parquette is one of a kind: the material of the game embodies the problem that gave rise to it (ideal plans in an environment devoid of context) and is, at the same time, the instrument to counter it (a simulation of history and conflicting interests). The game is tailored for what Venhuizen wants to achieve with it: 'plans [...] able to adjust to constantly changing demands, as they were also once shaped by history during the design process, and had to demonstrate flexibility in the course of their development' (2010:68). And this is but the playing field—in later versions players also deal with detached homes and residential blocks to increase density in a plan area. However, more rules apply here: something that rarely occurs in construction toys but is distinctive for a genre of games discussed in the next chapter.

62 Interview with Hans Venhuizen on 21 July 2021.

C

THE DOS AND DON'TS OF THE PERFECT CITY

Choices and Ideologies in City Building Games

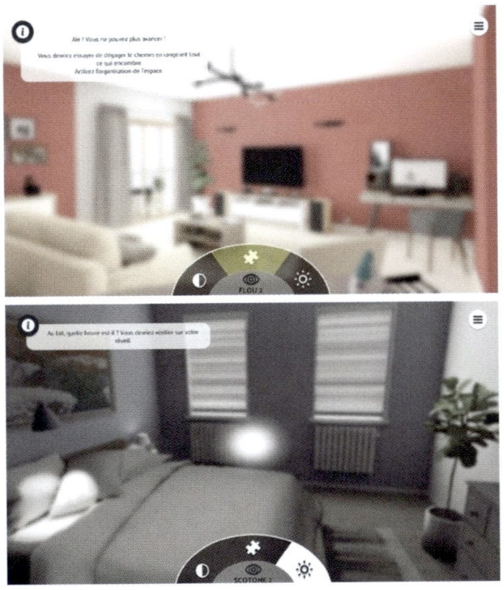

01

A game in which anything goes and no rules apply can be intimidating. That preoccupied game developer Thomas van den Berg when he was working on his sandbox game *Cloud Gardens* (2020). In order not to scare off players, he devised a second mode with over one hundred levels (or mini-games), which gradually increase their familiarity with various materials and actions. Casually nudged into creativity through these little experiments, players would hopefully manage to find their way to the sandbox. Developer Pierre-Alain Gagne also considers competitive elements and rewards as prerequisites for 'real' games. Even so, *Sensivise* (2020)→01, from his company DOWiNO, contains none; it is essentially a simulation of the problems faced by visually impaired people in their living environment—for example, reading the time with a scotoma, or finding things despite tunnel vision. The DOWiNO website lists *Sensivise* in the category 'serious games', but Gagne hesitates to call it a game: 'There is a challenge, but that is limited.'[1] Players can activate a magnifying glass or contrasting light, and then they have to cope on their own. That is exciting, but 'there are no levels, rewards, scores or competition', all those aspects that are so fundamental to tabletop games (board games and card games), which are the subject of this chapter.

Board games that deal with architecture and city development are often called 'city building games'. They offer a simplified, abstracted version of urban environments, in which players compete for the tallest towers, the most efficient or lucrative infrastructure, or the greenest residential areas. The key difference with doll's houses and construction toys is that rules frame the play behaviour. They determine what is allowed and what is not, under which conditions and for whom. Some choices or actions are rewarded, others punished. The winner is the player who is best at observing the rules or cleverest at dealing with them.

A game is a form of empowerment: players can grasp and control situations that remain inaccessible in normal life. At the same time, the developer also exerts a considerable influence on the course of the game through the material and rules, in which he embeds—consciously or not—messages and ideologies. How to decipher those? Can they also be sidestepped? Are they questionable manipulation techniques, or are they mostly deployed in meaningful ways?

THE ROOTS OF CITY BUILDING GAMES

Compared to doll's houses and construction toys, modern board games are a recent genre. Classics such as go and chess are centuries old, but the first 'Eurogames' and 'thematic games' (sometimes called 'Ameritrash') date from the second half of the twentieth century. It is a large and multifaceted world in which you can easily drown, but an entertaining chapter by Greg Costikyan in *Tabletop: Analog Game Design* (2011) offers some guidance.[2] Costikyan paints portraits of five types of player and how they view one another's preferences. 'Abstract strategy gamers' swear by no-nonsense, cerebral games like go or chess, in which nothing is left to chance. For them, a theme serves no purpose—that only distracts or conceals a bad game concept. A second group of 'board wargamers' views those classics as bland and meaningless: they prefer realistic simulations of real conflicts, including some measure of chance and good fortune. As long as a game is firmly anchored in reality, they gladly accept lengthy rules or somewhat shaky game mechanics. To 'Eurogamers', the degree of realism matters far less. They want, first and foremost, clear and accessible games that you win through tactical choices, but without the headaches caused by abstract classics, or the soured atmosphere that arises when simulated war turns into bickering. They like to be

1 Interview with Pierre-Alain Gagne on 4 November 2021.
2 Tabletop games can be either board games or card games. This chapter mostly discusses board games, but city building games also exist in the form of cards, for example *Machi Koro* (2012) by Masao Suganuma and *Sprawlopolis* (2018) by Steven Aramini, Danny Devine and Paul Kluka.

surprised, but chance may not determine the outcome of a game—strategy is what counts. The theme is of minor importance to them, or only relevant insofar as it makes the playing experience more enjoyable: it often remains relatively independent of the game mechanics, but strongly influences the design and style of the game figures. That is unthinkable for a fourth group, the 'Ameritrashers':[3] what matters most to them is the theme, and in a good game the mechanics align with it. If there is no cohesion between the two—or if the theme is even decorative—you are dealing with a superficial marketing strategy. For these players, chance and luck are not taboo, nor is conflict, as long as the latter is limited to negotiating, colluding, breaking promises and arguing. Finally, there are 'Beer-and-Pretzels Games' that Costikyan does not connect with any specific fans: such brief, simple, funny games appeal to a broad and motley group.

Besides the Blockbusters

Many of Costikyan's definitions crop up in *Eurogames: The Design, Culture and Play of Modern European Board Games* (2012), written by Stewart Woods, one of the few academic studies of the history of board games.[4] Woods begins with board games in general and gradually zooms in on the area that interests him. As far as 'classical games' go, one can no longer determine who devised them. They have been passed down over many centuries—some since antiquity—from generation to generation and have undergone steady change. More recent 'mass-market games' such as *Monopoly*, *Scrabble*, *Trivial Pursuit* and *Pictionary* are the blockbusters in the land of board games. They fly off the shelves year in and year out. To the general public they illustrate what a board game is and what you can expect.[5] Major game publishers like Hasbro and Mattel are not inclined to search for innovations outside that safe market. Woods' interest, therefore, largely centres on a third category of board game: the 'hobby games' from the mid-twentieth century on, within which he distinguishes a number of genres: 'wargames' since the 1950s, 'role-playing games' since the 1970s, 'collectible card games' since the 1990s, and most recently Eurogames, which are the subject of the rest of his book (2012:17–20). *(The Settlers of) Catan* (1995) by Klaus Teuber is often seen as the first full-fledged representative of that genre and a milestone in the history of modern board games, but there have been predecessors dating back to the 1960s.

In the 1970s and 1980s, it became clear that major manufacturers had neglected adults. Small publishers and shops compensated for that, especially in the United States and the United Kingdom, with an alternative range of innovative board games. Concepts shifted 'from lengthy two-player games towards multiplayer games with an emphasis on sociability and playability over simulation' (2012:45). Participants still competed and measured themselves against one another, but usually without direct confrontations: 'Players win or lose depending on *their own decisions*; combat in the game can be kept to a minimum' (Booth 2021:30). Those shifts found very fertile ground in Germany, and within a few decades the country acquired the status of 'acknowledged center of board game

3 The definitions 'Eurogame' and 'Ameritrash' suggest that those game genres appear on one continent or another, though that is not the case. Indeed, though many early representatives of Eurogames come from Germany, the roots of the genre lie in the America of the 1960s. To avoid misunderstandings, the term 'thematic game' is often used as an alternative to 'Ameritrash'.

4 Woods provides an overview of the publications that preceded his book (2012:7–10) and concludes that 'to date there are no substantial critical works that address the topic of modern board games, much less Eurogames' (2012:10). Indeed, most studies of popular culture ignore games, bemoans Mary Flanagan (2009:67). According to Vincent Berry (2021:4, 13) that omission still exists today, except for historical research into classical board games, with as platform the periodical *Board Games Studies* from 1998 to 2004 and the *Board Games Studies Journal*, founded in 2016. Paul Booth makes particular mention of the periodicals *Analog Games Studies* (founded in 2014) and *Games Studies* (since 2017) (2021:5), but he, too, notes that 'board games [...] are a remarkably understudied phenomenon' (2021:3).

5 Woods sees these games as modern classics, since they are now known to young and old, and 'the rules to these games have become a part of the Western cultural lexicon'. But unlike their predecessors, they owe that status largely to 'a combination of manufactured nostalgia and effective marketing' (2012:18).

02

design innovation worldwide' (Woods 2012:47).[6] That explains the term 'Eurogames', which evolved over the course of the 1990s into zero-conflict 'accessible games that privilege the role of mechanics over theme, [...] deemphasize the role of chance, offer predictable playing times, and are usually of a high standard in terms of component quality and presentation' (2012:79).

Today, a large and lively culture of fans and experts centres on contemporary board games. Academic researchers have perhaps a tendency to ignore them, but the game world itself contains plenty of expertise. An illustration of that is BoardGameGeek, an online platform launched in 2000. Covering tens of thousands of games, the database is an invaluable source for finding out anything at all about city building games, new or old.

Reconciliation between Theme and Mechanics

In many ways, the relationship between theme and game mechanics is crucial to players, developers and researchers alike, but it is also a constant cause of contention—concerning what is vital for a good game, or how best to analyse games. For 'narratologists', games are all about the theme and you have to think of them as a narrative medium. 'Ludologists' think that is nonsense: games are an autonomous medium with a dynamism all of their own. Numerous authors have undertaken attempts at reconciliation, among them Henry Jenkins, who contends that although not every game tells a story—some abstract games do not do that at all—that is no reason to throw out the baby with the bathwater. Sometimes, 'narrative elements might enter games at a more localized level' (2004:121), without the entire game immediately forming a coherent story. All the same, a game experience always consists of more than simply narrative aspects. And to the extent that games tell a story, they do not do that in the same way as other media (2004:119). Paul Booth also seeks a way out of the 'narratologists versus ludologists' debate: Games 'act like media texts by creating an

6 Avoiding direct conflict and socially sensitive themes aligned with coming to terms with the war legacy during the post-war reconstruction years in Germany. Military simulations, even in the form of games, would quickly balance on the edge of what was (legally) admissible. But the country also had a 'lengthy history of excellence in toy and game production' and an 'established cultural disposition towards gaming' (2012:61). Besides widespread media attention, starting in the 1970s and 1980s, leading institutions lent official credence to games as a form of cultural expression with broad support within society: for example, the *Spiel des Jahres* ('Game of the Year')—the Oscar in the world of board games—from 1978 on, and also the games fairs in Nuremberg (for professionals only, since 1950) and Essen (for everybody interested, since 1983), as well as the German Games Archive, established in 1985: a research and documentation institution that, like the Toy Museum, falls under the Nuremberg Municipal Museums.

03

alternate world for viewers/players to mindfully inhabit' (2021:8), but you should never lose sight of the recipients of those stories, because 'the rhetorical arguments that board games make are always tempered through the choices taken and not taken by players' (2021:11). Booth therefore combines both sides in a 'ludo-textual analysis'.

The relationship between game mechanics and game theme is also what distinguishes Eurogames from thematic games (or Ameritrash). Eurogames have efficient, well-balanced, entertaining mechanics: they unfold easily, are challenging, and also remain interesting while you wait for your turn and after being played numerous times. The theme is of secondary importance. The opposite is true when it comes to thematic games: first a theme, then suitable mechanics. Unfortunately, there is no comprehensive book on thematic games like that by Woods, who does not even mention them. Perhaps that is because he has in mind a sliding scale rather than two strict categories. Indeed, though the theme in Eurogames is usually general and rather superficial—because sensitive, socially critical or more complex issues would hinder the dynamics of the game—it nonetheless has added value: '[It] serves not only to make the game more readily understandable, but also provides the player with a role around which their actions within the game can be contextualized' (2012:105).

City building games occur in almost all modern board game genres. Sometimes, city development is overlaid as an inviting, familiar layer on a dynamic and balanced game concept, which could just as easily be about, say, vegetable cultivation or archaeological excavation—the link between game mechanics and theme is practically zero. But sometimes, extensive research has been carried out, and the structure of the game faithfully reflects reality. City development is a theme that lends itself to interpretation in such diverse ways that one can link it to almost all game mechanics. That has been done on numerous occasions since the 1970s.

Early City Building Games

Skyscraper (1937) →02, by Karl Smith, is the earliest dated city building game on BoardGameGeek.[7] Every player receives a simple plan of a neighbourhood, with sites on which you can place wooden houses, shops, churches and public buildings for a fee. Everybody plays a different role (Tax Receiver, Home Builder, Public Utilities or Insurance Agent) and receives income at various moments, depending on the buildings that he or she possesses. The winner is the first player to complete a skyscraper or place a building on each site within his or her Business District, Municipal District and Residential District. But just like in 'real' life, the best strategist also suffers setbacks: personal plans are thwarted by a cyclone, tornado or fire. The game principle of *Skyscraper* is fairly basic, but for its time it was very innovative for each player to receive their own game board and their own role. Players of city building games value that: what you build is yours.

Three years later, architect Charles Deaton made his first board game, *Gusher* (1940) →03, in which players compete against one another in a search for petroleum. In terms of theme, it is not a pure city building game, but the game board does show a landscape divided into plots, with farmsteads, a small lake, an airport and a railway track. It has an ingenious mechanism with a double floor, which generates a different starting situation every time: punched through the upper board are almost 150 openings that represent drilling locations. Searching for black gold, you insert a drilling tower into them.[8] Success is determined by wooden planks between the two layers, which are shaken around at the start and block different openings on each occasion. The form and contents of the game correspond nicely with each other, but this remarkable board would also be suitable for other themes and situations, creating a random pattern of 'yes' or 'no' in a landscape in a predetermined relationship.

04

Housing Drive (1948) →04 is, like the other two, a typical game from the pre-television era, with carefully designed packaging and high-quality material (wooden houses, coins with the logo of the manufacturer Pepys Games, and engraved metal dice featuring symbols in six different colours). The principle is fairly straightforward: You have to gather labour, material and power in order to realize property according to a building licence. That is almost impossible without at least some government subsidy. At the same time, you have to be frugal, because the game does not reward the biggest builder, but the one who uses the least subsidy per house. *Housing Drive* is a child of its times. Although it is not known if it was commissioned by the government, it is typical of the post-war reconstruction era in the United Kingdom, when the government did everything it could to generate public support for inevitable reforms.[9]

Starting in the early 1960s, European and American board games increasingly developed into the modern versions we know today. In 1962 the collaboration between a scientist (Olaf Helmer) and a game developer (Reuben Klamer) resulted in the city building game *Square Mile* →05, notable for the quality of its material and a pioneer in terms of complexity, depth and, especially, 'replayability'.[10] That last aspect is on account of the modular composition of the board,

7 Karl Smith (1895–1986) obtained in 1937 a patent for the game, which was marketed by Parker Brothers (the publishers of *Monopoly* since 1935). From 1925 on, this company regularly launched educational games for children and adults, on themes such as property, transport and current affairs. Smith was a publicity manager and cartographer, and occasionally he made a game—including, a year earlier, *The Little Colonel* for Selchow & Righter, which along with Parker Brothers and Milton Bradley made up the top three in the American board game industry.

8 See the YouTube review on The Dice Must Flow channel: https://www.youtube.com/watch?v=IFhgNM4YrB8 (last consulted on 7 May 2022).

9 *Housing Drive* was released in the same year as *Charley in New Town* (1948), the first in a seven-part series of educational cartoon films by John Halas and Joy Batchelor commissioned by the Central Office of Information. The film promotes the New Towns that were intended to reduce overpopulation in major cities after the war. An Austrian game with comparable intentions to *Housing Drive* is *Die klugen Staatsbürger* ('The clever citizens') (1956) by the educational Jungbrunnen Verlag publishing house. Here, too, the richest are eventually denied victory because—wholly in line with the fiercely socialist bias of the publisher—praise is reserved for whoever invests most in public institutions.

10 *Square Mile* appeared two years before *Acquire* (1964) by Sid Sackson, which Woods considers to be the starting point of the development of modern board games (2012:33–35).

05

a wonderfully illustrated landscape of 4×4 square plots. There are a total of 24 such squares, which means that the structure can vary. Moreover, in the first phase of the game the plots are randomly assigned their future function, which means that the industry, the school, the shopping centre and the church are distributed differently around the landscape. That also makes it interesting to play *Square Mile* multiple times.[11] Step by step, the 'modern age pioneers' transform the virgin landscape into a 'thriving community': they surround each plot with connecting routes, expand them with a more finely grained road network and finally place the miniature building that matches the designated function. The best player is the cleverest at juggling the buying and selling prices and making most profit. In that regard, *Square Mile* is more of an economics than a planning game, but through its variable combinations of three layers (landscape, zoning plan and road network with buildings), it simulates realistic city development. Such game mechanics lend themselves well to generating discussions and exploring different scenarios.

YOUNG AND TALKATIVE: MODERN CITY BUILDING GAMES

Board games have flourished continuously since the 1970s. They 'are becoming more ubiquitous, are taking up more leisure time, and are becoming more thematically complex and rich' (Booth 2021:7). Players—especially of what Woods calls 'hobby games'—form an active community. They test and discuss games in smaller groups and clubs and on social media and have 'a clear tendency to experiment with rulesets, expecting input into the kinds of games they wanted

11 See also: Orbanes 1989 and the review of the virtual Board Game Museum, a YouTube channel devoted to vintage board games: https://www.youtube.com/watch?v=Cy9XtTiXrEk (last consulted on 7 May 2022).

06

to play and experimenting with the form as a part of their involvement' (2012:30).[12] Unlike the previous chapters in this book, it would be strange to stick to a division between precursors and contemporary versions. The history of city building games is still young, and some early innovations from the 1970s or hits from the 1990s are a match for the latest arrivals. Certain themes or game mechanics run like a connecting thread through all those decades, without having lost any of their topicality or popularity.

Apparent Architecture: 3D Skyscrapers on Grids

The most eye-catching city building games feature a game board on which a skyline full of competing skyscrapers appears. The best-known of them is *Manhattan* (1994) →06 by Andreas Seyfarth, a typical Eurogame and winner of the internationally coveted *Spiel des Jahres*. The board contains six grids, each containing 3×3 squares. Each grid represents a metropolis on which players, each in their own colour, can build towers out of blocks. They can also continue to build each other's towers—whoever placed the final floor is the owner. It is a low-threshold, dynamic and appreciated game, with simple rules and a well-thought-out and balanced scoring system. But it has little to do with architecture: the game mechanics are independent of the theme. For example, you are only allowed to continue building another player's tower if that makes your portion of the construction at least as big as his. That encourages players to place blocks with lots of floors on

12 Some game reviewers have built up an international reputation on YouTube over the years; for example, in German-speaking countries Hunter & Cron (Johannes Jaeger and Jan Cronauer)—recently renamed Hunter & Friends—and in the United States there is The Dice Tower, headed by Tom Vasel.

07

08

smaller blocks, which would not be logical in the real construction world. And why do you get extra points if your towers in a particular city are in the majority, but not if they are distributed evenly across the entire area? Moreover, you might expect something different to happen on the Manhattan grid than on that of Sydney, Hong Kong or São Paulo, but the names of the cities are totally irrelevant, and are even omitted in the reissued game, where the grids float on colourful tropical islands in an ocean. Games of this kind have the advantage that they are highly appealing visually and that they incorporate the tangible and modular qualities of construction toys. The colour and size of the blocks indicate which moves are and are not allowed, and the aim is to combine them tactically, but in terms of contents the relationship with architecture and urban design is often negligible.[13] The game would still work if the modules were lumps of sugar to make sticks of candy.

Alex Cutler partly addresses that drawback in *Expancity* (2018) →07 by combining high-rise fever with 'tile placement': the towers are placed on a board composed of separate tiles, which is gradually extended. With each turn you first place a square site and after that a building block. Adjoining sites determine which place is suitable: they provide amenities for the users of the towers and influence the property prices. Parks are always good: they generate additional profit for both residential towers and companies. Education or healthcare is very positive for whoever lives beside them, and a police station or church offers a slight improvement, but for other amenities, the underlying idea is not always clear: shops are surprisingly irrelevant and cafés and sports facilities even quite frankly bad for the *Expancity* housing market. Companies benefit enormously from nearby shopping centres, but have to avoid hospitals and churches—why? Those illogical connections between game mechanics and theme make it difficult to play *Expancity* intuitively as a one-day planner: You cannot rely on your common sense or experience in the 'real' world, but you have to constantly check which

13 Both before and after the appearance of *Manhattan* there have been comparable games, with a gridded board for building skyscrapers. They include *Manhattan* (1986) by Karl-Heinz Koch, *Skyline* (1988) by Roland Siegers, *Hong Kong* by Reiner Knizia (1999), *Project Skyline* (2004) by Jung Je Ho, *Skyline of the World* (2005) by Hans van Tol, *Skyliners* (2015) by Gabriele Bubola, *Cloud City* (2020) and *Neoville* (2021) by Phil Walker-Harding. In other games the skyscrapers are built with dice, whose colours and/or values determine the construction sequence and permissible combinations; for example, *Skyline* (2012) by David Short and *Blueprints* (2013) by Yves Tourigny.

function yields what number of points for which type of tower. Even so, the game has a lot to offer and there are various strategies to win, not in the least through so-called 'contract cards'. They create links between the towers and reward specific constellations with bonus points. That encourages players not to focus blindly on individual buildings but to view the city at a macro-level too. The sometimes curious combinations provoke interesting discussions about the desirability of such urban policy and ensure a welcome light-hearted note: 'Second Communion' grants you bonus points if you own a building beside a church and a café; 'Exit through the Gift Shop' if you build a commercial tower beside a hospital; and 'Nosebleed Seating' if your residential tower stands next to a stadium.[14]

Miniatures with Meaning

In the mechanics of *Manhattan*-like games, building blocks mostly act as counters and markers. Other games feature principles with three-dimensional buildings or components, which relate more closely to architecture—for example *Megacity: Oceania* (2019) →08 by Jordan Draper and Michael Fox, a kind of construction toy in the form of a board game. Players receive construction assignments with various materials: glass, concrete and steel, symbolized by tiles of transparent, grey and black plastic in various forms. For example, they have to use a fixed number of components, reach a certain height or integrate a courtyard into their building. Progressively, Oceania emerges in the middle of the table: a water city of the early twenty-first century that aspires to solve the problems of 'overpopulation and rising sea levels'. The game components recall the design language of contemporary architecture and the emphasis is on creativity and dexterity, something unusual in board games. Theme, principle and appearance are more closely interwoven than in the *Manhattan*-like games, yet *Megacity: Oceania* is not a simulation: the actual complexity of metropolises and the environmental and population issues are not addressed.

Other games reflect reality more faithfully, among them *Big City* (1999) →09 by Franz-Benno Delonge. More than twenty years after its appearance, this classic among the city building games has lost none of its appeal.[15] A vibrant capital city made up of eight 'neighbourhood' cards, each comprising eight or nine plots, is created on the table, with a different urban plan every time. On these plots you can place not only houses and offices but also parks and 'special' buildings (department stores, post offices, banks, etc.). The more the merrier, and the bigger the better. As a smart entrepreneur you always take adjoining plots into account: greenery and public transport are good for extra points, but the arrival of a factory causes prices to plummet. Tactical thinking enables players to exert a lot of influence on development, and the numerous tiny buildings fire the imagination.[16] Where might Big City be located? The game is German in origin but the rigid grid, the little bungalows that yield more points if they are located on the edge of the city and the cultural offerings, limited to a maximum of three cinemas and three churches, call to mind American suburbia. At the same time, *Big City* is abstract enough to admit improvisation. With a little fantasy, the buildings could even be replaced by others, as long as their 'story' does not mess up the scoreboard.

14 Alex Cutler discusses the development of the game in an interview on: http://knowdirectionpodcast.com/2020/11/game-design-unboxed-001-expancity-with-alex-cutler (last consulted on 7 May 2022). *Zoned Out* (2020) by Keith Rentz appears to be heavily informed by *Expancity*, but is a watered-down version of the original.

15 In 2019, Mercury Games released a jubilee edition with somewhat bigger, updated buildings, a new graphic design and slightly adjusted rules.

16 In the early 1960s, *Square Mile* with its three-dimensional buildings of plastic was also a pioneer in this regard. In the Australian *Metropolis* (1976) by Maverick Marketing the function of the miniature buildings does not extend much further than their property value; their colour indicates who owns them. Another classic from those years is *Prize Property* (1974). Like *Square Mile*, it was released by Milton Bradley (name of the developer unknown) and has a high-quality illustrated double board: a landscape as top layer, which is removed to reveal sold plots. As its subtitle indicates, it is a *Land Development Game* about luxury property: ski condominiums and lodges, casinos, hotels, health spas, golf clubs and other sports venues. Money constantly plays a central role, as a result of which the focus is less on city development than on a *Monopoly*-like economic simulation. See a presentation by the online Board Game Museum at: https://www.youtube.com/watch?v=BUQv5Zi5F_8 (last consulted on 7 May 2022).

MIDTOWN 11
LINCOLN
MIDTOWN 14
WASHINGTON
LITTLEITALY 65
LITTLEITALY 61
ROCKY MOUNTAINS
AVENUE
LITTLEITALY 66
LITTLEITALY 62
EVERGLADES
EASTSIDE 79
FRONT
EASTSIDE 75
EASTSIDE 78
BOULEVARD
WALL
STREET
DOWNTOWN 26
PENNSYLVANIA
AVENUE
ROAD
ARIZONA
DOWNTOWN 25
OLDTOWN 52
BOULEVARD
WESTSIDE 85
MISSOURI
RIO GRANDE
QUEENS
NEW YORK
ROAD
AVENUE
BOULEVARD
WESTSIDE 83
CHINATOWN 46
CHINATOWN 42
STREET
LOS ANGELES
WESTSIDE 84
ROAD
SAN FRANCISCO
ROAD
AVENUE

10

11

12

Big City, just like the slightly older *Metropolis* (1984) →10 by Sid Sackson, is based on a framework of possible combinations between buildings, with an accompanying gain or loss of points. The game tells its story through that scoreboard. While powerful property developers pull all the strings in Big City, Metropolis looks more provincial with its pastel shades, the plentiful greenery and the river on the game board. The table indicates that houses and flats are more valuable if they are beside a park, and that shops, schools and houses benefit from being close to one another. It is best to build hospitals and department stores in the city centre, preferably without other development nearby. A factory belongs beside a river and is taboo near a school or hospital. It is all rather simplistic, but obvious, logical and accessible. And in Metropolis, any aggression is frowned upon; the aim is to 'build a habitable city and decent surroundings'. If a number of players have not enough land to build something bigger, they are even allowed to combine plots and share the profit with one another.

The landscape on the playing board, the connections between the various fields, the possible combinations between various functions and their positive or negative assessment with points: all these elements together are the building blocks with which *Big City* and *Metropolis* convey their message. More recent concepts are often more layered and abstract, in addition to which the assessment system no longer appears on a separate scoreboard but can be read from the game.

Layered Grids

Tile placement, like in *Expancity*, is very common in recent city building games. The mechanics align well with the theme of urban planning, since tiles affect one another just like the parts of a 'real' city. Three well-known and appreciated city building games based on that principle are *City Tycoon* (2011) by Hubert Bartos and Łukasz S. Kowal, *Sunrise City* (2012) by Isaias Vallejo, and *Quadropolis* (2016) →11 by François Gandon. All three have an appealing and accessible game dynamic that sustains interest, and architecture and city development are very much in evidence in terms of both visual language and presentation of the rules. But in terms of substance, the relationship with urban design remains remarkably

PALACE OF CULTURE AND SCIENCE
METRO
SIGISMUND'S COLUMN
WILANÓW PALACE
WATER FILTERS

13

HOTEL
SÄGEWERK
SCHATZAMT
DACHDECKEREI

14

superficial: the connections between cards have scarcely anything to do with reality. For example, while public services understandably score in *Quadropolis* if they are distributed evenly around the city, harbours must be arranged in rows for whatever reason, and what surrounds them is in both cases irrelevant. Buildings depend on one another because some of them generate the resources—inhabitants and energy—that others need. For instance, tower blocks generate inhabitants, which can be placed everywhere except in parks (!). Factories produce energy, which shops and tower blocks have to consume. Strangely enough, the factories and harbours themselves consume no energy at all. If you are left with a surplus, then parks function as rubbish dumps, because they 'absorb pollution'.[17]

The mechanics behind 'tile placement' are comparable to the tables from *Metropolis* and *Big City*: the combination of various buildings or their placement on certain sites is sometimes rewarded and sometimes punished. With each turn, players make choices on the basis of those rules. The more layered the game, the more options and the more comprehensive the consequences (extending deep into the following rounds of the game). The appearance of architecture and planning in tile placement games is more abstract than in *Big City* or *Metropolis* with their 3D buildings, and the efficiency of tiles with illustrated buildings generally allows for more dimensions and greater complexity. But if the game mechanics and theme are just tenuously connected to each other like in *Quadropolis*, discrepancies between the city in the game and its real counterparts are less apparent on abstract tiles. Take the example of the harbours: if they were 3D buildings, four in a row would look rather peculiar. And if the game encourages you to surround factories with shops and flats, 3D would make you frown more quickly. Games with a plan and three-dimensional miniatures are, in that regard, less forgiving if reality is distorted, or simply overlooked. But the latter is not the case in every tile placement game.

Suburbia (2012) →12 by Ted Alspach is a smash hit among city building games. As a big fan of *SimCity* (1989), the world famous urban design simulation video game by Will Wright, Alspach wanted to create a board game that would arouse similar enthusiasm: a game in which you are at the helm of a multifaceted organism, in which everything connects with everything else. In *Suburbia* every player develops their own city with the help of hexagonal tiles. That was crucial for Alspach, because each of the six edges facilitates possible interaction with the neighbours. Squares would have been too limited for the realism he had in mind. Each tile states what it must and can do and whether other tiles influence it positively or negatively; the game is crystal-clear in structure. What makes it so strong is that the connections between the various places stem very logically from the theme. They are expressed by three indicators: income, reputation and population size. For example, a freeway generates income if it is flanked by commercial areas, but it is bad for your reputation. A slaughterhouse or farm benefits from restaurants in any district (including those of fellow players), but a fancy restaurant makes a loss as soon as a second one opens, even if that is a fast food restaurant. Your reputation influences the population size with each turn—usually positively, because if people are happy, they attract newcomers. But conversely, a growing population also has a negative effect, because the city loses its valued, small-scale character. At certain stages of that trend, therefore, you have to return a reputation point.

17 In *Sunrise City* the relationship with city development is even more tenuous. While adjoining cards influence one another enormously, that is down to colour alone. They are nicely illustrated with buildings that align with the function symbolized by their colour (red for residential, blue for commercial, yellow for industrial, etc.), but in essence that is purely decorative. The same applies to the role cards, each of which depicts a character from the construction world (Architect, Tycoon, Zoning Commissioner, Lobbyist, etc.). Without that visual language the game would look very abstract, but it would still function well: the mechanics wouldn't be at risk. The theme is a bonus, and so it is in *City Tycoon*. In the instruction booklet for that game, a cigar-smoking magnate encourages players to think tactically and work hard. Illustrations of futuristic buildings and modern energy plants immerse you in a 'property atmosphere' awash with money. But here, too, everything visually supports the game mechanics, and those have hardly anything to with urban planning: *City Tycoon* is essentially a logical and economic game that demands a lot of strategizing to move sources as cheaply and profitably as possible from A to B.

The unique thing about *Suburbia* is that theme and mechanics go almost hand in hand: it succeeds excellently in simulating the multifaceted dynamics of city development.[18] While the theme here is derived from *SimCity*, other developers have devised a theme of their own and adapted or derived their game mechanics accordingly.

Ode to the Theme

Capital (2016) →13 by Filip Miłuński is a fine introduction to the built environment of Warsaw down the ages.[19] The game is structured around six historical periods starting in the late sixteenth century, when Warsaw became the capital of Poland. Each player builds their own city with the usual houses, industry and even culture, complemented with almost forty architectural icons. They are explained in the information booklet and lend *Capital* a distinctive, local appearance that corresponds with the progress of the game. The First and Second World War take place just before and just after the third period, and Miłuński has introduced a factor at those two moments that seldom appears in city building games: the destructive effect of war, by which first one tile, and later another two, must disappear from the urban landscape of each player.

Paul Sottosanti has in *Neom* (2018) →14 also incorporated negative events: not wars but disasters. Like *Capital*, it is a tile placement game with familiar mechanics and categories, but in each of the three acts ('generations') a special 'disaster tile' occurs to thwart other players. A flood, fire or 'crime spree' costs (a lot of) money or tiles, because destroyed buildings have to be rebuilt or removed. Not all lovers of city building games value such an extra dimension—after all, the genre is mostly associated with progress. But according to Sottosanti, all city development—including game versions—should take unpredictable events into account.[20] The 'disaster tiles' considerably strengthen the cohesion between game mechanics and theme: it is precisely those uncertainties that let a tile placement game flourish to the full. They make clear just how much all elements are intertwined and challenge players to anticipate, for example by not putting down too many vulnerable houses, or by providing protection with fire stations and police stations. Sottosanti has worked it out down to the details; for instance, 'crime spree' is the only disaster that has no effect on public buildings, because 'who's going to rob a government building or a power plant?' And fire is the only disaster by which not only building tiles, but also resource tiles can be swept from the board, because wood and oil can also catch fire. With its refined scenarios and multifaceted cards, *Neom* is less accessible than *Suburbia*, but an important step towards even more realistic simulations.

The graphic design of *Capital* and *Neom* is relatively pragmatic, but sometimes the theme leaves a very strong a mark on the appearance of a game. A case in point is the educational *Smog: The Air Pollution Game* (1970) →15 by Richard Rosen, in which players place houses and industry on a grid with tiny plastic pins. Factories are given ominous, dark-grey plumes of smoke of variable size that, depending on the wind, are carried far into one district or another, even

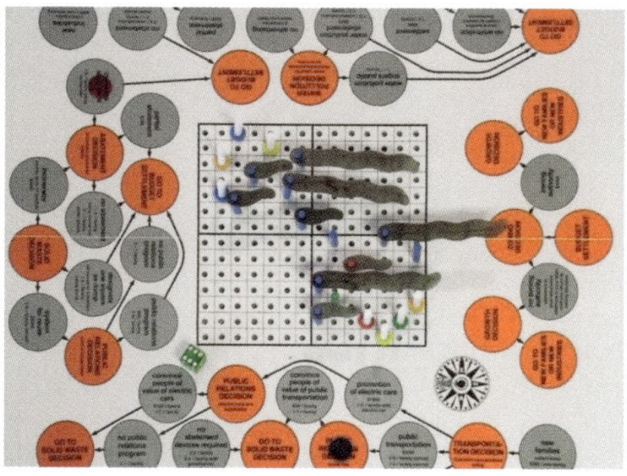

15

16 →134–135

18 Only the selection of buildings in each of the four categories (residential, industrial, commercial and civic) opens itself up to criticism. For example, in the first phase of play there are just two public buildings out of a total of 32—and they are mints. Culture has to make do until the end with two museums, complemented at most by two cinemas in the commercial sector. Hospitals and libraries are completely absent and, contrasting with the total lack of public transport, there are no fewer than six airports, two motorways, two car parks and two petrol stations. But it is not for nothing that the game is called 'Suburbia'.

19 In a much more superficial way, the simple, popular city building game *New York 1901* (2015) by Chénier La Salle can form an exciting introduction to New York architecture from the early twentieth century. The game mechanics involve a lot of juggling with the form logic of the tiles, but they are beautifully illustrated with the building style of the period.

20 Sottosanti's blog features an absorbing argument in favour of 'disaster tiles': https://interestingchoices.com/?p=1591 (last consulted on 7 May 2022). That prompted a lively discussion on BoardGameGeek among players about how those pictures could be taken from the game or adjusted: https://boardgamegeek.com/thread/2123908/houseruling-disasters-removing-their-destructive-nature (last consulted on 7 May 2022). Some players felt that they did not belong in a city building game at all, while others only regretted their excessive effect on the course of the game.

17

if there is little or no industry there. It is a very simple concept, which at a glance illustrates how directly, especially in an urban environment, everybody is confronted by the priorities and choices of others.

An equally spectacular game board that appeared more than a decade later is Frederic Vester's *Ökolopoly* (1983) →16: a detailed illustration of a city with all sorts of political, economic and ecological aspects connected to one another by lines. Revolving numbers are visible through twenty small windows: these are indicators for environmental pollution, population growth, political awareness, quality of life and so on. They can be operated with wheels on the edges of the board. As soon as you turn one, almost everything changes with it; the developer himself called it a 'paper computer' that simulates mutual influences, positive and negative developments in the short and long term.[21] The scoreboard and indicators on the tiles of other games have here become one with the board.

A contemporary game that is fully interwoven with its theme, and visually expresses that too, is *Bruxelles 1893* (2013) →17 by Étienne Espreman, about the heyday of Jugendstil in the Belgian capital. Every player is an architect: Victor Horta, Paul Hankar, Gustave Strauven, Paul Cauchie or Paul Saintenoy. To end up as the most illustrious designer, you have to balance between two boards: the 'Jugendstil board' and the 'Brussels board'. The first derives from the drafting tables of the times, with their sliding, perpendicular rulers, an essential instrument for architects back then.[22] A T-square limits the part on which you can realize your artistic ambitions: buy material (wood, stone or iron), use them to create new pieces of furniture or pieces of art, then sell them, or work on an iconic building. On the other board you are mostly networking: you show your face at a fair, at the

21 Frederic Vester also made computer versions of *Ökolopoly*, the first of them in 1985. *Ecopolicy: The Cybernetic Strategy Game* is available for contemporary Windows versions and is still used in workshops with school pupils and students.

22 Interview with Étienne Espreman on 15 December 2021.

vor
Sanierung
Sanierung
Produktion
Aufklärung
Lebensqualität
Vermehrungsrate
unkte
können verteilt
werden auf:
undenzähler
Vermehrun
Geburten, Sterbefälle,
Unfälle, Zu- und Abwande
Bitte malnehmen
nsfaktor

vor
Produktion
zurück
Lebensqualität
Gesundheit, Sicherheit,
sinnvolle Arbeit, Wohnqualität,
Naherholung, Freizeitangebot
13
12
11
10
zurück
vor

market, in the Jubilee Park… and make sure you leave a good impression on personalities such as Prince Albert, banker Georges Brugmann, entrepreneur and patron Édouard Empain or lawyer and politician Emile Vandervelde. The double game board guarantees a multifaceted play dynamic with lots of different options, and it is a striking reflection of the architecture scene of the time, personified by real figures. One half cannot exist without the other, and that ingenious game structure on two levels is an excellent way to convey the ambivalence that still confronts many architects today, forever searching for the right balance between artistic intention and provision of a service. That makes *Bruxelles 1893* a universal and timeless game, and to cap it all it is wonderfully illustrated by Alexandre Roche.[23]

18

Joining Forces

The relations not only between the various elements but also between the players are decisive for the course of a game. Which roles can they play? Do they have the same starting position or do they all have different skills? Are they diametrically opposed or can they maybe support one another? Among the early city building games there is one that stands out: *Our Town* (1978) →18 by Jim Deacove, with as subtitle: *The Co-operative Real Estate & City Planning Game*. Here, players complete not against one another but against the game. Sometimes—like in 'real' life—it can be useful to possess or control something together, for example a credit union, cooperative supermarket or public park. But collaboration is not easy: there is a lot of opposition from anonymous 'OBOCs' ('Owners Beyond Our Control') who seek monopolies. The only opportunity for the player collective to gain the upper hand is by remaining 'loyal, generous, entrepreneurial and far-sighted'.

Deacove was exceptionally early with *Our Town* and his many other cooperative games.[24] It was not until the twenty-first century that the genre found its way into the more commercial games industry, and even today it rarely occurs among city building games. In a competitive game, much revolves around secrecy: players conceal their cards and obfuscate their personal tactics as much as possible. That 'puts players on opposite sides of the board'. In a cooperative game, by contrast, there is 'a form of groupthink, where players work in sync to problem solve' and 'defeat a challenging system' (Booth 2021:32).[25]

19 →138–139

One of the bestsellers among the cooperative games is *Pandemic* (2008) by Matt Leacock. In terms of theme, the later version, *Pandemic: Rising Tide* (2017) →19, which Leacock made with Jeroen Doumen, is particularly relevant here. It concerns water management and landscape planning in the Netherlands: Players have to join forces to construct four hydraulic structures before the sea and rivers flood the country, a process they can temporarily slow down with dikes and pumps. The threat posed by the water is excellently simulated by the clear blue blocks: they constantly increase in number and the damage from regions badly affected spills over into neighbouring regions as soon as there is no dike separating them. Every now and then there are severe storms, causing sea levels to rise, dikes to burst and setting off chain reactions. The theme in this game is very tangible; the players are immersed in it and feel the stress of what the landscape does to inhabitants. As soon as they find ways to harmonize their special skills, things start to improve significantly. The pump operator has more flexibility in draining away water, the hydraulic engineer can build more dikes and the port master more ports. Everybody benefits from each other's work. The final goal is very clear: as soon as four hydraulic structures have been built, the country is

23 In 2019, Espreman made *Bruxelles 1897*, a slightly simplified card game version of *Bruxelles 1893*.

24 Since 1971, Jim Deacove and his company Family Pastimes have released more than one hundred cooperative games for all age categories. The slightly simpler precursor to *Our Town* was *Community: A Co-operative Game about Love & Peace* (1972). This was followed by games with comparable themes for younger children: *A Beautiful Place: A Co-operative Ecology Game* (1981) and *Home Builders: A Co-operative Building Game* (1997).

25 See also: Allen & Appelcline 2018 and the online platform Meeples Together, with essays on and reviews of cooperative games. An interesting side effect is that many cooperative games are also suitable for playing 'solo', because their mechanics don't require any competition between players: no matter what the number of participants is, the only opponent remains the game 'itself'.

20

protected and the game won. But if there are no cards left—if the players were not efficient enough—or if the water has caused so much damage that there are no blue blocks any more, then the whole team has lost the battle.[26]

Cooperative and competitive games differ greatly from one another in terms of goal and conclusion. For where lies the challenge if it no longer comes from facing opponents? That is very clear in *Rising Tide*, but in *Cities: Skylines* (2019) →20 by Rustan Håkansson it is less so—or at least different. In the latter game, the team of players realizes a sustainable city with a high quality of life, measured according to the satisfaction of residents.[27] If the money runs out, the happiness level becomes inadequate, or a player cannot make any move, then the game ends prematurely and the team has lost. Otherwise the balance is drawn up after the final milestone. If the team has less than 30 points, the result is ambiguous: the game is not lost, but the city is still 'unsuccessful'. From 0–10 it is a 'City of no importance', from 11–20 an 'Ambitious City [that] could become something', and from 21–30 a 'Busy City', where '[t]hings are starting to really get rolling'. Only above 30 can the team call itself 'successful', and even then there are gradations from 'Boom City' (41–50), via 'Grand City' (51–60) to 'Heavenly City' (61 or more), which '[c]itizens [...] wouldn't trade [...] for anywhere else in the world'. Such a conclusion is also known as 'cooperative scoring': the game ends with an assessment, which

26 A less well-known though equally successful cooperative game is *Flash Point: Fire Rescue* (2011) by Kevin Lanzing. It is thematically so convincing that you can almost play it intuitively as soon as you know a few basic rules—you can guess the rest. The game board shows the floor plan of a house, where fire has broken out. The players are firemen and firewomen tasked with saving residents from the flames. They can gain entry to closed rooms using their axe, but walls broken open do not contain any fire if the flames spread further, and if too many walls are lacking, the whole building collapses. It is not a pure architecture game, but it excellently conveys how the various parts of a house are connected and what the possible consequences are if something goes completely wrong.

27 Each new building or city district claims electricity, water supply and waste disposal, and if you provide them successfully, you make people happy. Environmental pollution, traffic congestion and crime also influence wellbeing. Unemployment should always remain close to zero, because either too many vacancies or too many job seekers put pressure on the city finances, and with no money you can do nothing as a developer.

LAND VAN HEUSDEN
N
W
O
Z
Oost-West
Thuis-Best
VOORNE-PUTTEN
HOEKSE WAARD
GOEREE-
OVERFLAKKEE
WEST-BRABANT
BEVELAND
DE ZOOM

(and resolve storms)
at all times
FRYSLÂN
KROMME
RIJN
UTRECHTSE
HEUVELRUG
VELUWE
LAND VAN
MAAS EN WAAL

the team can try to better in a following game or can use for comparison with others. That is very different to a 'cooperative victory' such as in *Pandemic*, where you either win or lose (Allen & Appelcline 2019:121–122).

So much freedom as in *Cities: Skylines* rarely occurs in a board game. The zones and buildings have various shapes that you can turn in all directions and their placement follows no strict rules. Moreover, players can fairly easily exchange their hand cards, which makes building projects flexible and each group can determine its own style. All that liberty does not come as a complete surprise, because the board game derives directly from the very successful 2015 video game of the same name, from developer Colossal Order. The translation was not straightforward, because there are big differences between city building board games and video games. The digital *Cities: Skylines* is a meticulous simulation: 'The computer simulates details down to an extreme level, with each inhabitant being born, going to school, finding a job, finding a place to live, having kids etc.'[28] All those minutiae give players the impression that their city is developing in a realistic way, but it is based on 'tiny random choices the computer does constantly for the inhabitants': an almost invisible simulation in the background, by refined algorithms. If you want something comparable in a board game, you run the risk that players are constantly busy with all sorts of cards, pawns and tiles to represent all those aspects. That is a disaster in terms of dynamics. Another main difference is that city building video games are often very open. Players do not receive tasks, the duration is not predetermined, and the conclusion is completely open-ended: 'You can play for hundreds of hours and set goals for yourself, yet the game does not end and tell you that you have won'. That is why the term 'sandbox' is often used, which would be nonsensical for a board game.[29] The commission given to Håkansson by board game publisher Kosmos, to turn the video game into a cooperative board game, was therefore not that straightforward at all. The result is a rather peculiar hybrid, trapped between two genres, and the question is whether it can appeal to players from both worlds. Gamers suddenly find themselves immersed in a simulation that they are accustomed to running silently in the background, while some board players will miss the well-oiled, perfectly attuned game mechanics and have the feeling that the spirit of the game eludes them.

THE UNFATHOMABILITY OF DIGITAL SIMULATIONS

In a board game there is no avoiding the message that the game is conveying: the scoreboard, the indicators and the points on the cards strike the eye immediately—they are the compass with which you navigate. In video games the underlying choices and ideas of developers are less visible: they are translated into algorithms, which steer the game in the background. The world-famous *SimCity* and *Cities: Skylines* appear perhaps like endless sandboxes in which 'everything' is possible, but developers have explored, orchestrated and incorporated into the game every probability in advance.[30] The more complex and

28 Board game developer Rustan Håkansson has explained the various phases of the process in 'Designer Diaries' on BoardGameGeek: https://boardgamegeek.com/thread/2279783/designer-diaries-index (last consulted on 7 May 2022). See: 'Designer Diary 1: Extremely detailed computer simulation'.

29 In some respects, digital city building games appear closer to analogue construction toys than to board games, but that comparison certainly does not apply everywhere: '[T]here is the crucial difference between the physicality of the first and the virtuality of the second. Whereas the first is more or less static, the second is dynamic and develops over space and time through a built-in feedback system. Whereas the first is a representation, a realistic mimicking, the second is a simulation that dynamically simulates not only the physical objects that make up cities but also the processes. Whereas the first might accommodate fantasy and role-playing when the construction process is finished, the second is focused almost exclusively on that very process of construction play' (Lauwaert 2007:199).

30 The original *SimCity* from 1989 is now also called *SimCity Classic*, to distinguish it from the 2013 *SimCity* (also known as *SimCity 2013*). *SimCity* and *Cities: Skylines* were the first two city building games in which every simulation resident is controlled separately. More and more city building video games have come on the market over the past fifteen years. Another popular example is *City Life* (2006) by the former software company Monte Cristo, which was followed by *Cities XL* (2009).

For its masters, the city was a matrix of financial abstractions.

Impossible prices drove old residents away and drained the ones who couldn't leave.

But in the craters left by the cyclical crisis, the Weird Folk settled.

The people gathered their power and used it to curb the swelling prices of their homes.

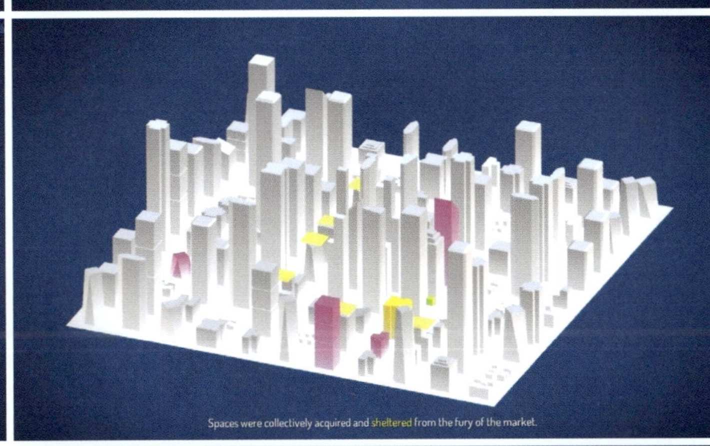

Spaces were collectively acquired and sheltered from the fury of the market.

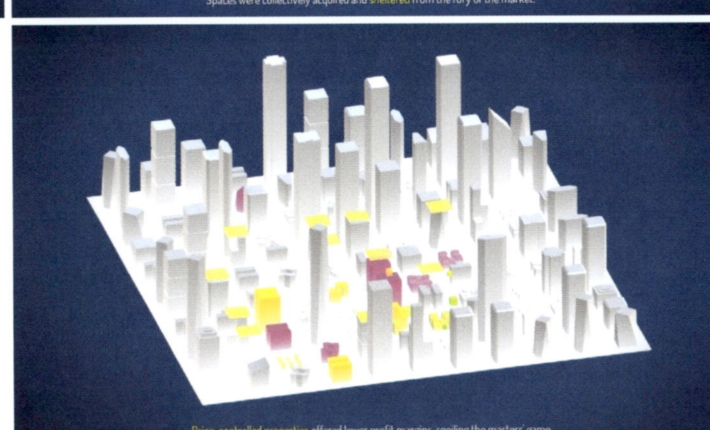

Price-controlled properties offered lower profit margins, spoiling the masters' game.

But their enduring resistance prevented the city from becoming their enemy.

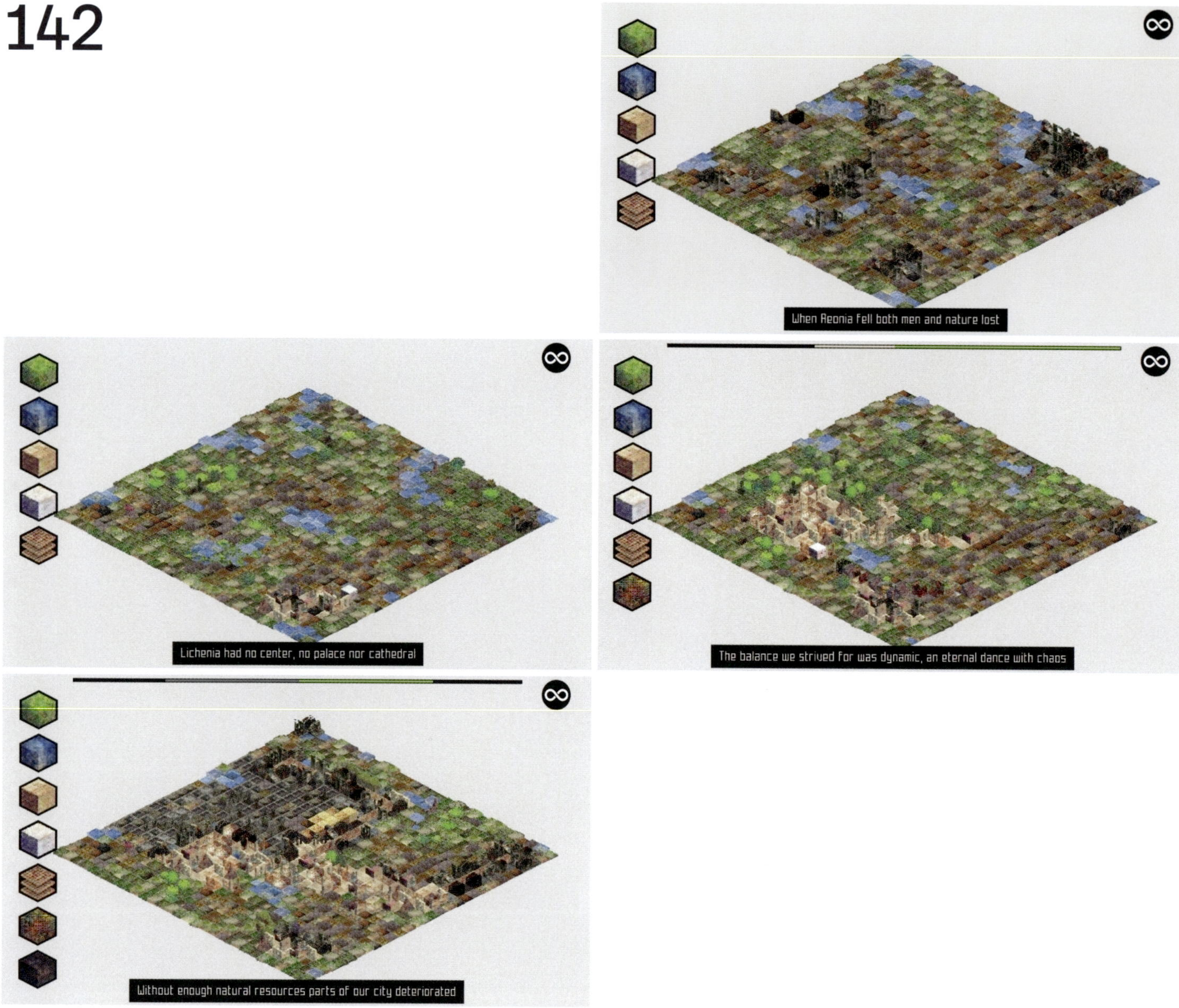

22

deep a simulation, the more unfathomable their choices. At the same time, virtual cities look increasingly 'real', reinforcing the impression that they imitate reality faithfully—in terms of substance too. That does not encourage one to verify the digital cogs of their black boxes. Moreover, 'most players have no formal training with which to identify and contextualize biases woven into the game mechanics' (Bereitschaft 2015:51).

Much has been written about the educational potential of *SimCity* and of its limiting ideology.[31] On the one hand, the game offers infinite possibilities: '[Y]ou can see your game evolve over time, there are wide-ranging environments to play in, more "pieces" to play with, more options, variations, and possible selections to make than when playing with a nondigital construction toy' (Lauwaert 2007:195). Digital city building games present a comprehensible picture of the complexity of urban structures and the mutual interdependence of their components. That helps in gaining insight into real city development and stimulates the problem-solving capacity of players. At the same time, critics worry whether digital city building games 'may communicate an incomplete and ideologically-biased view of urban systems, especially the nature of urban planning, politics, and power' (Bereitschaft 2021:6). Players govern like gods over their urban creations, from a top-down, technocratic perspective: '[N]ot only can they destroy an entire city and start over on a whim, they make their decisions in a virtual political vacuum

31 For a good overview of existing literature on the pedagogical potential of city building games, see: Bereitschaft 2021. For two complementary explanations of the criticism of *SimCity*, see: Bereitschaft 2015 and Lauwaert 2007 (or the later revised text: Lauwaert 2009:73–83). See also Pedercini 2019 for references to various internet sources on the same theme.

with no [...] democratic processes to contend with' and 'the only hard limits are finite space and financial resources (which may be overcome with a variety of cheat codes)' (Bereitschaft 2015:53).

A game session begins with a virgin landscape. Reward mechanisms and feedback stimulate economic expansion and population growth, preferably through high (and rising) property prices, limited crime (thanks to plenty of police) and low taxes (i.e. few collective amenities).[32] A city is composed of residential, industrial and commercial zones. 'Mixed use' means additional hassle; it is easier to let inhabitants commute by car between discrete, uniform zones to meet their daily needs. Other means of transport also exist, but you solve a traffic problem with a few mouse clicks by widening the road, so why make things difficult? The style of architecture, finally, is reduced to the greatest common denominator—in *Cities: Skylines* 'a kind of generic Euro-American contemporary blend [...] lacking the layers of history and heritage that enhance a city's unique sense of place' (2015:54). On balance, *SimCity* is not a 'boarderless playground' but rather a 'large playing canvas within a closed, rule-bound system', which allows for almost no latitude to play 'outside of the box' (Lauwaert 2007:209–210).

All colour and diversity is also erased from the 'sims', the simulation residents. City building games 'have altogether ignored the issue of race and ethnicity' (Bereitschaft 2015:56). Various artists have addressed these dubious social aspects. Matteo Bittanti, for example, who with his book *How to Get Rid of Homeless* (2015a) responded to the 'homeless scandal' after the launch of *SimCity 2013*. That version of the game featured a strikingly large number of homeless people—as yellow, anonymous silhouettes who carry around heavy black bags. Many players wondered whether it was because of a software malfunction, and internet forums quickly filled with speculation and solutions for the 'problem'. Some were suggestions to help the poor 'sims' find a job or a rental home, but there were also offensive comments and proposals to flatten parks occupied by homeless people. Bittanti compiled two volumes filled with countless unedited conversations between surprised, distraught and outraged players. He wrote an accompanying introduction, but he chose not to include it in the publication, and thus the two books became a 'literary game without instructions' (Bittanti 2015b:9), which deliberately raises all sorts of questions in the minds of readers.[33] In book format the casual, intangible, digital exchange of views acquires a different connotation: '[I]t attributes value and relevance to content normally deemed trivial and irrelevant' (2015b:11).[34] The posts become fascinating research material that provide immediate insight into how players deal with, view, and try to understand the simulation. They illustrate just how interwoven the game is with reality. Forums are the perfect place for 'the interplay between play and society, politics and entertainment'. They 'forcefully introduce—or, rather, *reintroduce*—a highly political vision that the alleged "neutral" algorithms were supposed to overcome' (2015b:1).[35]

Political facets are also a feature of the work of Paolo Pedercini, a critical enthusiast who has spent years studying the underlying messages of *SimCity*. In response to the opaqueness of contemporary city building games (and other video games), he made minimalist, abstract simulations that reveal and question

32 The feedback consists of virtual advisors, opinion polls, newspaper headlines, statistics, graphs and fluctuations in the number and behaviour of inhabitants (Lauwaert 2007:207).

33 Bittanti's work is often cited in texts about the socio-cultural background to *SimCity* and other city building games, but the most interesting explanation of it is his own text, on his site: https://mattscape.org/text-slideshow (last consulted on 7 May 2022).

34 The postings are a form of 'external gaming' (Lauwaert 2007:201–202): activities directly related to the game but taking place outside of it, for example in chatrooms or in program software for creating changes or extensions. External play allows for more variations than internal play, but it remains limited as long as a game is not open source (like *SimCity*).

35 Another project often cited in relation to *SimCity* criticism is *Magnasanti* (2014) by Vincent Ocasla. From 2006 to 2010 the artist-architect explored how far he could drive up the number of residents in *SimCity*. He achieved the best result by endlessly repeating the same pattern with optimal efficiency. It became a terrible city with scarcely any public amenities, lots of pollution and unemployment and a life expectancy of 50 years, yet the population remained at 6 million for 50,000 *SimCity* years.

certain dynamics one by one. *Nova Alea* (2016) →21, for example, deals with property speculation and gentrification. It is set in a city filled with white skyscrapers. The player is a speculator who acquires buildings cheaply and sells them expensively before the property bubble bursts. Resistance gradually emerges from 'below': protest groups demand rent control, social housing and anti-speculation measures. But the players, alias investors, have no choice but to cling to their position. *Nova Alea* makes clear that 'out of the box' thinking is not valued in city building games.

Pedercini's alternative games distinguish themselves from regular city building games not only through their simplicity but also through a clear story, in the style of Italo Calvino's *Invisible Cities* (1972): 'When Aeonia fell, both men and nature lost. The elders left, so it was our time to start over. We had to unlearn master plans and grow our cities like gardens [...] to reclaim the detritus of the old world. [...] Our city was born in the shell of the old one.' Thus begins *Lichenia* (2019) →22, a 'city building game for the Anthropocene' that zooms in on the tabula rasa with which almost all city building games begin, but which in reality does not exist. By contrast, in *Lichenia* you are immediately burdened with rubbish left behind by others: 'stalagmites of crystallized straws and stirrers', 'a monumental formation of memory foam mattresses', 'a meteorite of congealed baby diapers', etc. You try to clean up that junk with mysterious blocks, without fathoming their exact functioning, orienting yourself to a score line to balance green (nature) and beige (civilization). In the meantime, the landscape is developing and, as a player, you are 'in a constant state of fixing things'.[36] Pedercini knows perfectly well what he wants to achieve here: 'This is not a game that tries to be liked. You need to interrogate the object you're confronted with and compare it with your mental model of a city or nature. It forces you to approach systems in an ecological and holistic way.'

That bigger picture also preoccupies other authors and developers. McKenzie Wark notes astutely that in most city building games just one city is built. And even if the cities of multiple players grow side by side, 'there remains an outside', and that equates to 'somewhere to displace your problems' (2015:5). Jose Sanchez distances himself from such a NIMBY attitude. In his *Block'hood* (2015) →23 players cannot remain fixated on their own constructions. They have to become aware of the mutual interdependence of various elements and the ecological impact of their actions. In developing the game the architect was inspired by The Plant, an urban farming facility in Chicago that aims to achieve complete circularity: every form of waste created through a production process must be recycled elsewhere on the site. Sanchez translated that principle into a digital tile placement game. Every block (tile) in *Block'hood* is dependent on others, whether as suppliers of specific sources (input) or as recipients, and usually both. Even the tiny neighbourhood of the first challenge, *It's All about Water*, is a complete ecosystem, which becomes increasingly complex with every additional block: If you want to supply your neighbourhood with 250 water units, a 'Water Tower'-block can be an option, but it costs money. A 'Corner Store'-block can generate that, provided it is supplied with labor, electricity and, especially, enough consumers. Those people have to live somewhere, but even a 'Small Apartment' needs fresh air, electricity and 'leisure'... and also consumes some of the water. Fresh air and leisure come from trees, but they only grow if they receive groundwater... Over the course of the game almost 200 types of blocks appear, each with its own black box in which the production rate of input to output is determined. Besides water, money and electricity, those flows can consist of food, manpower, knowledge, pollution, animals, culture, etc. (almost 80 types in all). As soon as a block is surrounded by the right requirements, production can start. But should something be lacking, production will suffer and, in the worst case,

36 Interview with Paolo Pedercini on 2 October 2021. See also: Pedercini 2019.

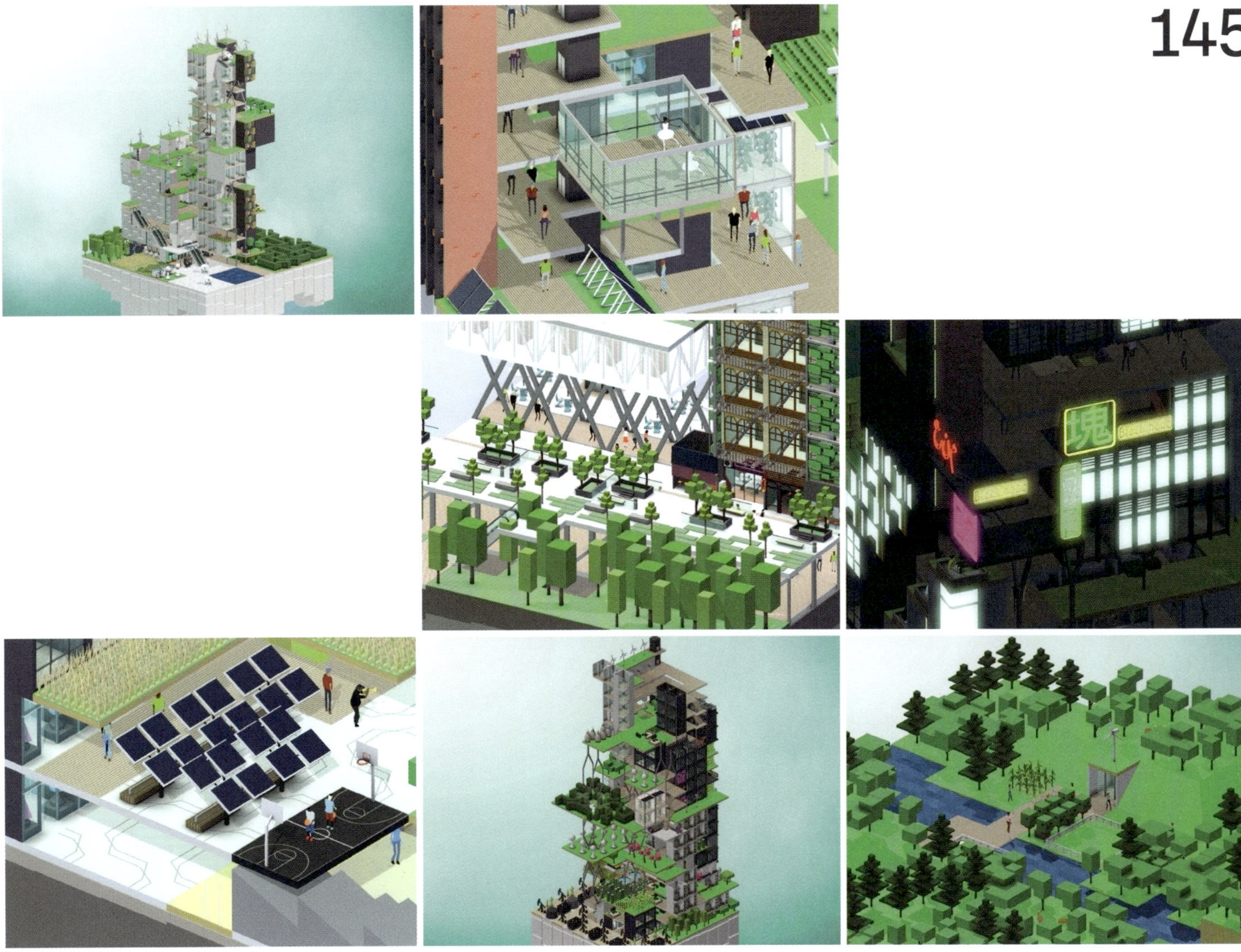

23

the block will acquire its 'decayed form'. The resilience factor determines how quickly that occurs, and the regeneration cost how much effort it requires to reverse the process.

Both in the challenge mode and in the sandbox mode of *Block'hood*, players aim for 'design patterns' of well-functioning combinations of blocks. The game is a research instrument: a toy and a tool at the same time. It does not prescribe one best way and it has an explicitly open source philosophy. Players share results with one another and can even create their own blocks or resources with a wizard (Sanchez 2015:95). In customary design software a design can only be evaluated afterwards, but *Block'hood* gives players information throughout the construction process. That makes them directly responsible for their choices: '[P]layers realise that every action in the game has a consequence, and that blocks will eventually die if they do not meet their required ecological dependencies' (Sanchez 2016:51).[37] Sanchez sees in this a possible future for the design disciplines, in which designers have to redefine their role: 'a new kind of distributed urbanism based on participation and emergence, [...] a dialogue across a city that consistently grows and is developed in spite of architects' (2016:51).

Sanchez and Bittanti both address social issues: the work of Bittanti focuses attention on the residents of simulation games, 'the figure of the human within the algorithm' (McKenzie Wark 2015:4). Who are they? What happens to them? How do they relate to their 'real' alter egos? What are the connections between those two worlds? Sanchez highlights social aspects by appealing explicitly to the personal responsibility of players.

37 Jose Sanchez founded in 2011 the design office The Plethora Project, 'to accelerate computational literacy in the frame of Architecture and Design' (cited from https://www.plethora-project.com, last consulted on 7 May 2022). In the early years he concentrated mostly on education and research, but design and software development gradually gained in importance. In 2022 he releases *Common'hood*, his second video game.

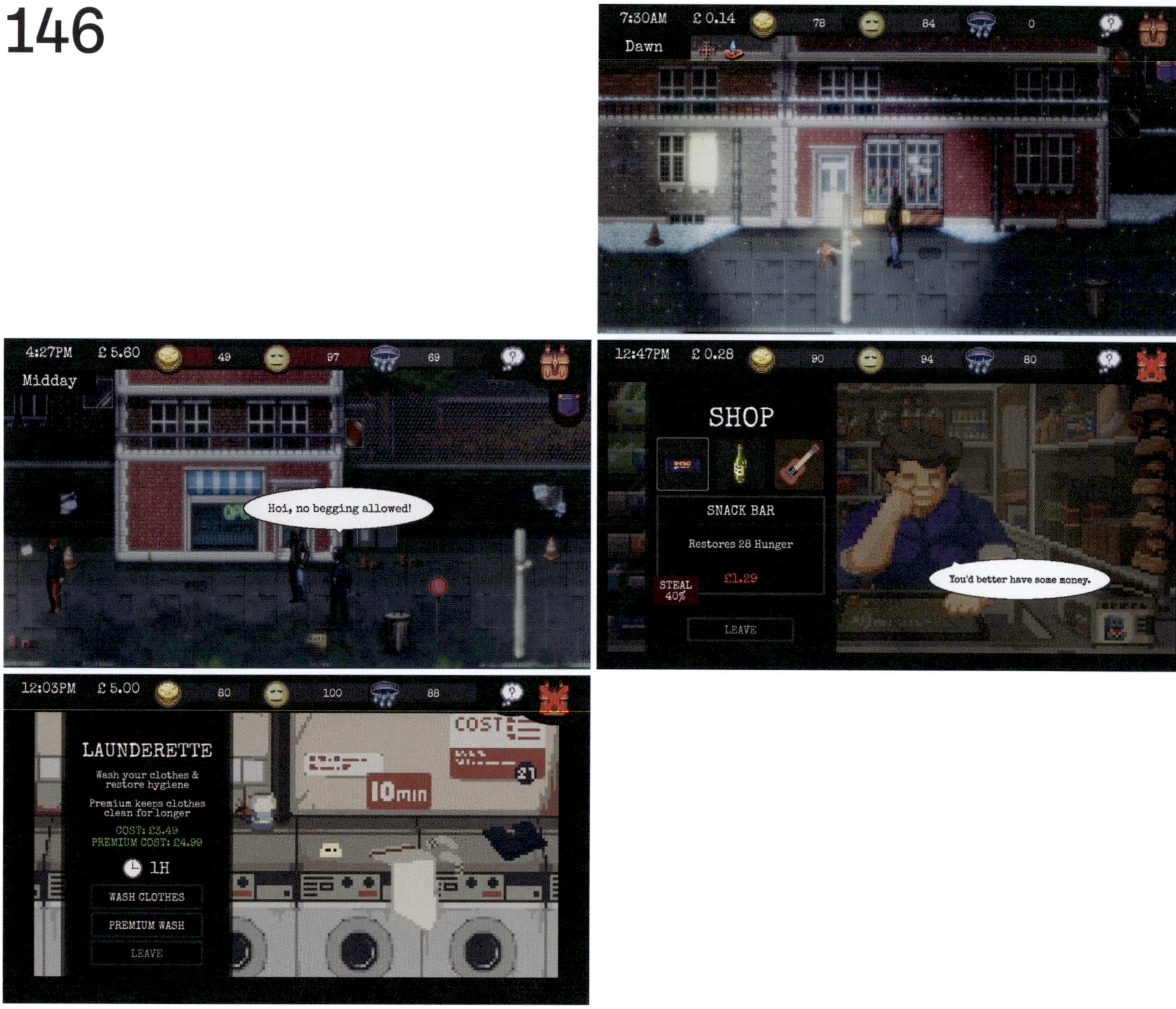

24

PLAYING TO MAKE A DIFFERENCE

City building games are usually rather impersonal. The figures are 'flat characters', and subjective approaches rarely occur. According to Bittanti, the homeless in *SimCity*, with their anonymous forms, are perhaps 'one [of] the most life-like aspects of the game' (2015:3). By contrast, other games centre on personal experiences and narratives, especially in socio-critical 'games for change'. Sometimes referred to as 'serious games', they 'are not necessarily meant to be fun, though fun may be a side effect, and are rather meant to make people think' (Flanagan 2009:249). Players are usually knocked off their all-powerful thrones and thrust into an uncomfortable, uncertain position: a war, a threatening environmental catastrophe, a homeless existence.[38] Jesper Juul writes about that vulnerability in game format in *The Art of Failure*. Although he focuses on video games, analogue games also have that potential to a certain extent: '[F]ailure has the double function of creating in us a feeling of being flawed and forcing us to

38 The online platform Games for Change specializes in 'impact-focused games and immersive experiences'. It organizes an annual festival and supports young makers in particular in the area of knowledge sharing and professional networking. The impact of environmental issues on the (built) environment is a recurring theme, for example in *Stop Disasters* (2007) by Playerthree, *SimCityEDU: Pollution Challenge!* (2014) by GlassLab (discontinued in 2018) and *Plasticity* (2019) by Plasticity Games. Also on this theme, 2022 sees the release of *Terra Nil* from Free Lives and Devolver Digital, a 'reverse city builder about ecosystem reconstruction'. Another theme that surfaces repeatedly in Games for Change is the personal perception of the (built) environment through the filter of a specific limitation, such as post-traumatic disorder (*Nevermind* (2015) by Flying Mollusk), depression (*Please Knock on My Door* (2017) by Levall Games) or loneliness (*Mosaic* (2019) by Krillbite Studio). The celebrated *This War of Mine* (2014) by Michał Drozdowski and Przemysław Marszał is about daily life (and survival) in a city during a war. Like *Cities: Skylines* it has also been translated into an eponymous cooperative board game, in 2017 by Michał Oracz and Jakub Wiśniewski.

reconsider our strategies in order to escape that feeling. [...] [It] connects us personally to the events in the game; it proves that *we matter*, that the world does not simply continue regardless of our actions' (2013:116, 122).[39]

Ghetto (1967) by Dove Toll is an early example of this: a board game to make the better-off aware of the problems of residents with very low incomes in American city centres. For example, you are given the profile of a single mother on social security with six children, and you have to survive in a simulated deprived neighbourhood. The structure of the game is rather didactic (with a 'Coordinator's Manual' for use in schools), but it promises unforgettable experiences—'What does it feel like to live in a slum?'—and insight into complicated issues: 'Some slum neighbourhoods improve. Others deteriorate. Why?' More than half a century later, that theme is as topical as ever, as demonstrated in *Taudis-Poly* (2019) by Fathi Bouaroua. The 'slum'-poly arose after the collapse in 2018 of a neglected block of flats in Marseille that killed eight residents. Over the following months, it was revealed just how many people in the southern French city lived in inhumane and unsafe conditions and how many indications of the impending drama were ignored by so many people. Expert activist Bouaroua intervened with his *Monopoly* satire. He replaced the chic streets and boulevards of the classic game with the addresses of dilapidated rental dwellings, dubious communes, sleazy hotels, slums and encampments. But none of that deters die-hard capitalists, for they even manage to make plenty of money from miserable living conditions. Except, in this game, they can only buy something after reading newspaper articles about the dramatic conditions in the places in question. Every resemblance to real events and/or characters... is purely intentional. So any defence along the lines of 'How could we possibly have known?' is no longer tolerated.

The housing shortage is also the theme of the impressive video game *Change: A Homeless Survival Experience* (2018) →24 by Danny Hayes, which begins with the telling: 'Click to lose everything'. You experience the urban surroundings from the perspective of a homeless person who roams the streets, tries to collect a few cents to buy a sandwich with returnable bottles and old newspapers, arrives just too late for a bed in a homeless shelter, and goes in search of a bench as the first snowflakes fall. The police station, the real estate agency, the temping agency, the late-night store, the recycled good store, the public toilets, the laundrette, the bus stop: all of these are stations that you repeatedly pass on your endless wandering through the comfortless city. It's enough to drive anybody mad: No home of your own without a job, and no job without an education, but if you want to study in the library you need a permanent address, and you can only get that after five nights in the shelter. If you finally manage that but you look unkempt, you have to first find somewhere to wash. In the meantime, your stomach is rumbling and all that traipsing around is tiring you out; it is cold, passers-by react abruptly to your questions, people behind counters usually cannot help you further. But you cannot simply resign yourself to the situation either: if your 'Happiness' drops to 0 (through a combination of hunger, dampness, cold, illness), then you have lost the game.

Change: A Homeless Survival Experience is not a city building game, but it does feature some familiar mechanisms, such as resource management: collecting, controlling and balancing resources, with an eye on the indicators. Clearly it is no sandbox game: it is composed of increasingly challenging levels, and you have no influence on the structure of the city. But you are constantly screening the built environment and its inhabitants for ways to rescue yourself from your unfortunate position. This city is a long way from SimCity: no objective grids, productive zones or sleek transport routes, but the downside of all this—a depressing street in a deprived neighbourhood. You play a character with a clear identity and a story, which is told in short episodes. That provides insight into and

39 See also Deslongchamps-Gagnon & Poirier 2016.

25

lets you experience the dramas and dilemmas of a real homeless existence.[40] The game developer found out for himself what it is like to suddenly have to balance on the edge of poverty. He conducted research among homeless people and at charitable organizations and wove much of his own findings into the game. *Change: A Homeless Survival Experience* is not specifically about architecture or urban design but it conveys in a much more tangible way than a city building game what the city 'does' to people who find themselves on the edge and try to survive there.

PROMISING HYBRIDS

Of all the aspects that characterize analogue and digital city building games, many have found a direct application in design practice. *Rezone The Game* (2012) →25 by Rolf van Boxmeer and Tessa Peters is a fine illustration of that. The possibilities of board games and video games are brought together in an original and powerful way in this early 'hybrid' game.[41] The playing field is a 3D model of a neighbourhood in Den Bosch, which struggles with vacant buildings (as was genuinely the case when the game was made). An occupancy rate of between 4 and 0 for each building is constantly indicated on a screen. If it nears 0, that has consequences for neighbouring buildings: vacancy begets more vacancy. Four players or teams try to solve the problem together. Their actions in the game are registered via a QR code on the top of the props by a camera. As a result, the game app 'knows' the situation on the board at all times. Each player has their own role, with their own priorities and skills: owner, mayor, designer or citizen. Nobody can act in isolation: If a designer wants to build something, he needs permission from the owner and mayor. And if the citizen is not interested, all the effort was for nothing. Those dependencies promote mutual understanding and collaboration. *Rezone The Game* is a form of empowerment: participants are deployed in the game as expert co-designers of their own living environment. The hybrid concept helps to build bridges between experts and lay people, politicians and citizens, manufacturers and consumers. The next chapter looks at games specially devised for use in design practice. That is no easy task, for as soon as a game is applied to a concrete issue, its very playfulness is threatened.

40 The first level tells the story of 'Poverty', but after that you can choose for a Veteran or Addict, somebody with Mental Illness or an 'Abandoned'.
41 An earlier though less advanced hybrid game is *GO ECO* (2007) by Lilian Ball.

D

RISKING PLAYFULNESS FOR A GREATER GOOD

Applied Games in and from Design Practice

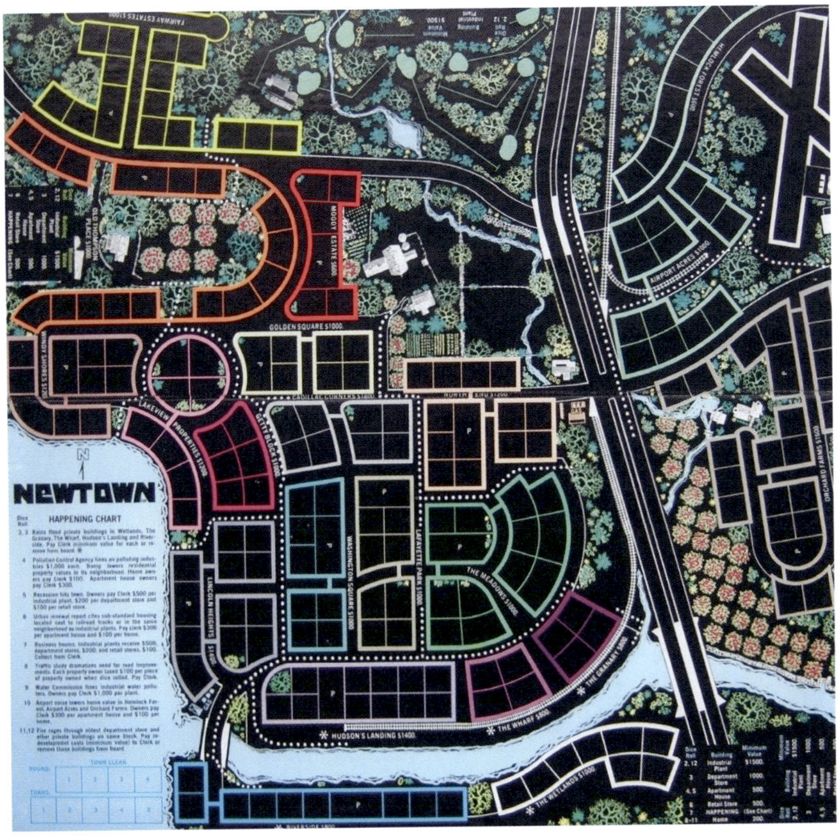

01

Among the historical city building games on the online platform BoardGameGeek, *New Town* (1967) →01 by Barry R. Lawson stands out on account of its unusual description: With this 'modern teaching aid in leading university city planning departments', Lawson promises 'an experience unlike any other game'.[1] *New Town* is an 'Action Game With Debate', in which players plan a new city. Whoever becomes the richest is the winner. But if the city as a whole becomes 'attractive and prosperous', everybody wins. With *New Town*, Lawson not only wanted to entertain but also teach players that: 'A Beautiful Community Takes More Than Money'. According to the packaging, even the entire United States ultimately wins 'when your family and friends learn that community cooperation builds great new towns'.

New Town is an applied game: an instrument to introduce people to planning processes. In 1972 Budd Hebert wrote a review about it that illustrates the sort of problems such games often face: First, the mechanics are not as well-oiled as they are in the exhaustively tested versions of experienced developers. It can take a long time before players master the rules. Conversations are important of course, but if it takes more than three hours to complete four of the five rounds and players have to look up information all the time, that can prove 'too cumbersome' even for motivated people. That does not benefit the replayability either (1972:352). Moreover, *New Town* has a number of conflicting goals: If you aim for personal gain, then 'town meetings bec[o]me quite a rousing affair', but if you primarily want to do something positive for the community without all that much competition, then it quickly becomes 'a bit dull' (1972:352). That is also a recurring question with applied games: Should they essentially be exciting and compelling, or rather educational and substantive? Finally, according to Herbert, *New Town* faltered when it came to determining the target group: '[I]n attempting to reach as large an audience of users as possible, the publishers sacrificed some strengths of the game. […] These are part of the strategy of marketing the game to "general" audiences; specifics must be sacrificed for the sake of generality' (1972:360).

1 See: https://boardgamegeek.com/boardgame/6505/newtown (last consulted on 30 June 2022). Lawson first made a version for professional planners and educators, later a simplified, commercial version for secondary and higher education (1971), and finally a family version (1972).

Despite all reservations, Herbert viewed *New Town* as 'a success' (1972:359), because Lawson made complicated planning processes tangible and comprehensible, especially for students starting out. He is not the only person to have taken on that challenge. Examples date back to the 1960s, and interest from within design practice has been growing right up to the present. What motivates developers to tackle projects by means of a game? What potential do they see in games compared with other media? And what happens with the playfulness when a game serves to support some underlying agenda? This chapter focuses on contemporary examples, both analogue and digital, or combinations of both. What are their strengths, what does each offer, and how to they complement one another?

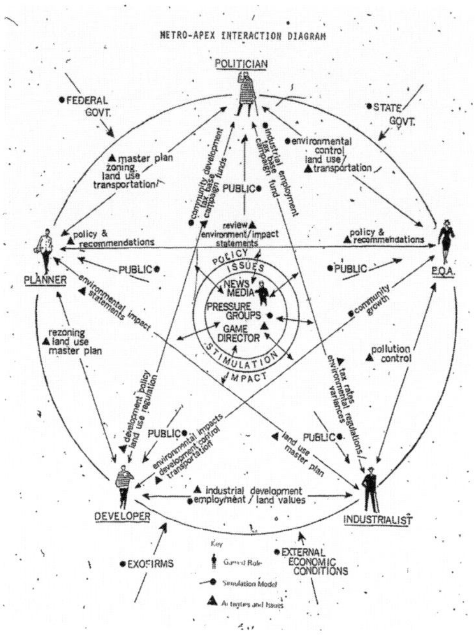

02

SIMULATIONS THAT KNOCK DESIGNERS OFF THEIR PERCH: GAME APPLICATIONS IN THE POST-WAR DECADES

During the Cold War designers became interested in simulation games that the American military used in order to replicate and understand real conflict situations and test various scenarios. If those games were diverted to peaceful missions, the idea went, they could make a constructive contribution to, say, urban development. Elizabeth Keslacy wrote a fascinating overview of how various designers tried to do just that in the 1960s and 1970s: 'From military games, urban planners took on the goal of *optimisation* rather than solution in the face of competing objectives' (2015:103).[2] That could only be achieved by working together: '[U]rban planning games were designed with an ethos of *cooperation*, promoting dialogue and encouraging empathy and understanding of other stakeholders' perspectives' (2015:104). Those initiatives align with a wider trend that undermined the authority of designers: architects and urban designers no longer stood at the helm but were simply one of the links in a complex chain.[3] Moreover, attention shifted from the production of architecture to how it was received by users and other parties: '[G]ames exposed the wide latitude with which architectural readers could understand and interpret designs, demonstrating the importance of reception in the creation of meaning' (2015:105).

More and more designers realized that games could represent real situations simply and tangibly, and, on top of that, could be challenging, exciting and motivating (Tóth 2015:73). By the end of the 1970s there were so many initiatives in that area that the *Journal of Architectural Education* (JAE) devoted an entire issue to them in 1979. It featured the most important examples and initiators from the 1960s and 1970s, which also appear in the later surveys by Keslacy (2015) and Eszter Tóth (2015). One of the pioneers was Richard Duke. With his *Metropolis* (1966) →02 he wanted to introduce budding architects to the decision-making entailed in urban development. In the role of city councillor, politician or property developer, they were playfully confronted with imaginary proposals, budgets and newspaper headlines and had to negotiate with others about investments through

03

2 Simulation games since the 1960s have been well documented, but architectural archives probably contain earlier examples. For instance, in as early as 1938–1939, Le Corbusier had plans for a game to elucidate his concept for the 'Cité radieuse' ('Radiant City'). It was not realized, but he discussed the idea with Albin Peyron, a key figure in housing projects for the Salvation Army in Paris. On the basis of their notes and sketches, Daniel Siret, Ignacio Requena-Ruiz and Arnaud Dercelles (2020) came up with a detailed description of what was to have been a huge box of building blocks measuring 120 × 95 × 15 cm, with a game board measuring as much as 225 × 300 cm, numerous game pieces for the construction of 'Unités d'habitation' ('Housing Units'), roads, garages, landscapes and infrastructure, as well as figures to clarify their functions. Given the dimensions, it was probably intended as an exhibition object: one of Le Corbusier's many initiatives to explain and promote his urban design principles in an innovative way. In addition, he probably wanted to use the building modules within his office for experiments with solar radiation.

3 Keslacy describes how during the 1960s architects were increasingly seen as part of a wider design team that included engineers, urban designers and landscape architects. Under the heading 'Environmental Design', the focus shifted from individual buildings to complete cities, and psychology and sociology devoted more attention to users. Citizens were increasingly consulted in design processes, and the architect, previously a creative soloist, became more of a project leader with expertise and experience (2015:102–103), a 'collaborative figure embedded in a network of experts, participants and constituents' (2015:101).

04

their assumed character.[4] *Metropolis* was more an educational than a research instrument. It conveyed reality as it was, without the ambition to change it: '[It] treated the existing conditions of reality [...] as rigid, permanent, and unchangeable. [...] [It] was not to test out real decisions [...] but rather [...] to come away with an appreciation for the complexities of decision-making at the urban scale [...] and to realise the value of communication and negotiation' (Keslacy 2015:105).[5]

That was different with a celebrated contemporary of *Metropolis*, the *Community Land Use Game* (*CLUG*) (1965) →03 by Allan Feldt.[6] *CLUG* simulates, at a scale of 1:10,000, the expansion of an industrial city until it numbers a quarter of a million inhabitants. The players are property developers who compete for the best sites; they have to negotiate and collaborate with the city authorities and with one another. Juan Pablo Bonta, a big fan of *CLUG*, described the game as an introduction, especially for young architects, to 'the conflict between freedom and regulation that is typical of planning in democratic societies'. He saw unprecedented possibilities: 'The educational potential of CLUG has no limits other than the ability and imagination of the game director and the players' (1979b:12). The only aspect of *CLUG* that did not entirely convince him was the scale: A square on the game board stood for one square mile, or over 2.5 km^2. If one of them was earmarked for housing, for instance, that amounted to 10,000 units in one go,

4 In 2000 Duke looked back on those early years, in which he himself in the Environmental Simulation Lab at Michigan State University and colleagues at other American universities started to devise and use games. In the 1970s they organized conferences, established bodies (the North American Simulation and Gaming Association, followed by the International Simulation and Gaming Association) and launched magazines (in particular, *Simulation & Games: An International Journal of Theory, Design, and Research*). Their findings also exerted an influence on university education; manuals were even written and, in the early 1980s, new institutes founded (2000:81–83). Many of those initiatives were interdisciplinary, but planners and designers always played an active role.

5 From 1969 on, Duke also developed a (rudimentary) computer version of *Metropolis* with the name *Metro/Apex*, which like its predecessor concerned 'how alternative chains of decisions affect patterns of metropolitan growth over a period of several years' (Haney 1971:10). Players could choose from no fewer than 25 different roles (including that of Planner) and their decisions were entered into a computer at the end of every round, which also simulated influences from the surroundings. Just like reality, planners had no direct authority to take decisions: '[T]hey can succeed only by developing strategies for sound community development and then convincing others, particularly the Politicians and Developers, that their recommendations are reasonable' (1971:10).

6 Both *Metropolis* and *CLUG* had a big impact on the development of later simulation games, among them Barry R. Lawson's *New Town* (Summers 1979:3).

without any (architectural) differentiation. Moreover, the grid that determined the structure of the city was 'rigid and monotonous' (1979b:12). That is why Bonta looked for alternatives in other games, and also in his own games.

Cedric Green's *Instructional Housing and Building Simulation* (*INHABS*) (1970) →04 was one of the first games at a very detailed scale of 1:250. Featuring *Lego* blocks, it was set at the level of a neighbourhood or residential complex; that meant it was closer to architecture than large-scale urban development. Each block represented a space within a building and could be placed and combined much more freely than on the rigid *CLUG* game board. That stimulated the design skills of the players. For Bonta, *INHABS* had unique qualities because of its flexibility, yet in terms of scale he thought it had reached the limit for a simulation game. It was suitable for exploring some local problems, but if you were to zoom in further, then too many relevant factors would disappear from view. Hence, 'the way to go was not to continue reducing the size of the territory modeled, but to limit the simulation to just one area of concerns' (1979b:13). Bonta did that in *Thermal Design* (around 1979) →05, in which players had to limit the energy costs of one building over a period of thirty years: select a favourable location in the landscape, orientate the house intelligently for optimal insulation, take into account possible additions to families and (in anticipation of initial and maintenance costs as well as required energy sources) install the right heating and cooling.

All these games, irrespective of their scale and theme, emphasize that countless factors and interests come together in design processes and that an architect alone cannot control them all (Keslacy 2015:110). With *Semiotics* (around 1979) →06, Bonta gave one final push against the official authority of designers. In that game, half of the participants are tasked with designing a specific type of building out of blocks. They are guided by four adjectives, which remain unknown to other players—e.g. 'rational', 'functional', 'traditional', 'bold' or 'modern' (Bonta 1979b:15). The others then have to select four adjectives from a much larger pool that they think best suit the results. Naturally, in most cases those interpretations do not match, so who is proved right in the end? In the first version of the game, an 'interpreter' scored if his answer corresponded with the intention of the designer, but Bonta changed the rules later: He approved of choices that a majority of interpreters agreed on—a further step away from the assumption that 'buildings must mean what their designers want them to mean' (1979b:15).

One of the most spectacular projects from those years—not focused exclusively on architecture but originating from a designer—is Richard Buckminster Fuller's *World Game* (1969) →07. That did not zoom in but rather zoomed far out: City development had to be seen in the context of the entire planet. Buckminster Fuller did not agree with the population theory of Malthus, which stated that the world's population would always grow faster than the available food—the sources had only to be distributed more fairly and scientific progress could help that: '[T]he design science revolution [...] would provide ever more effective tools and services with ever less, real resource investment per each unit of end performance' (1969:286). In the long term, an extensive computer network would register, classify and visualize global information about the environment. An early version of that 'World Resource Inventory' was projected on an interactive map of the world during the *World Game*. In this 'Game That Has No Losers', narrow-minded national attitudes had to make way for a global cooperative approach (1969:287). For Buckminster Fuller the term 'game' was a political statement: '[H]e wanted it seen as something that was accessible to everyone, not just the elite few in the power structure who thought they were running the show'.[7]

05

06

07

7 Cited from: https://www.bfi.org/about-fuller/big-ideas/world-game (last consulted on 30 June 2022). The *World Game* was 'one of Fuller's more profoundly subversive visions. [He] wanted a tool [...] whose findings would be widely disseminated to the masses through a free press, and which would, through this groundswell of public vetting and acceptance of solutions to society's problems, ultimately force the political process to move in the direction that the values, imagination and problem solving skills of those playing the democratically open world game dictated'. See also: Buckminster Fuller 1971 and: Wasiuta 2009.

In the 1970s, many more applied architecture games appeared, with various intentions and target groups. A lot of them were deployed to educate future architects; others to test future scenarios with professional colleagues and decision-makers. Games were later also used to involve non-professionals in design processes and to promote equal communication. In the special issue of the *JAE*, developers and researchers discuss their experiments, experiences and findings from that time.[8] In her overview 'Potentials of Games in the Field of Urban Planning' (2015), Eszter Tóth extends the line far into the twenty-first century.[9] Architects and urban designers still see games as a way of reaching people outside their profession, conveying abstract or complex concepts, stimulating participation or promoting certain approaches.

CONTEMPORARY DESIGNERS FROM THE DRAWING BOARD TO THE GAME BOARD

The Routledge Companion to Games in Architecture and Urban Planning (Brković Dodig & Groat (eds) 2020) is a contemporary counterpart to the special issue of the *JAE*. More than forty years later, games are still deployed in the design disciplines as *Tools for Design, Teaching and Research*. The publishers of the volume spoke to more than fifteen individual and teams of developers about the motivations, considerations and issues they try to get to grips with through games. It is a lavishly illustrated overview of concepts, approaches and analyses. At the same time, some of the cases beg the question: Is this really a game? For example, Ali Javid (2020) discusses a grid that he uses with students to help them grasp the complexity of design assignments. He calls it a puzzle, but it is essentially a diagrammatic representation of recurring aspects of interest for anyone who is trying to align design and research. In another contribution, Linda Groat (2020) praises the sorting exercises used in psychology, which provide insight into the patterns of thought and preferences of participants. The results are efficient, reliable and meaningful. Naming, grouping and regrouping pictures and concept maps is playful and entertaining. But does that immediately turn a sorting exercise into a game?

More specific elements are probably needed for that, such as in *Lifestyle* (1989) →08 by Christian Raffeiner and Helmut Walch. Like sorting exercises, that game is based on the associations that people, depending on their socio-cultural background and personal taste, have with certain images. One of the players is given a question that he has to answer with photographs. For example, 'What place do you think is most suitable for practising your profession?' or: 'Where do you feel most secure?' or: 'Of which house would you most like to get to know the owner?' He orders from 1 to 4 the photos that to him best answer the question, without the others seeing his numbers. They then try to guess his preferences, and whoever does that best over several rounds wins the game. The discussions and considerations are very insightful. Players gradually get to know each other's style and taste better, even in other areas such as sports and leisure, cookery or travel. They have to both clarify their own preferences and see things from another person's perspective. This game principle could be extremely useful in the first phase of a design process, if the architect and client have yet to get acquainted and understand each other. The competitive element and the directness of questions such as 'Where would you make cutbacks first as minister?' are guaranteed to create a sense of dynamism that will not tire quickly.

8 For additional literary references, see: Keslacy (2015) and Tóth (2015).

9 Many of the aims from the early years still apply today. Tóth lists in her overview: 'education, professional education, [...] communication among stakeholders, citizen engagement'. Newcomers since the 1970s are: 'awareness raising [...] and data collection (2015:77). The latter in particular has become much easier with increasing digitalization.

Wohnküche

Bauernhof

Bootsküche

Wartezimmer

Peru, Pfahlhütten im Amazonas

Universität Bochum

Costa Rica, Villa

Alternatives Wohnen

Antikes Badezimmer

Altbaufassade

Amsterdam, schwimmender Bauernhof

Wigwam-Toilette

Modernes Holzhaus

Costa Rica, einfache Wohnhäuser

Swimmingpool

09

In their pursuit of more transparency, accessibility and participation, architects and urban designers see the added value of tools of representation and communication from other professional disciplines and sometimes make avid use of them—whether they are comic strips, films or games. Yet they sometimes have a simplified understanding of those other media and their realization. They set to work on something new with lots of enthusiasm and high expectations, only to then realize that they have underestimated its complexity.[10] Some dice and a few counters promptly give the impression of a game, just as a series of pictures with text balloons immediately suggest 'comic strip'. Such elements can easily be picked up and deployed in an easy-to-understand way, but the development of a fully functioning and successful game demands expert skill, experience and talent. Forty years ago Bonta wrote: 'Architects have a long-standing fascination with ready-made solutions borrowed from fields other than their own. Sociology, environmental psychology, cybernetics, semiotics have all had their day; perhaps gaming is next. Its impact could be particularly pervasive, because games are easy to understand and fun to play (which is not to imply that they are easy to design and use well). The problem with such fads is that expectations always outshine accomplishments' (1979a:1).

The previous three chapters examined characteristics from three classic genres (doll's houses, construction toys and city building games) that can be of relevance to designers. The fourth chapter discusses recent games that were either specially devised for design practice or that cast a particular light on the built environment, which can be interesting for architecture and urban design. What are the ingredients for a meaningful, refreshing, effective and enjoyable game? Can they be achieved together at all? Who has succeeded in bringing them together over the past twenty-five years?

10 Among architects who want to make comic strips, the text in particular can often prove an unexpected obstacle. When they notice that a comic calls for a totally different writing style than needed for a project presentation—and that they have usually not mastered that art—some of them team up with a professional writer. Others adopt a more pragmatic approach—Bjarke Ingels, for example, whose starting point for *Yes Is More: An Archicomic on Architectural Evolution* (2009) was to print out all his PowerPoint presentations and attach Post-Its to them with simple explanations. Skilfully combined in a composition of picture sequences with text balloons and an appropriate font, it soon looked very much like a comic strip and benefitted from the positive associations that readers have with that medium (van der Hoorn 2012:135).

10

Strokes of Luck: The Simplicity of Great Classics Surprises Anew

Two of the most surprising contemporary architecture games were not originally intended as games: *(Un)perfekt* (2014) →09 by Querkraft Architekten and *Mängel Quartett* ('Defects Quartets') (2012) →10 by Studio Karhard, two simple yet telling reinterpretations of the classic games 'memory' and 'quartets'.

(Un)perfekt begins as a standard game of memory: players discover the first cards, become familiar with the visual language, look for memory aids to remember which pictures are where. After a few rounds it gradually becomes clear that something strange is afoot: the pairs are not identical. Almost, though not quite. Half of the cards consist of photographs that architect Jakob Dunkl took of buildings, where something does not look right: a traditional pitched roof that appears as if something has been leaning against its left side for a little too long, the huge clock on a church spire that is pushed off its axis of symmetry by a tiny window, an oversized chimney that towers above a modest home like a triple telescope... All of them surprises that would be mercilessly banned from the drawing table of the architect but that occur naturally in the surrounding world. Dunkl started to 'correct' his discoveries in Photoshop. Then he used the pairs of authentic and airbrushed images in lectures to illustrate the philosophy of his office: Imperfections are (also) part of architecture and you shouldn't take yourself too seriously as a designer.[11] The idea for the memory game came later. Querkraft Architekten gave it away as a promotional gift and sold it in some Vienna bookshops and museum shops. *(Un)perfekt* would deserve much more attention, because it is in the form of a game that the pairs of photos work best: They no longer require any explanation; a game of 'spot the difference' automatically arises alongside the memory game. There is scarcely a better trigger imaginable to get players of all ages and backgrounds to look at architecture openly and with curiosity and generate informal conversation about what makes something 'beautiful' or 'successful'. At the end of the day, what do we expect from architecture: symmetry, sleek lines and logic, or rather (as the enclosed information leaflet suggests) something 'surprising, anarchic, illogical and [...] alive'?

Mängel Quartett also deals with imperfections, but they are even less planned than the previous ones and are not in the least valued: construction errors in brand-new buildings or renovations just completed. The game principle is that of a classical game of quartets: whoever collects the most quartets wins

11 Interview with Jakob Dunkl on 10 May 2016.

the game. But the photographs and texts on the cards ensure an exceptional combination of amazement and familiarity. In a kitchen, for example, the draining board is installed the wrong way around—and therefore cannot be used, because the opening for the tap is at the front. According to the game card, that creates a frustration factor of 1 on a scale of 5—in other words, a 'joke'—and the cost of remedying it amounts to 50 euros. Considerably heavier are bent pipes (200 euro to correct), a half-finished plug socket stuck behind a radiator (frustration factor 5), the hideous connection between a tiled and a parquet floor (a factor 5 that causes a 'headache') or tiles that block the hinges of a window (500 euro unforeseen). All situations are authentic. They were photographed by the architect Alexandra Erhard, who often had to supervise the completion of construction projects early in her career. That was largely a matter of guesswork: there were no official guidelines to present, compare and evaluate the defects clearly. So she compiled a databank and wrote a guide and checklist for homeowners, craftsmen and designers, with practical tips and well-founded background information. The *Mängel Quartett* was intended as a pleasant bonus, but its success immediately surpassed that of the other two.[12] The slogan 'Construction defects are not child's play' indicates a healthy dose of self-irony, something that Erhard thinks the design and construction world badly needs. Not just the built work but also those involved could fill a quartet game with their errors. Under the title 'Explanation by construction director', Erhard listed the excuses she regularly heard, such as: 'It was already late...' for the back-to-front sink unit. Or: 'What do you mean? It works, doesn't it?', for the winding mechanism for roller shutters that was very clumsily attached across a decorative tile edge.[13] The game does well both in trendy bookstores and at construction fairs: a sign that it is appreciated by people across the industry and everybody can identify with some part of it. Humour works wonders: it softens criticism and promotes mutual understanding and successful collaboration.[14]

Querkraft Architekten and Studio Karhard ended up in the world of games almost by accident. They benefitted from the strength and renown of the classics 'memory' and 'quartets' and gave them an interesting and clever twist. There is no lack of playfulness in what they do, but they were not influenced or hindered by a hidden agenda, and their games did not have to achieve any underlying goals. That autonomy was even greater in the creation of *Mystery on Fifth Avenue* (2008)→11, 12 by Eric Clough and his 'multi-disciplinary design firm' 212box. They made a large, wondrous and expensive one-off work for a private client for whom money seemed to be no obstacle: the renovation and refurbishment of a 400 m^2 apartment overlooking Central Park for him, his wife and four children. Clough integrated into his design a game in eighteen episodes, which explains the sources of inspiration for his architectural concept. Refined secret codes, delicate puzzles and precious implements to decipher them—all were incorporated into furniture and wall coverings, tucked into secret pockets and concealed behind double doors. The occupants knew nothing, until they received a mysterious letter that launched the start of the game. Inside they found a poem, which led to the hiding place of a novel specially written for them, *In These Rooms of Wood and Stone*, to accompany them along the eighteen stages of the journey of discovering between their own four walls. After the eighth mystery they received a CD with original music. Step by step, the history of the building unfolded, historical figures and artists told their stories, and the family was swept along on 'a journey of wonder derived from things that inspire: music, history, story-telling, mystery, and the very craft of making things'. In this project, architecture and

12 Interview with Alexandra Erhard and Thomas Karsten (Studio Karhard) on 6 July 2021.

13 *Mängel Quartett* is also suitable as a game of trumps. Players try to win cards from other players by overtrumping them with a bigger frustration factor or higher costs. Whoever has amassed the biggest amount of damages at the end wins as the 'defect expert'.

14 Architects also frequently use comics to voice criticism with a smile. See: van der Hoorn 2012: 95–122.

Clue #1
Salamander, Salamander, Where Are You?

Clue #2
For Cherubs

Clue #3
Chamber Cipher Mathematics

Clue #4
Astro Heat

Clue #5
Rose Stone

Architecture and Interiors of the Residence.
The 4200-square-foot apartment is strategically split into two territories — kids' land and then the rest of the apartment — marked by a threshold that features a stone family crest. With its stunning view of Central Park, the once misdirected foyer is now a large library room that serves as a pinwheel to the living room, dining room, kitchen, and master suite. Similarly, a homework den and a pajama room in the children's wing provides circulation to two large two-room suites, each split between the boys, Cavan and Owen, and the girls, Kiera and Ella. Space between rooms serves as a functional bridges rather than a void of hallways; thresholds house storage, butler's pantries, wet bars, linen rooms, bathrooms, and dressing rooms. Additional features include a sleeping den and a home office with a terrace.

Kick-Off Letter
The entire journey kicks off with an envelope addressed to the family that contains six Russian doll-style letters, one for each family member and each in additional, progressively smaller envelopes. Collectively the letters make up a larger poem, which is based on Yeats's poem "To Be Carved on a Stone at Thoor Ballylee". The stanzas lead the family to congregate around the secret panel in the library/dining room threshold, which contains the book. Notice the vintage stamps: one two-dollar, two one-dollar (a 1912 Benjamin Franklin), two one-cent and one two-cent, both a reference to the 212box name and the equivalent of four dollars and four cents, a nod to 212box's project code of 0404 (fourth project of 2004).

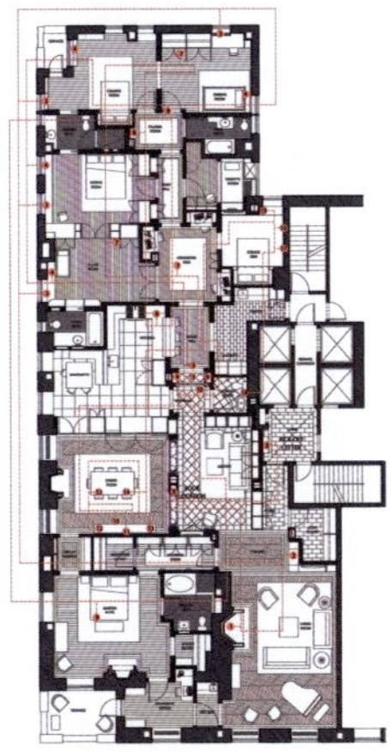

Clients Inspire
Inspiration is drawn from many sources. In the case of renovating an apartment on the Upper East Side of Manhattan, there was inspiration in the fourteen-story view of the Central Park Reservoir and the city's skyline that acted as a backdrop to the palatial space. And there was the apartment's unique history of once being the thirty-two servant's rooms for a triplex penthouse belonging to Marjorie Merriweather Post and E.F. Hutton. And, of course, there was the attractive challenge of everything an architectural gut renovation and a full-interiors package can entail. While all of these aspects of the project certainly stirred our team creatively, the true inspiration was looking into the eyes of four brilliant children and realizing that this apartment could make a lasting impression on their imaginations.

So 212box set out to not only fulfil the functional and spatial requirements of the renovation, but to also create an experience for the family of six that led them through a journey of wonder derived from things that inspire: music, history, story-telling, mystery, and the very craft of making things.

Clue #6
Modular Vitruvian Treasure Chest

Clue #10
Loud Cranks

Clue #11
In Regards To Its Use

Clue #12
Draw à droit

INSPIRATION
in•spi•ra•tion, n.
1 stimulation or arousal of the mind, feelings, etc., to special or unusual activity or creativity.
2 the state or quality of being so stimulated.
3 someone or something that causes this state.
4 an idea or action resulting from such a state.
5 the act or process of inhaling; breathing in.

Clue #7
Galileo Galilei

In These Rooms of Wood and Stone
To inspire Cavan, Keira, Owen, and Ella, 212box created a story that fictionally traces "inspiration" through forty historical figures, beginning with Francois I and ending with Marjorie Merriweather Post. The book is segmented into five parts with two chapters per section. The odd chapters contain the story of two young friends, Ricky and Elynn, who discover long-lost clues and who embark on a wonder-filled adventure; each of their episodes is followed by a series of clues, which lead the family through their own apartment of discoveries. The even chapters feature segments about fictionalized historical figures, who at young ages undertake their own personal paths of inspiration and talent; these sections are followed by biographies and contextual information. Throughout the book, illustrations, diagrams, definitions, and factoids make the journey both educational and fun.

Clue #13
Draw à gauche

Clue #14
Inspiration NRG

Clue #8
Salamandre

A Unique Historic Context
Aligned with the Central Park Reservoir, the residence at Fifth Avenue is rich in history. An excerpt from:
"Built to Suit: Custom Planning at Fifth Avenue", Luxury Apartment Houses of Manhattan by Andrew Alpern

Marjorie Merriweather Post and E.F. Hutton spurred one of the first cooperative apartment buildings in New York after they met with a construction company and a real estate firm in 1923. Having complained about the traffic noise and gasoline fumes, Mrs. Hutton said that she wanted to have her home rebuilt at the top of an apartment house. Tearing their existing mansion down and capitalizing on the significantly appreciated value of their property, a new thirteen-story (plus penthouse) building was planned. The top three levels and a portion of the ground floor were devoted to the Huttons' "relocated" mansion. The public entrance was placed on Fifth Avenue to permit a private driveway and lobby to be constructed on East 92nd Street for the exclusive use of the Huttons and their guests. Upstairs, a grand fifty-four-room residence was created that holds the record as the largest apartment ever constructed. The apartment included a silver room, a wine room and cold storage rooms for flowers and for furs, along with a self-contained suite of rooms for closer family members.

Clue #15
Magnet Poem

Clue #9
Scytale

Clue #16
LightBox

Clue #17
Letter Puzzle

O DEAR ME, HARD MATCHED
REFRESHMENTS AND VEHEMENT THRILL
PANCAKE DAY OF MONDAYS CHAMPION
PADDLE I'M BAD HONEST TO
GOODNESS RUN OF THE MILL
NOTATION OF OVERSHADOWED
I AM THE HIGH SOULED ALARM CLOCK
AND NON OBVIOUSLY GUARANTEEING

HERE THE TRAVELLERS S AND M
AND THE CHILDREN MADE FROM THEM
C AND K AND O AND E
COMPOSE A HAPPY FAMILY,
AND IN THESE ROOMS OF WOOD AND STONE
SET FORTH TO BUILD A LOVELY HOME.
MAY THIS GOOD LOVE AND LUCK REMAIN
THROUGH ALL BE RUINS ONCE AGAIN.

A Journey of Inspiration
The book (the nature of it is unbeknownst to them) is presented to the family. It invites them to explore their newly renovated apartment by supplying them with clues about hidden architectural details, codes, ciphers, and tips about secret passages, sculptures, and original products created for and from the story. In addition to originally scored music and songs, the book also included fictional letters from Marjorie Merriweather Post and an educational story that teaches them about the history and genesis of inspiration through politics, art, science, and much more. It is our hope that we will inspire them to do great things.

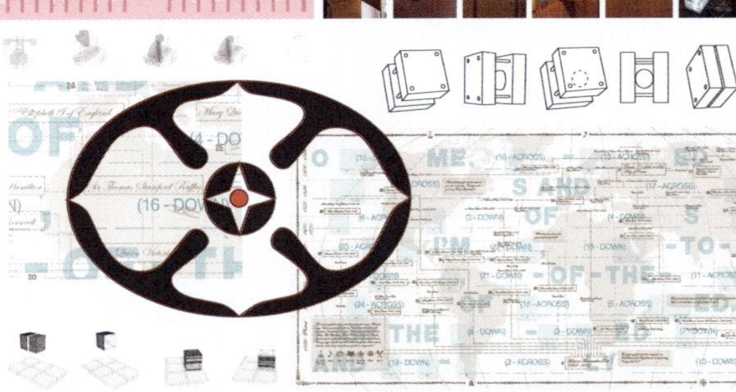

Clue #18
Salamander Cipher

Architect:
212box Architecture PC

Project Team:
Eric Clough
Eun Sun Chun
Erik L'Heureux
Heather Bensko
Robert Mastro
Aida Ly
Kevin Bell
Tania Chau
Travis Jackson
Todd Nickey
Amy Kehoe
Joanna Katz
Isabella Bruno

Final photography © Jeff McNamara, © Fred Conrad and © Jody Kivort

All graphic & editorial content © 212box Film LLC

11

FDYDQ,WKHDUFKHU'VFKLOG;
FXULRXP,EULJKW -- BRXU
TXLFHJLOGSLYRWVDOG
OHDSVOLNHDGDOFHU.
WKHNHBWRSUHVHUYLQJ
FXULRXPLWB'VOLJKW
DVPXFKDVWKHDQVZHU.

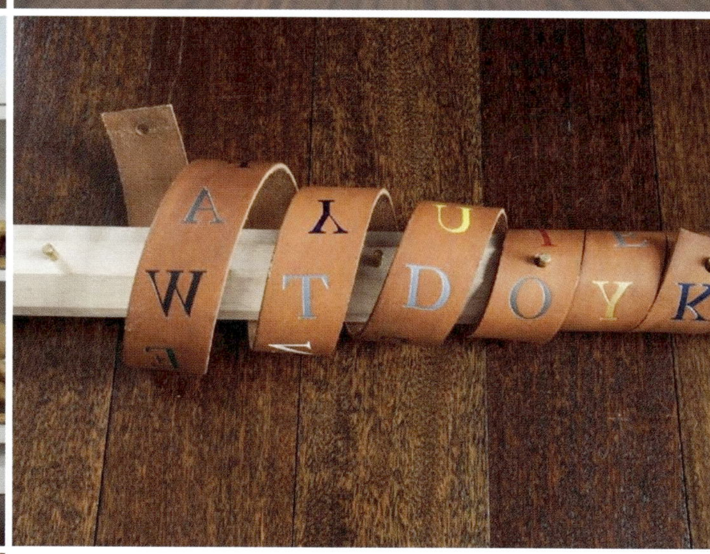

STEVESDEN SOUTH WALL
LEFT OF WINDOW MIDDLE PANE

games are interwoven like never before.[15] The game explains the genesis of the design, but it also influences the design: it is ever-present in the architecture.[16] *Mystery on Fifth Avenue* is an impressive yet very unusual project, because almost everything was possible. In most cases designers are limited by all sorts of concrete conditions in the development of a game, especially when it is intended as an instrument to improve a specific situation.

Pragmatism and Realism

Most games created for design practice are exhaustively described subsequently by their makers. Evidently there is a need for explanations in a field that is still relatively new and developing rapidly.[17] Ekim Tan, the founder of the office Play the City, which has been developing game applications since 2010 to support participatory planning processes, explains that she initially faced an 'image problem' and even wondered: 'Was it really a good idea to call our method a game?' (2019:268). And more recently, '[o]ur designer colleagues often ask: Can we design and build cities through a city game? [...] Can such "playful" meetings about serious city challenges change the behaviour of involved stakeholders?' (2017:302). In response, Tan and other makers explain that games can rival established forms of communication and representation as 'real-world problem solvers' (2019:268).

Invite

First,—quite apart from their contents—for most people games evoke pleasant associations and memories because of their appearance. A game board, coloured cards and a few counters are often enough to get participants in a cheerful mood: '[W]hen negotiations take the form of a game with a hint of playfulness, lugubrious discussions [...] can be avoided; and a conflictual situation can be turned into a constructive one' (Hofmann 2020:18). Not only the inviting appearance but also the legibility, accessibility and tangibility of the material have a positive influence on the course of the exchange of views. While fifty years ago developers of applied games had to rely on A4 sheets from the photocopier and cut-and-paste work from their own studio, they have now been able to copy so much from the commercial games industry in terms of design and durability of materials. The effectiveness of applied games as communication tools is increasingly recognized—and with it the importance of careful, attractive

15 The following citation from the project description by Eric Clough illustrates how the game permeates every corner of the apartment: 'A longer intertwined clue involves, in part, removing a leather strap embossed with lettering from the crown moulding of the pajama room and wrapping it around an octagonal-sectioned rail detail on the 212box custom-made master bed. [...] Decrypting the riddle on the strap leads one to the rose stone and two decorative door knockers from two hallway doors, which fit together to make a crank, which in turn opens hidden panels in a credenza in the dining room. The panel of the credenza then reveals multiple keys and keyholes [...] and, when the correct ones are used, yields a hidden magnetic sculpture and two hidden drawers containing acrylic letters and a table-size cloth inspiration map' (2009:93, 96).

16 Eric Clough is an important and original representative of the architecture game. Scarcely hindered by financial restraints, he could realize an exceptionally large number of ideas in *Mystery on Fifth Avenue*—and all that for a small circle of just six people. Games subsequently remained an important part of 212box's work. In 2012 Clough started *Into Mystery*: another riddle game, though much more ambitious. It is being released in regular episodes—11 of the 18 up to now—by Kickstarter. This time the target group is unlimited: the games focus on all interested parties across the world. *Into Mystery* gives them access into the sources of inspiration and philosophy of the office. It promises to be 'a monument to creativity and human inquiry', a project that has to lead to the construction of a veritable tower, 'the first structure of its kind', because: 'Not built by governments or private corporations, this building's creation relies solely on those with a passion for puzzle solving, architecture, and the future of a new creative, global community. [...] It will be one of the first buildings with such a close relationship between those who get to explore it and those who made it happen'. See: https://www.kickstarter.com/projects/1400869672/into-mystery-reveal (last consulted on 30 June 2022).

17 All the makers of the games discussed in this section published about them subsequently. See: Hofmann 2020, Tan 2017 & 2019, Venhuizen 2010, Gugerell, Jauschneg et al. 2017 and Gugerell, Platzer et al. 2018. In their professional practice, games are not always taken seriously; that is why they often emphasize what 'fun' can contribute to 'seriousness'. A case in point is Susanne Hofmann: 'Of course, building is a serious matter. It is about costs, resources, social acceptance, and the sustainability of what is built. [...] [B]uildings [...] not only determine our social environment, but they also shape our cities, villages, and landscapes. That's where the fun stops. Or maybe building starts with fun? [...] [A] game is perhaps the key to a more socially engaged architecture and urban planning' (2020:30–31). Architects who make comic strips also often see the necessity to legitimize what they do because they fear not being taken seriously. See: van der Hoorn 2012:10–12.

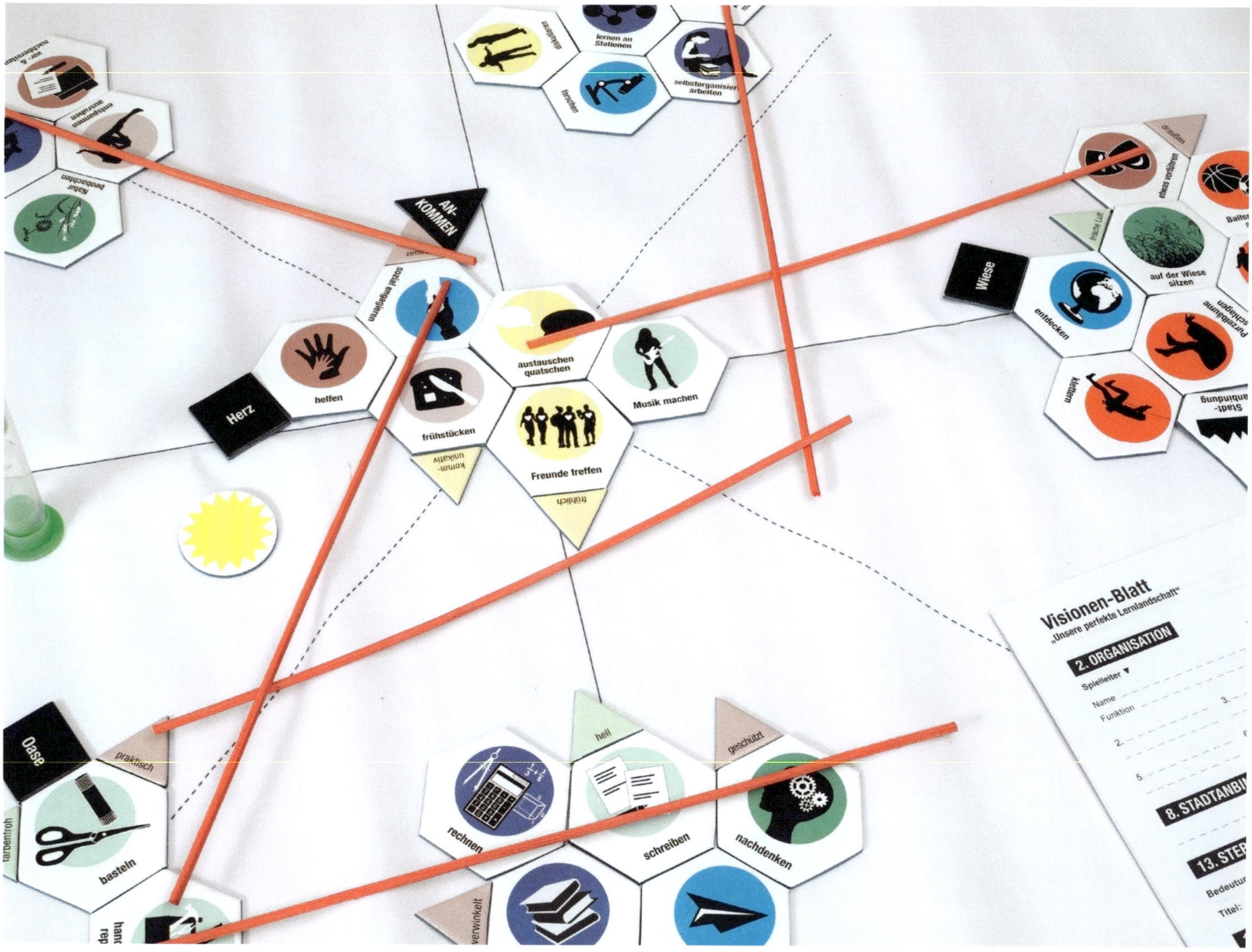
lernen an Stationen
forschen
selbstorganisiert arbeiten
AN-KOMMEN
sozial engagieren
helfen
Herz
austauschen quatschen
Musik machen
frühstücken
Freunde treffen
kommunikativ
fröhlich
Wiese
entdecken
auf der Wiese sitzen
frische Luft
draußen
etwas verändern
klettern
Natur beobachten
entspannen ausruhen
Oase
praktisch
basteln
hell
geschützt
rechnen
schreiben
nachdenken
verwinkelt
farbenfroh
Visionen-Blatt
„Unsere perfekte Lernlandschaft“
2. ORGANISATION
Spielleiter
Name
Funktion
8. STADTANBI
13. STE

Schul-Visionsspiel
„Unsere perfekte Lernlandschaft“
dieBaupiloten
1
START

design.[18] In that regard, the *Schul-Visionenspiel* ('School Vision Game') (2018) →13 by die Baupiloten was one of the most fully developed games of recent years.

Colourful triangular and hexagonal cards of laminated cardboard, with clear icons and easy-to-understand concepts, appear from sleekly designed packaging. In addition, a playing surface, hourglasses in red, blue and green, red sticks, explanatory cards and sets of forms, everything in a clear, inviting graphic look. Die Baupiloten are specialized in supervising participatory building processes and their game helps school communities, prior to the construction of a new building, renovation or extension, to formulate their needs and aspirations. The desired functions are selected, clustered, connected to one another and given their own atmosphere in 17 steps and around 100 minutes. That has undoubtedly contributed to a positive start to construction projects for many schools, but is the *Schul-Visionenspiel* really a game? It derives its playful appearance from elements from the games world, especially the distinctive hexagonal cards, but it contains no scoring mechanism and none of the participants or team members is ultimately declared the winner. Nobody would come up with the idea of playing it outside the context of a workshop or for any other reason. Nor is it a construction toy: it specifically does not focus on the appearance of buildings and spaces, but on their atmosphere and substantive characteristics.[19] However, it is a constructive and motivational instrument developed over many years of trial and error, which has now acquired a generic form, suitable for schools of any imaginable type, size or location.[20] It only seemed logical to release a commercial edition, but die Baupiloten had not considered the fact that in the process they were in danger of losing one of their unique selling points: the contribution of office chief Susanne Hofmann as moderator.[21] She halted the process when she realized that, with the sleek *Schul-Visionenspiel* under their arm and after thorough preparation, competitors could just as well offer their services as games moderator in schools.[22]

Connect

In addition to their accessible and positive appeal, games are appreciated because they can make participants aware of the motives of others, and thereby cultivate mutual understanding and collaboration. To that end, the division of roles among the players is particularly important. Tan devotes a lot of time to that aspect with Play the City.[23] In the first project by the office, *Play Almere: Wierden* (2009), everybody played the same role (a resident), with identical skills. Players had a strong tendency to compare themselves and compete with others, which did not help the dynamics. In response, Tan introduced more differentiation in later projects, 'reminding players that their powers are limited and different, and that they need to work with others to succeed' (2017:295).[24] Over the years, diversity proved to be increasingly important: 'The more stakeholder interests

18 '[G]ames and game-like participatory co-design tools provide communication tools *par excellence* for architects to better understand user wishes and perspectives about their built environment' (Hofmann 2020:18).

19 According to Hofmann, one of the biggest disadvantages of standard architecture representations is that they present 'an image of a space, not its intended effect' (2020:19). The latter is her goal with the *Schul-Visionenspiel*.

20 For other game experiments by the office, see: Hofmann 2014:108–115.

21 Interview with Susanne Hofmann on 14 January 2020.

22 Upon request, the *Schul-Visionenspiel* can be borrowed from die Baupiloten or from the Hans Sauer Stiftung, which helped to finance the development of the game. Interested parties must first explain their motivations on a form: Why, where and with whom do they want to play the game?

23 In the early years Tan drew inspiration from such role-playing games as *Dungeons and Dragons* (1974). In it, 'many characters [...] come together to build a collective adventure and carry out careful research before they meet to play; for instance, they determine the era and location of the adventure, their character's powers, and who they need to supplement to reach their goals' (2019:266). In a comparable way, in *Play the City*-workshops, 'play becomes much more advanced when players [...] are given the chance to develop, expand, and apply an evolving understanding of their roles in an interactive, creative setting with other players' (2019:267).

24 In *Play the City: Games Informing the Urban Development* (2017), Tan looks back at seven intensive years with countless game sessions in twenty different cities. In addition to her own projects and methodology, she has facilitated exchanges between game developers with, for example, a database of game applications and the organization of congresses. See: http://gamesforcities.com/database (last consulted on 30 June 2022). Her book includes the *Play the City Game Manual* and an extensive overview of seven projects by the office and explanations of thirteen games by other developers, interspersed with interviews with parties involved and experts.

included in a game, the more intricate and valuable the game becomes' (2017:74). Other developers also see that multiplicity has a positive influence on the result of an applied game. The *Schul-Visionenspiel*, for example, is played in mixed teams of 4–7 participants: teacher, administration, director, pupil, parent, etc. That is in order to avoid one table coming up with a typical 'teacher proposal' and another with a 'pupil concept'. But what developers sometimes disagree on is whether everybody has to play 'themselves'. Participants themselves generally prefer to do that, because they expect that the game will yield more for them if they stick close to reality. Susanne Hofmann is adamant: If they swapped roles in the *Schul-Visionenspiel*, then they would have to speculate about the ideas and wishes of others... That inaccuracy would prove counterproductive as a preparation for actual building projects. For Tan, it differs per situation and participants sometimes do have to be coaxed out of their comfort zone, because 'playing with roles that are too familiar can also restrict the creativity and innovativeness' (2017:297). In a polarized context in particular, it can be good to change roles in order to gain a better understanding of other positions.

14 →168–169

Weighing Up Options

Play the City →14 game sessions always concern a 'real life challenge', ideally a 'multiplayer, multidisciplinary and unpredictable process' (Tan 2017:47). The plan of a neighbourhood or region on the table or on the floor serves as a game board. On it, the players place all sorts of 3D miniatures to visualize their proposals: tiny buildings in all possible forms and sizes, green areas, roads, wind turbines, solar panels, infrastructure and so on. Those items are not as abstract as they are in the *Schul-Visionenspiel*—in fact, over the years they have become increasingly realistic. With each new game session, new elements are added to the Play the City Game Library; it already contains a few thousand and also includes specific functions such as a local brewery, a women's refugee centre and a hammam. Those three-dimensional, recognizable props with colour codes and a font of their own have become the signature of Play the City. Like in classical construction toys and board games, they make a complex situation tangible and comprehensible. They enable participants to join the discussion and help reach a decision, irrespective of their professional background. For most buildings and expansion plans, Play the City has also collected research data, so-called 'datasets': information about the costs and benefits of specific infrastructures, best practices from various countries and so on. These are mostly presented on 'Technology Cards' and 'Innovation Cards' so that players can take well-considered 'data-driven decisions'. Therefore the placing of blocks is not a simple construction project, but a conscious selection and activation of specific 'policies, strategies and actions' associated with the chosen items.[25]

A big advantage of games is that participants can make choices without fearing the consequences and then receive feedback about their course of action and decisions. In standard games, the latter lies in the balancing of resources, points, bonuses and penalties. That is not always possible with applied games, yet it is still a key aspect because '[i]t is the game mechanics that make the serious game fun, not the topic. [...] Game-based learning is fun because it provides players with choices and allows them to experiment, to play' (Platzer, Stowasser et al. 2018:30). How is that in Play the City? The props call to mind analogue city-building games, and players can step into the shoes of others involved, but just like die Baupiloten there is no scoring system or winner. According to Tan, what turns a Play the City session into a game are the negotiations between the players, the voting and prioritizing at the end of every workshop and the 'reality check' by an expert who passes judgement on the resulting proposals. In terms

25 Interview with Ekim Tan on 17 February 2022. The principle of 'data-driven decisions' is reminiscent of the modules in Jose Sanchez's *Block'hood*, discussed in Chapter 3. An input and output of specific sources is indicated for each of the modules; placing a block always has consequences for the surroundings.

15

Groen/blauw dak
Green roof
Groen/blauw dak
Green roof

15 min
+
4 min per
team

EFF
eindhovenfilmfestival.nl

of dynamics and motivation, those challenges are comparable with scoring in standard games. For even if there is no winner, participants still want to know whether they have played 'well' or 'badly'. In applied games with an open end, that feedback can only surface on the spot, while in more general 'serious games' or exhibition games it is sometimes embedded in the game itself.

In 2021 Hans Venhuizen made an autonomous exhibition version of his game *Parquette* (2009) →15, with integrated scoring and feedback. The very first *Parquette*, from 1991, is discussed at the end of Chapter 2. The playing field of herringbone parquet that he designed became the basis for the 2009 version used for workshops at Museum de Paviljoens in Almere. The landscape, which represented the coastal zone of the Dutch new town, filled the entire floor of a hall.[26] Participants had to build 1,500 new housing units. They visualized their proposals with blue houses in three sizes, in contrast with the existing landscape of natural wood. There were four interest groups: Administrators, Builders, Present Residents and Future Residents. They had to consult, negotiate, protect their own interests and consider one another.[27] Venhuizen explained, clarified, moderated, kept an eye on the time and chaired discussions. Profit, Satisfaction and Trust were evaluated at the end of each round and the roles rotated.[28]

In 2021 Venhuizen made a single-player version for the Architecture Centre Vienna with a playing time of twenty minutes, without a game moderator. The distinctive landscape with small houses and trees of natural wood no longer represented a polder, but an 'agricultural community with a rich history'.[29] The field of play was much smaller, and visitors had to plan just 300 new living units. Of particular note were the alternatives for Venhuizen's own role as game moderator: The feedback remained hidden behind four hatches until the end; it consisted of responses from four political parties from the (fictive) city council concerning the plans to increase density. What mattered for the Greens was a valuable yet unprotected piece of nature in the middle of the landscape. If it contained more than five housing units, they gave the one-day planners a minus; if it was left intact, they gave them a plus. The Liberals, by contrast, wanted to stimulate living in attractive surroundings, so they rewarded 30 or more units in the valuable area with a plus. Players received a plus from the Socialists for more than 50 per cent social housing and a plus from the Conservatives if more than half aligned with existing development patterns. This response phase had something very dynamic and exciting: players walked through the landscape once again, counted their houses and hoped for the required three plusses for a green light from the city council.

Feedback

Participants expect immediate feedback at the end of a game session, but what yield can you expect from an architecture game in the long term? Planning researcher and game developer Katharina Gugerell is candid on the matter: 'Nobody actually knows that exactly. There is not enough empirical data, and evaluations are often implemented right after a game is played. I often read in reports about "attitude change" and "behavioural change", but the latter in particular revolves around deeply rooted, fundamental values—you certainly cannot change

26 Interview with Hans Venhuizen on 21 July 2021. Venhuizen also calls the 2009 version *Urbanists*, to distinguish it from the original *Parquette* of 1991 (Venhuizen 2010:128).

27 They had to define a course with respect to four aspects: Type of Expansion (organic, overlapping or nearby); Type of Development (high-rise, free-standing or mixed), Density (8, 32 or 80 dwellings per hectare) and Location (coastal zone, forest zone or scattered) (Venhuizen 2010:130–131).

28 If a Builder made a loss, he went bankrupt and was replaced. If an Administrator met the needs of Residents inadequately, then he too had to make way for another. Future Residents could become Present Residents by settling, and Present Residents could become Future Residents and look for a new home in another city district.

29 What was a dike in Almere became, in the Austrian context, a motorway doubled with a railway line. Venhuizen rewrote the complete case history as a (fictive) Austrian post-corona context with rising property prices, legible on a big board. Visitors could play just one role (individually or as a team), and the choices concerning Type of Expansion, Type of Development, Density and Location were reduced to three ready-made packages plus a free option.

them that quickly'.[30] Like, Gugerell, Venhuizen warns against false expectations: 'It is not the case that you can lift things one by one from games and implement them directly in a design. You shouldn't trust anybody who claims that'. Yet Gugerell has no doubts: 'Serious games touch on a sensitive issue: when it comes to transferring knowledge and stimulating participation, we're still living in the Stone Age and new formats are badly needed. Games are no longer a side issue; they reach a broad audience. And it is fascinating how strongly they can trigger people to engage with a theme. That works incredibly well'. Venhuizen explains: 'The game is part of the creative process and not of the design. It's not about the exterior, the facade, but about *how* something arises'. That also applies to later games by Venhuizen: 'I facilitate the participatory formulation of a brief aimed at achieving change. My games are about understanding decision-making and your position in relation to that—and from there you can contribute to clearly formulating the brief for the designer'. Play the City occasionally dares to engage with current developments, but that involves more than is the case when setting up something new: '[W]hile the city gaming method allows players to generate alternative and innovative plans, influencing ongoing plans is a longer-term process' (Tan 2017:306). In such a case it can help to train local game moderators who can continue to monitor the development: 'Creating ownership for the game as a platform for open exchange between local stakeholders [...] helps the longer-term existence and penetration of the game, and thus, its potential links to reality' (2017:307–308).[31]

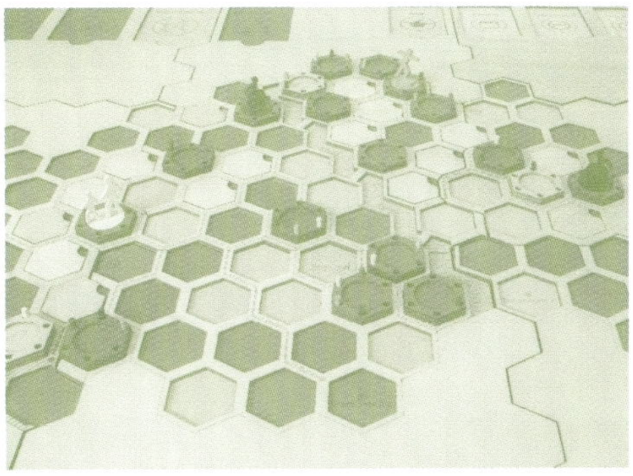

16 →172–173

Whether a game is educational, contributes to participatory planning or raises participant awareness of a particular problem, a moderator can help to translate the game experience into a long-term effect. Gugerell has examined this aspect in depth in response to *Mobility Safari* (2017) →16, which she developed with architect Martina Jauschneg, Ludwig Grimm and Mario Platzer.[32] That game brings together much of the foregoing. First, it is a feast for the eye: a hand-made unique object in wood, which depicts the plan of Vienna in a colourful hexagonal pattern. Players can choose from four roles: cyclist, pedestrian, skateboarder or wheelchair user. From that perspective they realize projects for sustainable mobility by bringing together permits, allies and resources. They score on a financial, ecological and social scale for each completed project, and finally there is a winner in each of the three sections. The connections with the immediate surroundings become clear thanks to the recognizable board and the concrete game mechanics that imitate local bureaucracy, networks and finances. But a game moderator is needed in order to anchor that awareness more deeply and to stimulate participants to undertake something, because otherwise the step to concrete behavioural changes remains too great: '[T]he game [...] falls short regarding triggering the players for active participation and behavioural change' (Gugerell, Jauschneg et al. 2017:418).[33] This is where the moderator can make a difference: '[T]he debrief is the crucial moment to transform the gaming experience into a deeper learning experience' (2017:419). Developers increasingly seek advice in the digital world for improvements in that area.

30 Interview with Katharina Gugerell on 16 July 2021.

31 Tan notes that more than 1,000 people played *Play Oosterwold* (2012) over a period of two years: 'Continuous player feedback collected systematically and reported back to the local planning teams helped the plan mature both during draft design as well as during the legalization process' (2017:306). See also the detailed description: Tan 2017:152–183.

32 A precursor to *Mobility Safari* is *Energy Safari* (2016) by Christina Ampatzidou and Katharina Gugerell. See: Ampatzidou & Gugerell (2019) and Ampatzidou 2020. Both games arose within *Playing With Urban Complexity: Using Co-Located Serious Games to Reduce the Urban Carbon Footprint Among Young Adults* (abbreviated as *Play!UC*), an international collaborative project by the University of Groningen (NL), Hasselt University (BE), the University of Applied Sciences Upper Austria and Green City Lab Vienna (AT) between 2014 and 2017. In that project, analogue and digital games were analysed and five prototypes for 'participatory, game-based urban development scenarios' were developed. They are documented on: http://play-uc.net (last consulted on 30 June 2022) and in: Platzer, Stowasser et al. 2018.

33 Three learning objectives emerge on the basis of individual research by Gugerell and of the *Play!UC* project: '[S]hould the players be informed about a certain policy topic (single loop learning), should they question existing models and concepts (double loop learning) or is the goal that they are engaging in problem solving and developing ideas and processes (triple loop learning)—or should it be a combination of all three?' (Platzer, Stowasser et al. 2018:29). See also: Gugerell & Zuidema 2017 and Gugerell, Platzer et al. 2018.

innovativ & bildend
Startposition 5
U-Bahn

Joker
Ereignis
Quiz (schwer)
Quiz (leicht)
U-Bahn
Donau
Startposition 2
Startposition 3

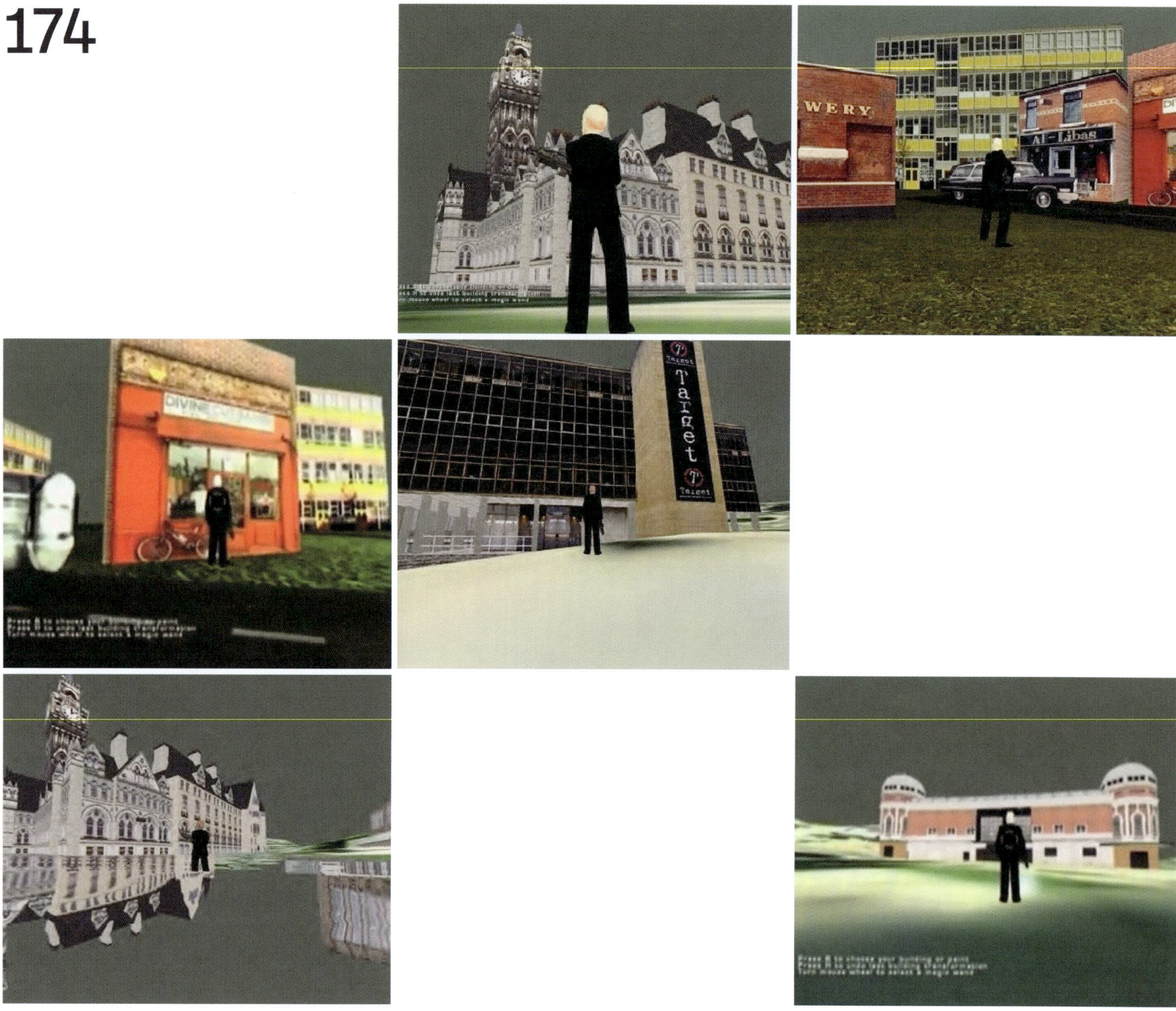

17

BRIDGES BETWEEN WHAT 'IS' AND WHAT 'COULD': DIGITAL APPLICATIONS

Hofmann, Tan, Venhuizen and Gugerell focus mainly on analogue games, but they also keep an eye on the digital world. Tan, for example, deliberately opts for board games on account of their 'superior flexibility to player inputs, and [...] ability to generate and galvanize meaningful relationships between players' (2017:298–299). Yet she is also aware of the potential of digital and hybrid variants, such as 'improved data processing power, speed and accuracy, or access to a wider range of players online through seamless integration with social media platforms' (2017:298). How do game developers navigate between the two worlds? When do they choose one or the other? What combinations exist?

The Power of Shooting and Running: Gaming Engines Diverted

Various authors have considered the potential of digital games for the design disciplines. *Space Time Play: Computer Games, Architecture and Urbanism—The Next Level* (von Borries, Walz & Böttger (eds) 2007) is a particularly impressive and extensive collection of project descriptions and essays by dozens of authors that address the questions: 'Why should an architect care about computer games?' and: 'What can a game designer take from architecture?' Later articles complement that overview with more recent examples (Poplin 2011 & 2014, Tóth 2015). Two of them are especially interesting on account of their uncommon, innovative approach: the game prototype *PlastiCity* (2005) →17 by Mathias

Fuchs and Steve Manthorp, and the digital game application *Participatory Chinatown* (2010) →18 by the Engagement Game Lab headed by Eric Gordon.[34]

PlastiCity is an early example of digital 'critical play', which playfully invites participants to reflect. The genre is comparable to that of Paolo Pedercini's games discussed in the previous chapter, but then focused on a real urban plan: William Alsop's masterplan for the city of Bradford in England. His 2004 proposal to demolish historical buildings to create space for a lake proved highly controversial: To what extent can or should designers intervene in existing structures with their urban development proposals? The makers of *PlastiCity* asked that question with what was a fairly new game technology at the time, Unreal Engine (1998). Like in a third-person shooter (TPS) game, you walk with a gun through a virtual environment, which is clearly recognizable as the centre of Bradford because of its Centenary Square, City Hall, Police Station and former Odeon Cinema.[35] With the same ease and flippancy as in a shooter game, you can clear away buildings or breathe new life into them: reduce or increase their size, relocate or paint them. There is something diagrammatic about all of this: developer Mathias Fuchs writes that 'some of [Alsop's] ideas have been exaggerated and take the form of a cartoon style attitude' (2006:4). It does indeed call to mind some architecture comic-strips in which exaggeration, humour and self-irony help to express criticism 'with a smile'. Architect and cartoonist Wes Jones calls it 'sugaring the pill' (van der Hoorn 2012:96). *PlastiCity* is not a reproach to Alsop, but an invitation to players to view city development without prejudice: To what extent does the shooter metaphor reflect reality? Are evildoing urban planners really so easy when it comes to erasing existing structures? How does that square with the creativity and working methods of someone like Alsop, which were 'more often ludic than constraint-bound'?

PlastiCity was an experiment, 'a comment on a city regeneration plan rather than [...] a tool for urban planning' (2006:5).[36] This distinguishes it from *Participatory Chinatown*, a customized video game for a participative planning process in Boston. Participants could play that in multiple groups of 10 to 15 people, each on their own computer but in a 'shared virtual environment' and a 'shared physical space' (Gordon & Schirra 2011:180–181), while talking about what they were doing. They could choose from 15 characters of varying ages and backgrounds and set off in that capacity through the virtual Chinatown of Boston, in search of a job, a place to live or a place to socialize. Along the way, they passed places and institutions that also exist in the real city: a real estate agent, a McDonald's as a cheap, low-threshold meeting place, the Chinese Evangelical Church as a provider of childcare, language and citizenship courses and so on. Not everything was suitable and accessible to every character: some places were unsafe or open at unfavourable hours, and some services were too expensive or tied to specific language knowledge or skills. All of that was described on 'Decision Cards', nine of which each player had to collect. Whoever found the most appropriate for his alter ego received a bonus. Information exchange, card swaps and comments in the chat also yielded additional points. It would be much more difficult to represent the built environment and social structure in an analogue game. The simulation would demand a constant shifting of cards and characters, which would significantly impede the dynamics. Now the software did that administrative work. *Participatory Chinatown* is one of the most well-thought-out role-playing games in the field of city development. It invited players to explore the surroundings from the perspective of someone else and address their needs. Two aspects helped in this process:

34 Eszter Tóth (2015) analyses twenty games from between 1999 and 2013. Alenka Poplin (2011 & 2014) describes several online urban planning games and then zooms in on *B3—Design Your Marketplace* (2009), a digital game prototype developed by students at Florida Atlantic University and HafenCity University Hamburg, to support resident participation in the establishment of a marketplace in Billstedt, a district of Hamburg.

35 In a third-person shooter game the player (the 'third' person) sees his avatar in the frame; he looks over his shoulder and determines his actions, but is not fused with him.

36 *PlastiCity* unfortunately never made it beyond a pre-alpha prototype that could be played but was not yet finished. Mathias Fuchs made a video of the end result achieved: https://www.youtube.com/watch?v=V8Fo8j5BZR4 (last consulted on 30 June 2022).

18

the biographical sketch that gave each character a concrete figure and the connection with the surrounding, familiar environment. Because of this, 'it was not just a disembodied character, but a character contextualized within the familiar space of the neighborhood' (2011:183). During the ensuing discussion the moderator continued to address the players using the name of their avatar. It was not until midway through the workshop that the name-boards were removed and the participants became themselves again. All of this ensured 'a strong feeling of connection to the neighborhood and a deep understanding of the issues in play' (2011:183).[37]

Excite, Visualize or Simulate?

PlastiCity and *Participatory Chinatown* emerged from design practice or were specially developed for it, but experiments have also been carried out with existing commercial video games in city development. Almost ten years after the book by von Borries, Walz and Böttger, Anders Eklund drew up the balance in his documentary *Gaming the Real World* (2016). It holds up the *Minecraft* application *Block by Block* as explicitly innovative, versatile and successful. Pontus Westerberg, digital projects officer at UN Habitat, recalls the past struggles with plans by architects and the spectacular impact when a *Minecraft* model was deployed in a project in Nairobi: 'It was like a lightbulb came on all the people in the room. […] As soon as they were able to walk around in this three-dimensional *Minecraft* model, there was a new kind of energy. People started expressing their ideas in a different way'.

Block by Block is both a fantastic and low-threshold instrument to get a varied group of people to brainstorm about projects of limited scale, but a designer is needed for the concrete implementation and the *Block by Block* team would probably be unable to tackle more ambitious and complex assignments. Gamer David Bergström, closely involved in the *Block by Block* pilot projects, notes that in *Minecraft*, 'you can't simulate things; you can only visualize things'. *Cities: Skylines* offers more possibilities: 'It's basically the same thing as *Minecraft* when it

37 With *Participatory Chinatown* it still remained quite difficult—just as with *Mobility Safari*—to achieve long-term behavioural change on the basis of the game: 'While playing a character clearly made an impression on players, one that manifested in an emotional connection to a neighborhood and its community, it did not translate to an immediate, rational reframing of the issues within the meeting itself' (Gordon & Schirra 2011:184). In the second half of the workshop the players quickly resorted to reasoning from their own point of view again. According to Gordon & Schirra, future research should therefore examine 'how game-based role-play can *reframe* issues for decisionmakers', because that is 'about changes in the context of the decision-making process and not the actual decision itself'. The effect of that is slow to materialize; it is 'a gradual process, not an immediate reflection of an experience' (2011:184).

comes to visualization, but it adds another layer of simulation. It's alive. There are citizens walking around, there are cars driving around, it feels like a real town'. The only marginal note is that video games, even if they can technically simulate reality excellently, are almost always based on strongly simplified information, calculations and models. 'It might look like [good cities], and you might be so convinced by the power of the simulation that you think it's the truth, but you really need to tweak and change it to a more realistic outcome', warns Jakob Munthe, Brand Manager for *Cities: Skylines* publisher Paradox Interactive. The commercial games sector, focused on entertainment, has no interest in making adaptations itself, but 'modders' (derived from: 'modification') like to do just that. They are gamers who expand and adapt existing software, as Bergström and his friend Emil Andersson did in 2017. For a workshop about the development of the Royal Seaport in Stockholm, they aligned traffic flows and the public transport network with the actual situation.[38] Jose Sanchez, architect and developer of *Block'hood*, enriched his game right from the start with solid data, because he wanted to simulate the functioning of a real city. There was a lot at stake: for him it was about nothing less than tackling climate change and building ecologically, so his game could not fail to make the grade at the very first reality check. He made optimal use of the possibilities of the digital medium to link data to his building modules, and one of the first reviews immediately lauded *Block'hood* as 'Minecraft For Real Life'.

Seeking for the Best of Both Worlds: Hybrid Architecture Games

Can the efficiency and dynamism of digital simulations also be combined with the tangibility, accessibility and social advantages of analogue games? A number of such hybrid games have appeared over the past decade—*Rezone The Game* (2012), for example, with which the previous chapter concluded. The colourful, three-dimensional plan of part of the town of Den Bosch is an attractive eye-catcher. Participants stand around the table, hand game characters to one another and discuss where to place them. The app informs on a big screen in real time about the level of vacancy in each of the neighbourhoods and the places where the players are active. If a city district does not receive the right input, it starts to decline. Finally, the screen shows which 'rezoned' neighbourhoods have survived and which have 'failed'. The game is cooperative and the app facilitates that: In a concept in which participants are not opponents but partners, it ensures excitement and competition (against time, vacancy and decline). *Rezone The Game* is highly suitable for breaking the ice at the start of a participatory planning process. It is accessible and amusing and is directly related to the surrounding reality and problems, but it has neither the ambition nor the potential to convey complex subject matter in an educational way or to offer concrete solutions.[39]

The educational aspect is more explicit in *Ré-Générations* (2017) →19. That spectacular installation measuring over 9 × 5 metres was inspired by Buckminster Fuller's *World Game*, but then slightly more pessimistically.[40] A transition area between city and countryside is represented on the floor, on which players have to add between 10 and 40 living units (10 cm tall cubes). They can choose between meadow or forest, high-rise or low-rise, by a river and/or close to the city, but no matter what, it will have an impact on the planet. We find ourselves in

19 →178–179

38 For a much more detailed technical description of necessary alterations, see: Pinos, Vozenilek & Pavlis 2020.

39 A highly original hybrid project was *Vienna All Tomorrows* (2018) by game developer Georg Hobmeier and his boutique game development studio Causa Creations. In it, players could help determine the future of Vienna after a fictive, satirical 'Öxit' (Austrian variant of Brexit) and 'Wixit' (Viennese secession from Austria). A huge city plan was projected on the floor and all sorts of project proposals, which players could vote on, appeared as augmented reality on tablets. Their choices influenced health, infrastructure, safety and atmosphere in the city, registered live in tables projected on the wall. The game was not a realistic simulation but essentially a critical statement full of local humour.

40 Interview with Bart Akkerhuis, Damien Charpentier and Alex Arnou on 30 June 2021. *Ré-Générations* arose out of the collaboration between the architecture office Studio Akkerhuis and a number of researchers in the area of gaming, simulation and new media. The simulation data was based on a large-scale study, conducted by the Institute for Sustainable Development and International Relations (IDDRI) in Paris, about the ecological footprint of five possible lifestyles in France in the lead-up to 2050. *Ré-Générations* was presented at the Architecture Biennale in Lyon in 2017 and the following year at two architecture centres in the same city.

SOCIÉTÉ SOBRIÉTÉ PLURIELLE
SCORE 2046
Jour du dépassement
06/01 12:54
Vous avez repoussé la date du jour du dépassement de
04j 08:52
Date
La population mondiale a augmenté de
9.93 millions
Population
Vous avez réduit les émissions de CO2 de
35.4kg éq CO2/pers
Empreinte carbone

VIVANT

VIVAN

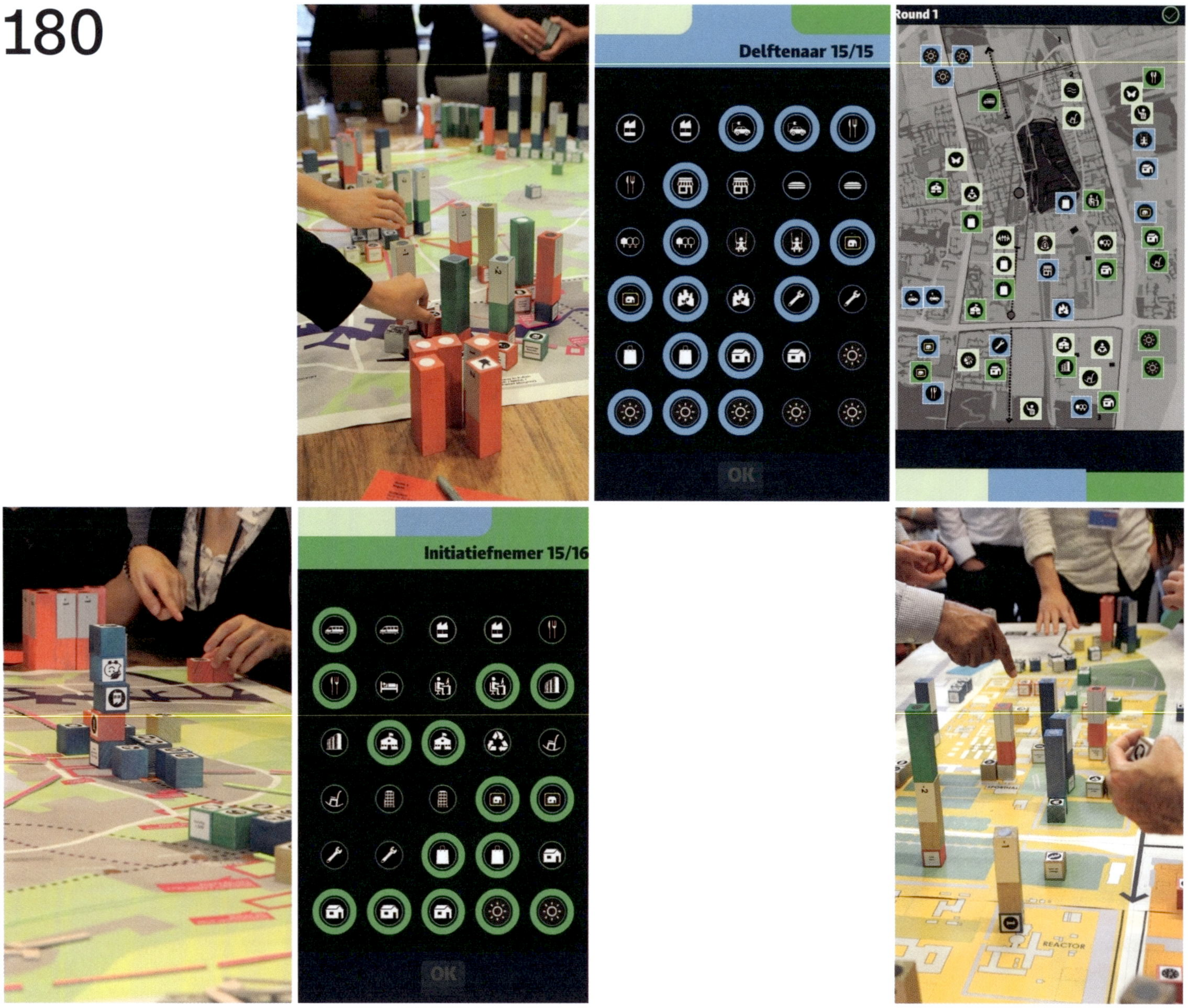

20

the Anthropocene and the Earth Overshoot Day (EOD)—'the date when humanity's demand for ecological resources and services in a given year exceeds what Earth can regenerate in that year'—arrives earlier and earlier: on 29 July in 2021. The blocks and the landscape on the floor appeal to the imagination and offer visitors easy access to the theme, but a purely analogue game would be unsuitable for such a complex situation. As soon as the blocks are standing, they are registered with an iPad and the players are presented with the bill: No matter what they do, their actions generate CO2 emissions and bring forward the EOD. The game then jumps from local to global and sounds the alarm about one of the five elements (water, soil, energy, air, or flora and fauna). For example, a shortage of sand means that no concrete can be produced, or the energy supply is overburdened, deforestation causes problems, or there is a period of extreme drought. Short films advise the participants about circular economy, sustainable mobility, water purification and so on as compensation for their preceding actions. CO2 emissions, EOD and the level of the world's population are constantly projected on the wall, updated all the time by the data processing in the background. The digital part relies on an extensive database of parameters and research results and the accompanying expertise of engineers. It determines the whole tension of this cooperative game. What matters in the end is the EOD that all players manage to achieve together: The entire duration of the exhibition simulates a period of 50 years, and the closer the EOD is to 31 December in 2067 the better.[41]

41 The duration of a round of the game corresponds with two and a half months in reality. A block in a forest area equals 2 million hectares less of afforestation around the world, and one game resident equals 500,000 'real' world citizens.

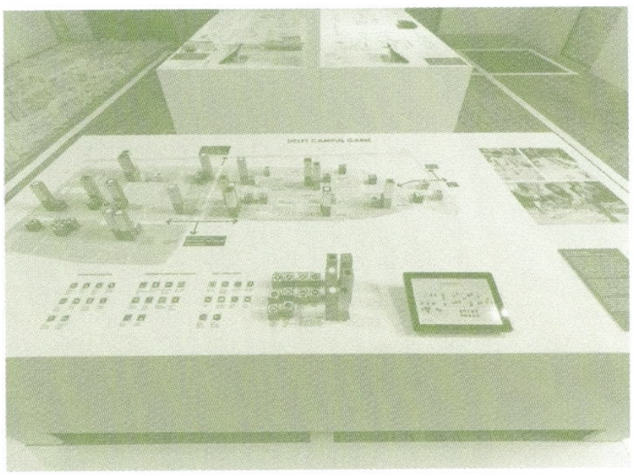

21→182–183

Rezone The Game and *Ré-Générations* were both devised for exhibitions, but hybrid game concepts also lend themselves well to participatory processes. The Rotterdam office Blok74 has specialized in this area since its foundation in 2011; *Delft Campus Urban Game* (2015) →20, 21 is a good example of their work.[42] The game board is a plan on which blocks with 'programmatic icons' are placed. Some of them are measurable and tied to a maximum: the number of parking lots, water and nature surface. They are 'a benchmark of the programme defined by various planning documents' (Ivković 2015:14). Other icons are intended 'to spark the creative brainstorm and discussion', or are even 'slightly "provocative" in order to stimulate "out of the box" thinking' (2015:14). A design phase and presentation by various teams is always followed by a vote, after which certain proposals are confirmed and others rejected. All those stages take place on or around the game board, vital for social interaction. But the icons and votes are also entered into an app, which then quickly presents an overview: which functions have been ditched, which have been retained and to what extent; which stakeholders were most successful with their proposals and which functions are located on what part of the site. That is how the digital component, just like with *Rezone The Game* and *Ré-Générations*, supports the competitive character of the game. According to Ivković, that helps 'both to keep the simulation close to the real planning situations, and as a motivation to get the best performance out of the players' (2015:20).[43] Moreover, the results are easy to share in digital form: during the game session with a projector and afterwards as documentation of the results for the client.[44] The app largely relieves the game moderator of the job of 'administrating' the game and it can be adapted relatively easily to new situations. In the future, Blok74 hopes to pursue that aim by replacing the manual entry on a tablet with smart blocks and/or digital tables.

Two issues crop up regularly: How to ensure playfulness if a game is also an instrument? And how to represent reality in a simplified yet accurate way: How to make a realistic simulation? That second question does not apply to location-based games, because they turn the built environment itself into the field of play and highlight hidden aspects of it.

PLAYFULLY EXPLORING THE SURROUNDINGS: LOCATION-BASED MOBILE GAMES

Location-based games are sometimes called 'spatially expanded games': '[They] are not [...] restricted to a set playground, game board, or online service. Instead, they venture into undefined and unlimited areas, sometimes incidentally or on the spontaneous initiative of the players. By doing so, they *appropriate* space, architecture, and objects to the game, making them parts of the experience' (Montola, Stenros & Waern 2009:77).[45] Usually it is not immediately clear which elements from the surroundings belong to the game—in theory, every item has 'potential game relevance' (2009:77) and it is often part of the game to detect the

42 Blok74 is a collaboration between urban designer Milena Ivković and programmer and game designer Stefan Nikolić. They made *Delft Campus Urban Game* for a two-day workshop at a congress of the International Society of City and Regional Planners (ISoCaRP). In that session, Delft University of Technology (TU), the Delft Design association and the municipalities of Delft and The Hague explored '[h]ow to create a sustainable knowledge region' (Ivković 2015:6), largely by bringing together science, knowledge transfer and local entrepreneurship on the TU campus. The game was later used on various other sites, and in 2021 Blok74 developed for the Architecture Centre Vienna a simplified, single-player version that can be played autonomously within 10–15 minutes.

43 According to Ivković, the competitive character does not get in the way of the aims of the game. There is ultimately a winner, but the proposals that are not voted away are also retained for all other players. The Final Design is therefore definitely the result of a 'collaborative effort' (2015:20).

44 Interview with Milena Ivković on 26 July 2021. For a comparison of analogue and digital game variants, see also: Platzer, Stowasser et al. 2018:35.

45 'Spatially expanded games' are an example of 'pervasive games', which exceed the usual boundaries of game concepts: 'A pervasive game [...] has one or more salient features that expand the contractual magic circle of play spatially, temporally, or socially. [...] The game no longer takes place in certain times or certain places, and the participants are no longer certain. Pervasive games pervade, bend, and blur the traditional boundaries of game, bleeding from the domain of the game to the domain of the ordinary' (Montola 2009:12).

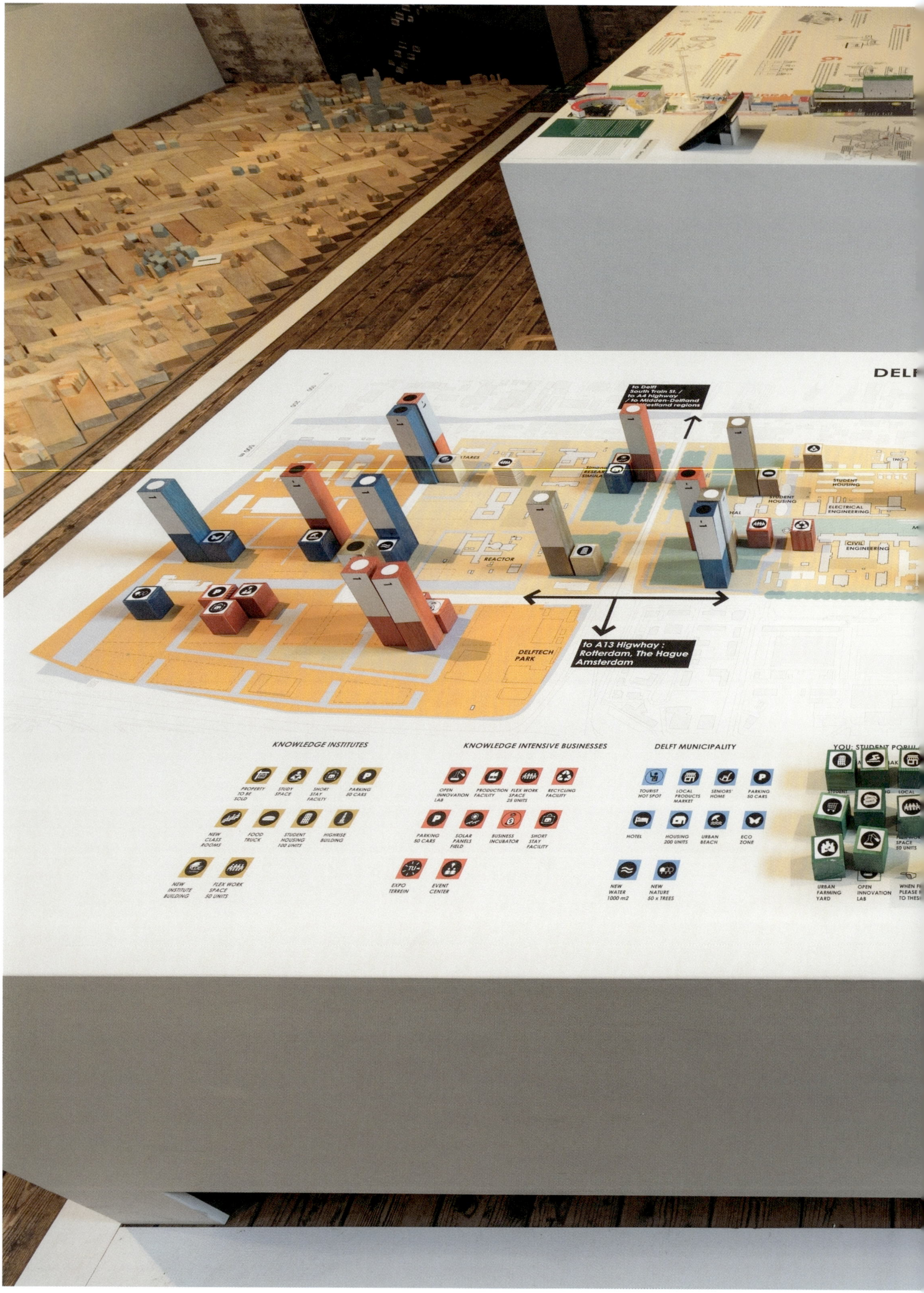
to Delft South Train St. / to A4 highway / to Midden-Delfland / Westland regions
REACTOR
DELFTECH PARK
STUDENT HOUSING
ELECTRICAL ENGINEERING
CIVIL ENGINEERING
to A13 Highway : Rotterdam, The Hague Amsterdam
KNOWLEDGE INSTITUTES
PROPERTY TO BE SOLD
STUDY SPACE
SHORT STAY FACILITY
PARKING 50 CARS
NEW CLASS ROOMS
FOOD TRUCK
STUDENT HOUSING 100 UNITS
HIGHRISE BUILDING
NEW INSTITUTE BUILDING
FLEX WORK SPACE 50 UNITS
KNOWLEDGE INTENSIVE BUSINESSES
OPEN INNOVATION LAB
PRODUCTION FACILITY
FLEX WORK SPACE 25 UNITS
RECYCLING FACILITY
PARKING 50 CARS
SOLAR PANELS FIELD
BUSINESS INCUBATOR
SHORT STAY FACILITY
EXPO TERREIN
EVENT CENTER
DELFT MUNICIPALITY
TOURIST HOT SPOT
LOCAL PRODUCTS MARKET
SENIORS' HOME
PARKING 50 CARS
HOTEL
HOUSING 200 UNITS
URBAN BEACH
ECO ZONE
NEW WATER 1000 m2
NEW NATURE 50 x TREES
URBAN FARMING YARD
OPEN INNOVATION LAB

to Delft Station
INDUSTRIAL DESIGN
to Old City
AULA
BK CITY
LIBRARY
Hello green player!
Reset

right objects or hints. That invites us to look at the surroundings in a new way: 'Spatially expanded games are inherently about *discovery* and *changing perception*. [...] Approaching a decidedly nonludic space with a playful mindset exposes the unseen and makes the familiar strange' (2009:89).

Location-based games have existed for a long time—the best known are scavenger hunts—but with the diffusion of digital media in the early twenty-first century, location-based mobile games (LBMGs) have also emerged, in which an app provides access to a game world 'behind' tangible and visible reality.[46] Troy Innocent was one of the pioneers in this area with *Urban Codemakers* (2010) →22. He set things in motion with a protest march against a general ban on games in the city, which the municipality of Melbourne apparently threatened to introduce. People wearing orange overalls carried banners with the slogan 'Stop the Ban on Play in the City!' through the streets. But the policy documents about the alleged ban (to be found on the game website) and the demonstration itself were a carefully constructed hoax to alert residents and arouse their enthusiasm for the game: 'disturbing or disordering the city's usual routines, engaging in activity not "sanctioned" by its authorities, [...] encourag[ing] participants to reflect on the authoritative control of urban space and [...] their role in the functioning of the city' (Leorke 2019:200–202). Interested parties could join Ludea, a 'micronation' of 'urban codemakers' with the special ability to anchor play in the city. They did that by collecting tags, which Innocent put up every week in the public space of Melbourne in 'often overlooked or "invisible" locations and infrastructure of the city usually taken for granted by passers-by' (2019:200). They came to places where they had never been before and developed an eye for all sorts of details. Each tag had a code that, entered on the site, attributed the finds to one of the three competing guilds: the 'Master Codemakers', 'Locative Urbanists' and 'Crossmedia Ecologists'.[47] The guild with the most points was eventually declared the winner. With *Urban Codemakers*, Innocent managed to involve residents in planning issues in a 'much more abstract, playful, and perhaps less proscriptive way than games like *Participatory Chinatown*' (2019:207) and 'without being reduced to a "gamification" tool or a heavily commercialised experience' (2019:234).[48] That autonomy is not a matter of course, because game development is often driven by external wishes and interests.

More than a decade after *Urban Codemakers* there is still plenty of interest in LBMGs, and new possibilities have emerged with the development of global positioning systems (GPS) and augmented reality (AR). Two recent examples are *Die andere Stadt* ('The Other City') (2021) →23 by Causa Creations and *Die Vergangenheit ist jetzt* ('The Past Is Now') (2019) by ArchäoNOW →24. The former illustrates the narrative possibilities of LBMGs, while the latter was a pioneer in the area of AR. Both are not only informative and educational, but also entertaining, surprising and exciting. They make players aware of places, histories and meanings that no longer exist or are inaccessible or overlooked, but that shape and/or enrich the city.

Die andere Stadt is an exploration of Vienna in the past, present and future, in three episodes and in different places around the city. It was devised by three artists with foreign backgrounds, under the supervision of game developer Georg Hobmeier.[49] The second part, *Unzustellbar* ('Undeliverable'), is set in and around the Reumannhof from 1926, a residential complex for workers that

46 Other examples of analogue location-based games are *Mystery on Fifth Avenue* (2008) by Eric Clough and 212box and the spectacular *Big Urban Game* (2003) by Nick Fortugno, Frank Lantz and Katie Salen, in which teams of players dragged huge inflated counters in red, yellow and blue through the Twin Cities of Minneapolis and St. Paul (Lantz 2007 & Montola 2009).

47 Players could choose between three guilds, each with its own medium to approach city planning: language for the 'Master Codemakers', technology for the 'Locative Urbanists' and nature for the 'Crossmedia Ecologists' (Leorke 2019:202). An extensive plan for the future of the city, in line with their ideology, stood on the site for each of the guilds.

48 From 2016 on, Troy Innocent developed *Wayfinder Live*, the successor to *Urban Codemakers*. See: Leorke 2019:195–240.

49 Interview with Georg Hobmeier on 3 February 2022.

STOP THE BAN
ON PLAY IN
THE CITY!

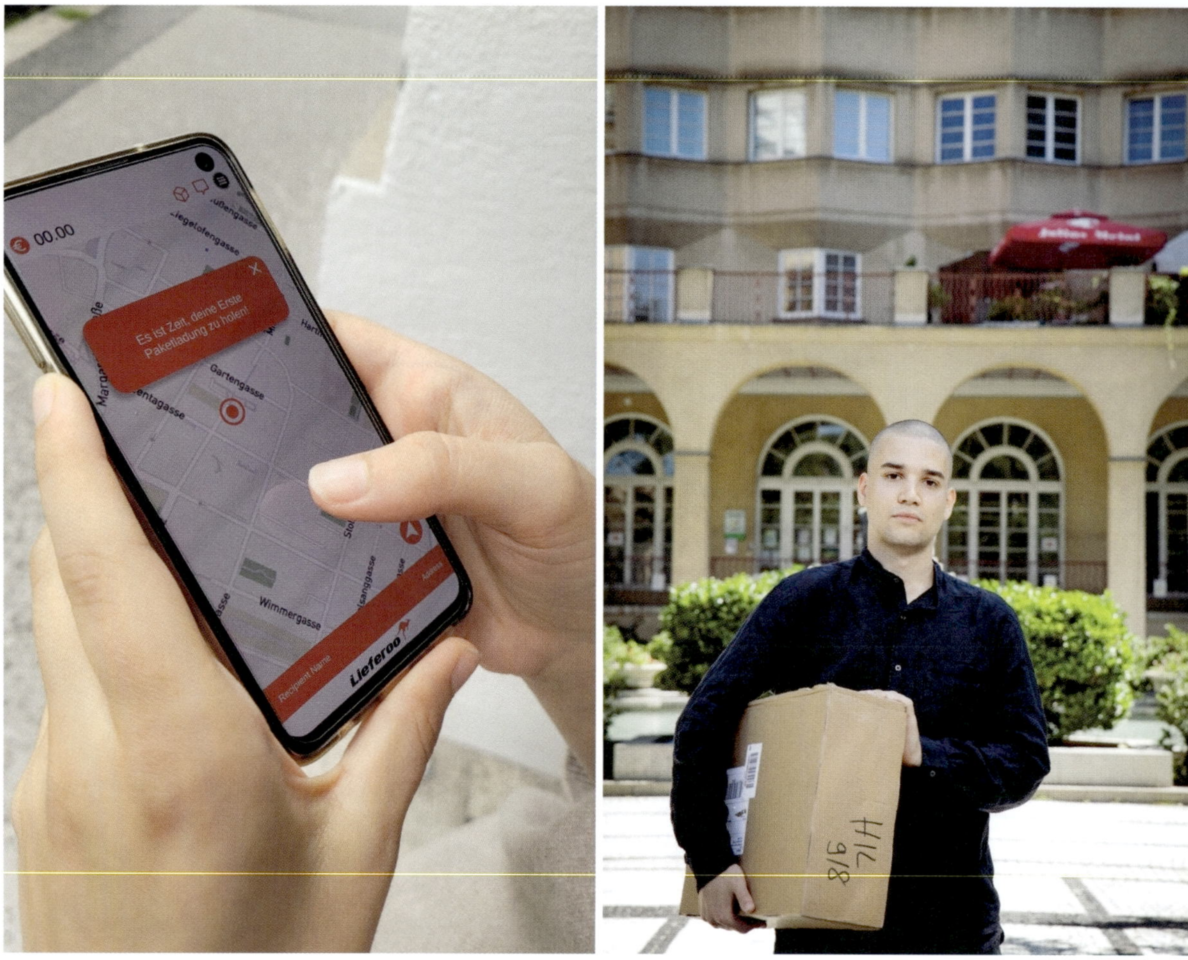
00.00
Es ist Zeit, deine Erste Paketladung zu holen!
Gartengasse
Wimmergasse
Lieferoo
Recipient Name
Julius Meinl

23

SOUVENIRS

24

embodies the heyday of socialism in the Austrian capital. The game does not offer specific information about the subject, but the story has a direct bearing on the significance of the place. Media artist Nestor Hiebl based the scenario on his personal experience working as a bike messenger: In the game a fictive company app sends you from A to B to pick up and deliver parcels. Every now and then, a message in broken German from a colleague flashes past, inquiring from another corner of the city about how things are going and asking if you can take on an order for him. But the boss is digitally breathing down your neck all the time, admonishing you to be even more efficient and unscrupulously venting his anger. In the meantime, the minutes tick by and a paltry few euros sporadically drop into your virtual wallet, only to vanish again quickly when you get blamed for late deliveries or damaged goods. Welcome to the world of the precariat: those countless underpaid workers who keep the machinery of modern metropolises running but are rarely noticed. *Unzustellbar* has a totally different genesis to *Participatory Chinatown*, though there are interesting similarities: Players merge with their characters and what occupies them; they move through the city to meet their needs. But in *Unzustellbar* the surroundings are no longer simulated—experiences, perspectives and points of view are shared in a realistic setting—and that has a huge impact.

Die Vergangenheit ist jetzt is a very different type of LBMG: The app does not provide an imaginary narrative, but a stunning spatial reconstruction of places that have disappeared from the centre of Vienna. The game is the result of a collaboration between the architect Franco Lanfur (with his firm VARS) and archaeologist Miriam Weberstorfer, founder of ArchäoNOW.[50] In this architectural and cultural-historical scavenger hunt, players search for certain symbols or details in public spaces. As soon as they scan them with the 3D camera on their mobile phone, an exact reconstruction of a disappeared building appears on the screen in AR. The virtual space overlaps exactly with the real environment that the camera films at that moment. Players can walk towards or around the building, explore it and search for clues to answer the question in the scavenger hunt. The game transports them directly into another time dimension.

The developers of *Die andere Stadt* and *Die Vergangenheit ist jetzt* make grateful use of recent technical innovations, such as increasingly accurate GPS and perfected AR. For the LBMG *Hello Lamp Post* (2013) →25, Pan Studio deliberately opted a few years earlier for the elementary technology: SMS. *Hello Lamp Post* is played all over the world, from Bristol to Malmö, Austin, Sydney and Singapore, for an average of six months per city. Banners inform passers-by that they can make contact, by SMS via a special number, with elements from the built environment such as lampposts, benches or manholes. No account or installation is required; a simple 'Hello kiosk number 271408!' is enough to strike up a conversation. The kiosk, bin or fountain contacted answers by SMS with a question: 'I can't turn. Can you tell me what's behind me?' or: 'If you listen carefully, what's the quietest thing you can hear?' or: 'How has the city changed, in the time that you've known it?' And thus a dialogue arises, to which players themselves contribute a lot, because their answers are reused: For example, they can read what a previous passer-by has heard, seen or shared, and conversations are reproduced on dashboards or presented to clients to give an impression of what is on the minds of residents.[51]

For Ben Barker, co-founder of Pan Studio, 'design is obsessed with performance; it is very rare that design sees it as its duty to have an experiential rather than a functional quality for people'. Things are no better in smart cities:

50 Interview with Miriam Weberstorfer on 21 December 2021.

51 Interview with Ben Barker on 22 June 2021. Each version of *Hello Lamp Post* consists of a 'generic default system' that remains the same for each city, plus a number of 'highly tailored custom objects that "know a lot about themselves" and ask managed questions'. Between them are 'different levels of granularity': Some types of object are already registered with a 'personality', but players can also add objects that the system does not fully know. For example, 'we don't have a basketball hoop as a personality type, so it would just talk like a generic object and say: "Thanks for waking me up. What brings you here?" But it wouldn't know how to behave like a basketball hoop'.

Good afternoon, we haven't met before. Can I ask, what brings you to this part of town?
I'm going home, you just happen to live on my route.
Oh right! The last person I spoke to said, "I was taking a short cut on my way to work, then I got distracted and started talking to a tree."

I'M A FIRE HYDRANT TALK TO ME
SMS:
HELLO
HYDRANT #6-9
TO 8514 8312
HELLOLAMPPOSTSINGAPORE.COM

Much revolves around efficiency, for example 'getting people from here to here as fast as possible with as few interruptions', while the journey itself can actually be an interesting experience—and play can certainly help in that regard.[52] As winner of the Playable City Award of 2013, Pan Studio was, with *Hello Lamp Post*, 'challenging everything that the smart city was: data, efficiency, taking out serendipity, focusing on making cities optimal rather than experiential...' In particular, smart cities have an overkill of 'data points: people putting sensors on top of lampposts and cameras on corners to optimize traffic flow or to always know how polluted a place is'. All those urban objects are given a new role in *Hello Lamp Post*. For Barker they are perhaps 'dumb' but also 'humanistic' and 'vulnerable' owing to their immobility. That evokes all sorts of things in players, who behave in a 'really supportive' way: 'either making jokes, or telling really sweet, sincere stories about what the place meant to them, or just observing: literally telling the object, almost in a nurturing way, about the place'.

FINALLY

The impression at the end of this exploration is that of extraordinary diversity. The generic term 'architecture game' comprises multiple genres. Doll's houses, construction toys, city building games: they are so unalike that they could almost be viewed as different media. That diversity is increased even further owing to the fact that analogue and digital concepts exist side by side and mixed up together.

Designers who experiment with alternative means of representation and communication often do so to reach a wider audience. The customary floor plans, sections, models and renderings throw up too many obstacles in communicating with people from outside the profession. Another medium can make for a more equal exchange of ideas. Moreover, attention shifts to experiences and meanings 'behind' the material and technical side of architecture. All those motivations and intentions surface in each of the three forms of expression in this trilogy: architecture comic strips, films and games. But they also differ from one another significantly.

Bricks & Balloons: Architecture in Comic-Strip Form (2012) consists of two parts: the first about architectural criticism, and the second about architectural design. The comic strips in part one are poetic or philosophical reflections on certain places or on architecture in general. That is also the approach of some filmmakers in *Spots in Shots: Narrating the Built Environment in Short Films* (2018): Struck by the beauty, mystery, excitement, multiple layers or contradictions of a place, they wanted to share that feeling—not by convincing the viewer of something, but by transporting them to another reality that would broaden their view of the place. Among the architecture games that come closest to that are such installations as Douglas Coupland's *Super City* (2005) and Chris Burden's *Metropolis II* (2010), as well as Rachel Whiteread's *Place (Village)* (2017), Alice Pasquini's *The Unchanging World* (2018) and Heather Benning's *The Dollhouse* (2007). The point of departure for those artworks is a doll's house or construction toy, but just like in the comic strips and films, the role of that architecture initially remains rather mysterious and the viewer has full scope to rely on their own perception, interpretation and imagination.

Among the comic artists and filmmakers who leave their public plenty of freedom for personal experiences and associations, some gave urban design analyses and architectural reviews a completely new twist by deliberately choosing an explicitly subjective point of view. Such a personal perspective also crops

52 '[T]he classic idea of portable games [...] is to fill idle moments of daily life with interesting game content'. But 'the choice between *move to play* or *play while moving* is central in spatially expanded games': 'Instead of making travel less bothersome and waiting less boring, many pervasive games require players to do *additional* traveling or waiting in order to succeed' (Montola, Stenros & Waern 2009:82).

up in games, with the added advantage that players can also temporarily assume other roles than their own. For example, Danny Hayes' *Change: A Homeless Survival Experience* (2018) gives an impression of life as a homeless person, the players of DOWiNO's *A Blind Legend* (2015) and *Sensivise* (2020) are suddenly blind or visually impaired, and in Causa Creations' *Unzustellbar* (2021) they feel what it is like to have to race from one address to another as a bike messenger. In applications specially devised for design practice, a lot of attention is devoted to assuming various roles. The expectation is that it promotes mutual understanding and collaboration. Sometimes participants play themselves, sometimes they do not, but almost always there is something that invites them to reflect on their own priorities, preferences and limitations and to seek to align them with those of others. That is perfectly illustrated by *Participatory Chinatown* (2010) by the Engagement Game Lab, but it also applies to the games by specialized offices such as die Baupiloten, Play the City and Blok74, and all the more so in cooperative games.

Comic strips and films that reflect on a building, concept or approach are often critical. The makers are touched by or indignant about a social or political issue; they want to shake up their readers or viewers and make them think. Critical works also appear in the form of games—for example Van Sowerwine's *Play with Me* (2002), Jon Haddock's *Isometric Screenshots* (2000), Sabine Bloch's *MärchenHaft* (2005–2006), Maykel Roovers' *Critical Blocks* (2012) and the work of Paolo Pedercini. However, they are mostly reflections on architecture as it appears in certain games, and only indirectly on the built environment around it. Other examples shine a light on real architecture or practices: Zupagrafika's *Blokoshka* (2016) and *Panelki* (2019) about former East Bloc architecture, or the critical distortions of *Monopoly*, such as Carl-Ludwig Reichert's *Provopoli: Wem gehört die Stadt* (1972) or Fathi Bouaroua's *Taudis-Poly* (2019). Those critical games rarely come from the design world itself. Maria Auböck, János Kárász and Axel Ott's *Capital Game* (1988) and Studio Karhard's *Mängel Quartett* (2012) are some exceptions, but their number is limited compared with critical comic strips. In architecture comics and films, criticism often occurs in combination with humour and irony, and the works often balance between fact and fiction. The makers deliberately put viewers on the wrong foot and stimulate an active attitude by not being specific about what is 'true' and what is imagined. Those two stylistic devices appear in You+Pea's *London Developers Toolkit* (2015) and Querkraft Architekten's *(Un)perfekt* (2014), but rarely elsewhere. A direct comparison of criticism in the form of a game and a film is offered by Mathias Fuchs and Steve Manthorp's *PlastiCity* (2005) and Squint/Opera's *Picture a City (Bradford)* (2004). Both concern the same master plan by William Alsop and in both works some buildings disappear with the ease of a mouse click. The film is described as 'an instrument to involve—even to provoke—a wider and diverse audience of citizens in the contemporary urban debate'.[53] The added value of the game is that the player becomes part of the story and sees his own avatar in the frame: he himself causes every change to the surroundings. That identification adds depth to the reflection.

The boundary between architectural criticism and architectural design is fluid, as already indicated in *Bricks & Balloons.* Authors expressed reservations about a building or a situation and naturally proposed an alternative concept. They used comic strips and films to communicate their own work in a convincing manner. Yet only very sporadically did a comic strip also influence the realization of architecture. The relationship is the reverse in the case of architecture games, where play is often deployed at the start of a design process in order to actively contribute to it. In The Why Factory's *Porous City* (2012), *Lego* provided the trigger for a very particular method of fundamental research into the integration of air

53 See the film description on Architecture Player: https://www.architectureplayer.com/clips/picture-a-city-bradford (last consulted on 30 June 2022).

26

and light in high-rise development. Damien Murtagh's *Arckit* (2015) emerged directly from a search to develop a modular construction system, for which models with flexible walls were needed. Construction toys have become part of daily practice at the office *El Equipo Mazzanti*. The miniature modules are translated directly into the construction world, and they help in solving real design problems and communicating concepts. Compared to construction toys, board games are usually too complex for direct applications because of the extensive rules, but their principles inspire the makers of games for design practice: in particular their ability to reflect a complex reality in a simplified way, to convey a specific message through a scoring mechanism, to bring various roles into line with one another and to stimulate players to pool their resources. Finally, hybrids of various genres regularly occur in practice: for example, construction toys that are tied to rules, or combinations of analogue and digital elements. Perhaps a real hybrid will eventually appear: as socio-critical as *Unzustellbar*, as responsible as *Block'hood*, as uniting as *Block by Block*, as interactive as *Hello Lamp Post*, as subtle as *(Un)perfekt*, as witty as *Mängel Quartett*, as spectacular as *Ré-Générations*, as enjoyable as *Rezone* and as elegant as *Mystery on Fifth Avenue*.

EPILOGUE: ABANDONING EFFICIENCY

In a book called *The Grasshopper: Games, Life and Utopia* →26, philosopher Bernard Suits once wrote: '[P]laying a game is the voluntary attempt to overcome unnecessary obstacles' (2005[1978]:55). Even after a number of years of research, that definition remains apt and refreshing, and perhaps it also clarifies what unites all examples. All players have some aim in mind: one wants to collect all pairs of cards, another wants to discover a story, and the next wants to locate a new hundred homes in a landscape. Such an aim is still independent of the game and it can also be achieved in other ways. That is why Suits calls it 'prelusory' (2005[1978]:51). A game only becomes a game when rules determine how that aim can be achieved—and then especially not in the easiest way (2005[1978]:54). Cards are deliberately shuffled and turned around; a story is packaged in riddles and hidden in the surroundings; some homes are not allowed in certain places in the landscape. And participants like the fact that they are bound by these rules. The 'lusory attitude' is 'that curious state of affairs wherein one adopts rules which require one to employ worse rather than better means for reaching an end' (2005[1978]:52). In other words, playing has a lot to do with abandoning efficiency. That is very liberating, yet also awkward and a little absurd. From the outside it can appear incomprehensible, but when a team steps into that same boat together, it can result in lots of humour and solidarity, and bring seriousness and fun together in unique fashion.

THE POWER OF PLAYFULNESS

01 *Destinazione Freetown*, TAM Associati, 2012
02 *Le giraffe hanno il collo lungo… e sono curiose*, TAM Associati, 2005
03 *Gioco Laguna*, TAM Associati, 2003
04 *Laguna Big Game*, TAM Associati, 2003
05 *Provopoli: Wem gehört die Stadt?*, Carl-Ludwig Reichert, 1972
06 *Buildings in Boxes: Architectural Toys from the CCA*, exhibition from 28 November 1990 to 31 March 1991, Photo: © Canadian Centre for Architecture, Montreal
07 *Imagination Playground*, David Rockwell, 2010, featured in *Play Work Build*, exhibition since 2012 at National Building Museum, Washington
08 *Architects at Play*, exhibition from 18 October 2019 to 9 February 2020 at International Centre for the City, Architecture and Landscape (CIVA), Brussels, Photo: © Filip Dujardin
09 *Social Design: Learning at Play*, exhibition from 23 November 2019 to 23 February 2020 at Design Society, Shenzhen, Photo: © People's Architecture Office
10 *Wait*, Lindsay Grace, 2005
11 *Dust & Dust Scapes*, Aram Bartholl, 2011 & 2013, featured in *Serious Fun: Architecture & Games*, exhibition from 16 March to 5 September 2022 at Architekturzentrum Wien (Az W), Photo: © Lisa Rastl
12 *The Continuous City*, Gareth Damian Martin, 2018
13 *Another Day of Depression in Kowloon* Yuk-Yiu Ip, 2012
14 *Down and Out in Los Santos*, Alan Butler, 2015
15 *Operation Jane Walk*, Robin Klengel & Leonhard Müllner (Total Refusal), 2018
16 *A Blind Legend*, DOWiNO (Games, Apps and Films for Change), 2015

A BEYOND THE PITCHED ROOF?

01 *Nuremberg House*, unknown, 1637, Photo: © Victoria & Albert Museum, London
02 *Little People Play Family House*, Fisher Price, 1969
03 *Mega Bloks—Lion's Kingdom*, Ritvik Toys, 1994, Photo: © Canadian Centre for Architecture, Montreal
04 *Mega Bloks—Build and Decorate Dream Home*, Ritvik Toys, 1993, Photo: © Canadian Centre for Architecture, Montreal
05 *Ultra Modern Dolls' House*, Tri-ang, 1937
06 *Whiteladies House*, Moray Thomas, 1935, Photo: © Victoria & Albert Museum, London
07 *Open-Sided Dolls House*, Roger Limbrick, 1962, Photo: © Victoria & Albert Museum, London
08 *Jennys Home Dolls' House*, Tri-ang, 1960s, Photo: © Victoria & Albert Museum, London
09 *The House of Viktor & Rolf*, Siebe Tettero, 2008, Photo: © Centraal Museum Utrecht / Ernst Moritz
10 *Dutch Design (Doll) House*, Gilian Schrofer, 2014
11 *Spiral Dollhouse*, Architecture BRIO, 2014, Photo: © Sebastian Zachariah / PHX India
12 *Arne Jacobsen Dollhouse*, Linda Stenberg, 2009, Photo: © Thomas Skyum
13 *Villa Sibis*, Wolfgang Sirch & Christoph Bitzer, 2004, Photo: © Fa. Sirch
14 *Modular House*, Ana Maia & Laurent Maes (Mini Archi), 2013, Photo: © Wolfgang Thaler
15 *Emerson Dollhouse*, Tim Boyle (Brinca Dada), 2010
16 *PoppenVilla*, Liliane Limpens, 1999
17 *My First Dollhouse*, PlanToys, 1990
18 *Slide N Go Dollhouse*, PlanToys, 2018
19 *Contemporary Dollhouse*, PlanToys, 2020
20 *Creative Play House*, PlanToys, 2004
21 *Victorian Dollhouse*, PlanToys, 2003
22 *Green Dollhouse*, PlanToys, 2009, Photo: © Wolfgang Thaler
23 *PowerHouse*, Rainer Köthe (Kosmos), 2010, Photo: © Wolfgang Thaler
24 *3 Huisjesspel*, Anne Kooijman (De Coole Kikker), 2011, Photo: © Wolfgang Thaler
25 *Kaleidoscope House*, Laurie Simmons & Peter Wheelwright, 2001, Photo: © Laurie Simmons
26 *Qubis House*, Amy Whitworth, 2012, Photo: © Wolfgang Thaler
27 *Play with Me*, Van Sowerwine & Isobel Knowles, 2002, featured in *Serious Fun: Architecture & Games*, exhibition from 16 March to 5 September 2022 at Architekturzentrum Wien (Az W), Photo: © Lisa Rastl
28 *Isometric Screenshots*, Jon Haddock, 2000
29 *MärchenHaft*, Sabine Bloch, 2005–2006
30 *Reflect Forward*, Lucy May Schofield, 2008
31 *Untitled (Dollhouse)*, Yinka Shonibare, 2002, Photo: © Wolfgang Thaler
32 *Place (Village)*, Rachel Whiteread, 2017, Photo: © Victoria & Albert Museum, London / Courtesy of the artist & Luhring Augustine, New York
33 *The Unchanging World*, Alice Pasquini, 2018
34 *Fallen Star 1/5*, Do Ho Suh, 2008-2011, featured in *Your Bright Future: 12 Contemporary Artists from Korea*, exhibition from 28 June to 20 September 2009 at Los Angeles County Museum of Art (LACMA), © Do Ho Suh / Courtesy of the artist and Lehmann Maupin, New York, Hong Kong, Seoul & London / Photo: © Museum Associates / LACMA

35 *The Dollhouse*, Heather Benning, 2007 & *The Dollhouse* (film), Chad Galloway, 2014

36 *Luisterhuis*, Machiel Spaan (M3H) & Rozalie Hirs, 2017, featured in *Serious Fun: Architecture & Games*, exhibition from 16 March to 5 September 2022 at Architekturzentrum Wien (Az W), Photo: © Lisa Rastl

B THE BLOCK AS TRANSFORMATION ARTIST

01 *Church and Sunday School*, Whitney S. Reed Toy Company, 1880, Photo: © Canadian Centre for Architecture, Montreal

02 *Stanlo nr 6*, Stanley Tool Company, 1933, Photo: © Canadian Centre for Architecture, Montreal

03 *Fabrik*, Josef Hoffmann, 1920, Photo: © Canadian Centre for Architecture, Montreal

04 *Stilspiel*, Hermann Finsterlin, 1921

05 *Dandanah*, Bruto Taut & Blanche Mahlberg, 1922, Photo: © Canadian Centre for Architecture, Montreal

06 *Supercity*, Douglas Coupland, 2005, Photo: © Canadian Centre for Architecture, Montreal

07 *Blockitecture—Habitat & Parkland*, James Paulius, 2013, Photo: © Wolfgang Thaler

08 *Uberstix—1600 Uberarc*, Dane Scarborough, 2008, Photo: © Wolfgang Thaler

09 *Arckit—Greenscape Village & GO Eco*, Damien Murtagh, 2021, Photo: © Wolfgang Thaler

10 *Bioblo*, Stefan Friedrich, Hannes Frech & Dietmar Kreil, 2014, Photo: © Wolfgang Thaler

11 *Minecraft*, Markus Alexej Persson, 2011, Screenshots: © Jonas Schwaiger

12 *Townscaper*, Oskar Stålberg, 2020, Screenshots: © Jonas Schwaiger

13 *Cloud Gardens*, Thomas van den Berg, 2020, Screenshots: © Jonas Schwaiger

14 *Capital Game*, Maria Auböck, János Kárász & Axel Ott, 1988, Photo: © Wolfgang Thaler

15 *Critical Blocks*, Maykel Roovers, 2012

16 *Critical Blocks*, Maykel Roovers, 2012, featured in *Serious Fun: Architecture & Games*, exhibition from 16 March to 5 September 2022 at Architekturzentrum Wien (Az W), Photo: © Lisa Rastl

17 *Blokoshka*, Zupagrafika, 2016, Photo: © David Navarro

18 *Panelki*, Zupagrafika, 2019, Photo: © Wolfgang Thaler

19 *Metropolis II*, Chris Burden, 2010, featured at Los Angeles County Museum of Art since 2021, Courtesy of the Nicolas Berggruen Charitable Foundation, Photo: © Digital Image Museum Associates/LACMA/Art Resource NY / Scala, Florence

20 *London Developers Toolkit*, Sandra Youkhana & Luke Caspar Pearson (You+Pea), 2015

21 *Porous City*, The Why Factory & KRADS, 2012, Photo: © Frans Parthesius

22 *Lego Towers*, Bjarke Ingels Group, 2006

23 *Block by Block*, UN-Habitat & Mojang / Microsoft, since 2012

24 *Forest of Hope*, El Equipo Mazzanti, 2012 & *We Play, You Play*, exhibition from 16 June to 29 September 2017 at Spazio FMG per l'Architettura, Milan

25 *Parquette*, Hans Venhuizen, 1991, Photo: © Thea van den Heuvel

C THE DOS AND DON'TS OF THE PERFECT CITY

01 *Sensivise*, DOWiNO (Games, Apps and Films for Change), 2020

02 *Skyscraper*, Karl Smith, 1937, Photo: © The Strong National Museum of Play, Rochester (NY)

03 *Gusher*, Charles Deaton, 1940, Photo: © Canadian Centre for Architecture, Montreal

04 *Housing Drive*, Pepys Games, 1948

05 *Square Mile*, Olaf Helmer & Reuben Klamer, 1962, Photo: © The Strong National Museum of Play, Rochester (NY)

06 *Manhattan*, Andreas Seyfarth, 1994, Photo: © Wolfgang Thaler

07 *Expancity*, Alex Cutler, 2018, Photo: © Wolfgang Thaler

08 *Megacity: Oceania*, Jordan Draper & Michael Fox, 2019, Photo: © Wolfgang Thaler

09 *Big City*, Franz-Benno Delonge, 1999, Photo: © Wolfgang Thaler

10 *Metropolis*, Sid Sackson, 1984, Photo: © Wolfgang Thaler

11 *Quadropolis*, François Gandon, 2016, Photo: © Wolfgang Thaler

12 *Suburbia*, Ted Alspach, 2012, Photo: © Wolfgang Thaler

13 *Capital*, Filip Miłuński, 2016, Photo: © Wolfgang Thaler

14 *Neom*, Paul Sottosanti, 2018, Photo: © Wolfgang Thaler

15 *Smog: The Air Pollution Game*, Richard Rosen, 1970

16 *Ökolopoly*, Frederic Vester, 1983, Photo: © Wolfgang Thaler

17 *Bruxelles 1893*, Etienne Espreman, 2013, Photo: © Wolfgang Thaler

18 *Our Town*, Jim Deacove, 1978

19 *Pandemic: Rising Tide*, Matt Leacock & Jeroen Doumen, 2017, Photo: © Wolfgang Thaler

20 *Cities: Skylines*, Rustan Håkansson, 2019, Photo: © Wolfgang Thaler
21 *Nova Alea*, Paolo Pedercini, 2016
22 *Lichenia*, Paolo Pedercini, 2019
23 *Block'hood*, Jose Sanchez, 2015
24 *Change: A Homeless Survival Experience*, Danny Hayes, 2018
25 *Rezone The Game*, Rolf van Boxmeer & Tessa Peters, 2012, featured in *Serious Fun: Architecture & Games*, exhibition from 16 March to 5 September 2022 at Architekturzentrum Wien (Az W), Photo: © Lisa Rastl

D RISKING PLAYFULNESS FOR A GREATER GOOD

01 *New Town*, Barry R. Lawson, 1967
02 *Metropolis*, Richard Duke, 1966
03 *Community Land Use Game*, Allan Feldt, 1965
04 *Instructional Housing and Building Simulation*, Cedrid Green, 1970
05 *Thermal Design*, Juan Pablo Bonta, 1979
06 *Semiotics*, Juan Pablo Bonta, 1979
07 *World Game*, Richard Buckminster Fuller, 1969
08 *Lifestyle*, Christian Raffeiner & Helmut Walch, 1989
09 *(Un)perfekt*, Querkraft Architekten, 2014, Photo: © Wolfgang Thaler
10 *Mängel Quartett*, Alexandra Erhard & Thomas Karsten (Studio Karhard), 2012, Photo: © Wolfgang Thaler
11 *Mystery on Fifth Avenue*, Eric Clough (212box), 2008
12 *Mystery on Fifth Avenue*, Eric Clough (212box), 2008
13 *Schul-Visionenspiel*, die Baupiloten, 2018, Photo: © Wolfgang Thaler
14 *Klimaatspel* & *Play the Koepel*, Play the City, 2019 & 2020, Photos: © Txell Blanco, Hyunyu Woo & Ekim Tan
15 *Parquette*, Hans Venhuizen, 2009 & 2021, featured in *Team Work*, exhibition from 31 October 2008 to 1 March 2009 at Museum de Paviljoens in Almere, Photo: © Gert Jan Van Rooij / featured in *Serious Fun: Architecture & Games*, exhibition from 16 March to 5 September 2022 at Architekturzentrum Wien (Az W), Photo: © Lisa Rastl
16 *Mobility Safari*, Katharina Gugerell, Martina Jauschneg, Ludwig Grimm & Mario Platzer, 2017, Photo: © Wolfgang Thaler
17 *PlastiCity*, Mathias Fuchs & Steve Manthorp, 2005
18 *Participatory Chinatown*, Eric Gordon (Engagement Game Lab), 2010
19 *Ré-Générations*, Studio Akkerhuis, David Malaud & Guillaume Dubois, 2017
20 *Delft Campus Urban Game*, Milena Ivković & Stefan Nikolić (Blok74), 2015, Photos: © Eranda Janku
21 *Delft Campus Urban Game*, Milena Ivković & Stefan Nikolić (Blok74), 2021, featured in *Serious Fun: Architecture & Games*, exhibition from 16 March to 5 September 2022 at Architekturzentrum Wien (Az W), Photo: © Lisa Rastl
22 *Urban Codemakers*, Troy Innocent, 2010
23 *Unzustellbar*, Causa Creations & Nestor Hiebl, 2021
24 *Die Vergangenheit ist jetzt*, ArchäoNOW, 2019
25 *Hello Lamp Post*, Pan Studio, 2013
26 *Grasshopper*, Drawing : © Caspar Schwaiger

Every book is a collective endeavour; one name graces the cover, but many others contribute behind the scenes. Critical readers and other experts who take the time to offer feedback and advice on a project as it evolves are especially valuable. Each of these interested observations and critical comments helps the book take shape. At the start of *Serious Fun*, they included the questions and suggestions from the Creative Industries Fund NL, which sharpened the theoretical and methodological approach and made image editing a key aspect from the early stages. How fine it is that a grant from the Fund comes with a wealth of useful tips. A committee that takes the time to put its recommendations on paper is not something that can be taken for granted.

In those early stages, when *Serious Fun* had yet to acquire a definitive name, other parties expressed their confidence and support in similar fashion, most notably the Van Eesteren-Fluck & Van Lohuizen Foundation and the Arts and Culture Division at the Austrian Federal Chancellery. Both of them also provided funding for my last publication, *Spots in Shots: Narrating the Built Environment in Short Films* (2018). The Creative Industries Fund NL has even been a loyal supporter of the complete trilogy, which started with *Bricks & Balloons: Architecture in Comic-Strip Form* (2012). None of these books would have been possible without their support.

From the summer of 2020 on, this present book developed in tandem with the exhibition of the same name for the Architekturzentrum Wien (Az W). Discussions about the subject had started some time earlier, and director Angelika Fitz's clear desire to devote attention to this unusual theme proved highly motivating. The collaboration with the Az W, from that point on with project leader Katharina Ritter and the rest of the team, was enjoyable and inspiring. Angelika's trust and receptiveness to unconventional insights, along with Katharina's ability to put things in perspective and her humour, carried the project at crucial moments.

The research phase gradually evolved into a number of individual, smaller projects. After all, a doll's house is poles apart from a board game in terms of genre, the analogue and digital variants of the same game concept can sometimes be highly dissimilar, and the developers of applied games often have very different intentions to those of people who devise conventional, commercial games. Exploring and understanding each type of game felt like learning the words of a new language, and it was a delight to be able to build on the work of others. For example, the Canadian Centre for Architecture has done pioneering work in researching, interpreting and presenting construction toys and doll's houses up until the 1990s. The warm welcome I received in Montreal when my project was still in its infancy unlocked an interest and enthusiasm that have stayed with me to this day. I was able to unpack, view, touch and try out dozens of historical construction toys. Opening a games box is and remains a magical moment.

At the start of the third chapter, it was a shock to discover that a comparable wealth of literature on the history of board games simply did not exist. Even before I could start my research into contemporary city building games, I first had to get a grip on the roots of that genre. That challenging quest once again made it clear that knowledge and expertise do not always originate in books. Anybody who wants to learn about the world of board games will discover a vast reservoir of useful information and astute observations in games libraries, in games reviews posted on YouTube, and on the worldwide platform BoardGameGeek. In particular, the games library in my home town of Vienna is run by a team of highly educated specialists who have personally tested a staggering number of games and can make all sorts of cross-connections between them. Many a time I returned home with bags brimming with new discoveries. Claudia Bayerl, Johanna France, Stefan Graf, Paul Gruber and Aaron Terzer not only guided me through their considerable collection, but also instilled in me a love of board games that I will have difficulty shaking off.

My research consisted of conducting dozens of interviews with almost all of the game developers represented in this book, and of carrying out countless test sessions with games. I am extremely grateful to all the game makers, architects and artists for taking the time to talk to me about their work; their input forms the core of this book. In some cases, the interview led to further discussions about how a particular game could be adapted for the exhibition. My thanks in particular to Gareth Damian Martin, Hans Venhuizen, Milena Ivković and Stefan Nikolić, who came up with revised versions of existing works specifically for that purpose. It was thrilling and instructive to witness that process at close quarters.

And what an incredible luxury: a project that lets you play for hours on end, under the guise of work. Jonas, Caspar, Adèle, Moritz and Milla often joined in. I cherish fond memories of many afternoons spent assembling games, when my office space was transformed into a photo studio, and later, in the lead-up to the exhibition, when we spent whole weekends at the Az W. What a joy that they were willing to be my 'guinea pigs' and helpers! I hope we will continue to play just as much after this project.

At the end of the process, I was fortunate to be able to fall back on the same dream team as I had four years ago with *Spots in Shots*, with photographer Wolfgang Thaler as newcomer. He immortalized dozens of games featured in this book. As an architectural photographer he was suddenly faced with a built environment in miniature, and that experiment proved a great success. His sensitive and patient eye never settled for partial solutions. 'Ich werde noch ein wenig herumdoktern...' ('Let me fiddle about with it for a bit...'), he would warn euphemistically—and some time later, after the umpteenth adjustment of angle, focus and lighting, came the liberating click of his camera shutter. Looking through his lens was an enriching experience for me. As in the previous book, translator Billy Nolan understood every nuance perfectly and succeeded in expressing it in English. I am extremely grateful that he did not throw in the towel in the final few months when tens of thousands of words were sent his way; I cannot imagine a better translator. Graphic designer Joost Grootens, working closely with assistant Julie da Silva on this occasion, succeeded in weaving together words and images to form a magnificent entity. This was no easy task, given the huge diversity of material and visual languages, but the result combines precise and subtle orientation points with refreshing and playful elements. Publisher Eelco van Welie, navigating calmly like a captain through rough waters, pinpointed with absolute accuracy the issues that still required attention, radiated composure and confidence, and always offered words of encouragement laced with humour.

Having to witness the making of a book at first hand can prove quite an ordeal for loved ones; I am therefore all the more thankful for every gesture of patience, understanding and interest shown to me throughout this process. And now that the end of the journey is finally nearing and the exhibition has generated plenty of publicity, it is tremendously uplifting to be approached by people who have become enthusiastic about architecture games because of this project. After all, there is no exhibition without visitors, and no book without readers. Every person who acquires a taste for architecture, games or architecture games through *Serious Fun* represents a small gift for the author.

Aarseth, Espen & Stephan Günzel (2019), 'Introduction: Space—The Theoretical Frontier', in: Aarseth, Espen & Stephan Günzel (eds) (2019), *Ludotopia: Spaces, Places and Territories in Computer Games*, Bielefeld: Transcript, pp. 7–9.

Allen, Christopher & Shannon Appelcline (2018), *Meeples Together: How and Why Cooperative Board Games Work*, Roseville: Gameplaywright.

Ampatzidou, Cristina (2020), 'Lessons about Learning from Serious Games: The Learning Potential of Co-Creation and Gameplay in Participatory Urban Planning Processes', in: van den Dool (ed.) (2020), *Strategies for Urban Network Learning: International Practices and Theoretical Reflections*, Cham: Palgrave Macmillan, pp. 281–305.

Ampatzidou, Cristina & Katharina Gugerell (2019), 'Participatory Game Prototyping—Balancing Domain Content and Playability in a Serious Game Design for the Energy Transition', in: *CoDesign: International Journal of CoCreation in Design and the Arts*, vol. 15, no. 4, pp. 345–360.

Arpa, Javier, Winy Maas & Adrien Ravon (2018), *Porocity: Opening up Solidity*, Rotterdam: The Why Factory & nai010 Publishers.

Balducci, Temma (2006), 'Revisiting *Womanhouse*: Welcome to the (Deconstructed) *Dollhouse*', in: *Woman's Art Journal*, vol. 27, no. 2, pp. 16–23.

Bereitschaft, Bradley (2016), 'Gods of the City? Reflecting on City Building Games as an Early Introduction to Urban Systems', in: *Journal of Geography*, vol. 115, no. 2, pp. 51–60.

Bereitschaft, Bradley (2021), 'Commercial City Building Games as Pedagogical Tools: What Have We Learned?', in: *Journal of Geography in Higher Education*.

Berre, Nina, Mélanie van der Hoorn & Anne Marit Lunde (eds) (2015), *Arkitekturstriper: Architecture in Comic-Strip Form*, Oslo: Nasjonalmuseet for kunst, arkitektur og design.

Berry, Vincent (2021), 'Que sait-on des jeux de société "modernes"?', in: *Sciences du jeu*, no. 14.

Bittanti, Matteo (2015a), *How to Get Rid of Homeless*, San Francisco: Concrete Press.

Bittanti, Matteo (2015b), *How to Get Rid of Homeless*, unpublished manuscript.

Bonta, Juan Pablo (1979a), 'Prologue', in: *Journal of Architectural Education*, vol. 33, no. 1, pp. 1.

Bonta, Juan Pablo (1979b), 'Simulation Games in Architectural Education', in: *Journal of Architectural Education*, vol. 33, no. 1, pp. 12–18.

Booth, Paul (2021), *Board Games as Media*, New York: Bloomsbury.

Bordes, Juan (2010), 'Building the Avant-Garde through Play: Nineteenth-Century Commercial Toys Derived from Educational Programmes', in: Stals, José Lebrero (ed.) (2010), *Toys of the Avant-Garde*, Málaga: Fundación Museo Picasso, pp. 16–51.

Botz, Corinne May (2004), *The Nutshell Studies* of *Unexplained Death*, New York: The Monacelli Press.

Brand, Jan & Minke Vos (2017), *1:12. Verbeeldingskracht in zorgarchitectuur*, Arnhem: ArtEZ Press.

Brković Dodig, Marta & Linda N. Groat (eds) (2020), *The Routledge Companion to Games in Architecture and Urban Planning. Tools for Design, Teaching, and Research*, New York: Routledge.

Brosterman, Norman (1991), 'Potential Architecture: An Infinity of Buildings', in: Canadian Centre for Architecture (ed.) (1991), *Potential Architecture: Construction Toys from the CCA Collection*, Montreal: Canadian Centre for Architecture, pp. 7–13.

Brosterman, Norman (1997), *Inventing Kindergarten*, New York: Harry N. Abrams.

Brosterman, Norman & Michael Lewis (1991), 'Notes on the Toys in the Exhibition', in: Canadian Centre for Architecture (ed.) (1991), *Potential Architecture: Construction Toys from the CCA Collection*, Montreal: Canadian Centre for Architecture, pp.15–36.

Bryan, James E. (2018), 'Material Culture in Miniature: Nuremberg Kitchens as Inspirational Toys in the Long Nineteenth Century', in: Brandow-Faller, Megan (ed.) (2018), *Childhood by Design: Toys and the Material Culture of Childhood, 1700-Present*, London: Bloomsbury, pp. 215–233.

Buckminster Fuller, Richard (1969), 'The World Game', in: *Ekistics*, vol. 28, no. 167, pp. 286–292.

Buckminster Fuller, Richard (1971), *The World Game: Integrative Resource Utilization Planning Tool*, Carbondale: World Resources Inventory, Southern Illinois University.

Canadian Centre for Architecture (ed.) (1990), *Buildings in Boxes: Architectural Toys from the CCA*, Montreal: Canadian Centre for Architecture.

Canadian Centre for Architecture (ed.) (1991), *Potential Architecture: Construction Toys from the CCA Collection*, Montreal: Canadian Centre for Architecture.

Canadian Centre for Architecture (ed.) (1992), *Toys That Teach*, Montreal: Canadian Centre for Architecture.

Canadian Centre for Architecture (ed.) (1993), *Toys and the Modernist Tradition*, Montreal: Canadian Centre for Architecture.

Canadian Centre for Architecture (ed.) (1995), *Dream Houses, Toy Homes*, Montreal: Canadian Centre for Architecture.

Canadian Centre for Architecture (ed.) (1997), *Toy Town*, Montreal: Canadian Centre for Architecture.

Canadian Centre for Architecture (ed.) (2000), *Cities in Motion: Toys and Transport*, Montreal: Canadian Centre for Architecture.

Clough, Eric (2009), 'Mystery on Fifth Avenue', in: Montola, Markus, Jaakko Stenros & Annika Waern (eds) (2009), *Pervasive Games—Theory and Design: Experiences on the Boundary between Life and Play*, Amsterdam, Boston et al.: Morgan Kaufmann, pp. 91–96.

Codognato, Mario (2007), *Whiteread*, Milano: Electa.

Cooper, Patty & Dian Zillner (2000), *Toy Buildings, 1880–1980*, Atglen: Schiffer Publishing.

Costikyan, Greg (2011), 'Boardgame Aesthetics', in: Costikyan, Greg & Drew Davidson (eds) (2011), *Tabletop: Analog Game Design*, Pittsburgh: ETC Press, pp. 179–184.

Coupland, Douglas (2005), *Super City*, Vancouver: Hemlock Printers.

Debik, Karl (1999), 'Mitteldeutsche Spurensuche', in: Leinweber, Ulf (ed.) (1999), *Baukästen: Technisches Spielzeug vom Biedermeier bis zur Jahrtausendwende*, Wiesbaden: VMA Verlag, Drei Lilien Edition, pp. 112–139.

Deslongchamps-Gagnon, Maxime & Alexandre Poirier (2016), 'L'expérience émotionnelle du joueur en échec dans l'art vidéoludique', in: *Sciences du jeu*, no. 6.

Döhl, Reinhard (1988), *Hermann Finsterlin. Eine Annäherung*, Stuttgart: Cantz.

Döhl, Reinhard (2000), 'Hermann Finsterlin. Spielsachen und Spiele', in: *Der Architekt*, no. 11, pp. 23–26.

Domsch, Sebastian (2019), 'Space and Narrative in Computer Games', in: Aarseth, Espen & Stephan Günzel (eds) (2019), *Ludotopia: Spaces, Places and Territories in Computer Games*, Bielefeld: Transcript, pp. 103–123.

Dousson, Xavier (2020), 'Les jeux de l'architecte Fabien Vienne. Des jeux à l'architecture, de l'architecture aux jeux', in: Prévot, Maryvonne, Éric Monin & Nicolas Douay (eds) (2020), *L'urbanisme, l'architecture et le jeu*, pp. 75–99.

Duke, Richard D. (2000), 'A Personal Perspective on the Evolution of Gaming', in: *Simulation & Gaming*, vol. 31, no. 1, pp. 79–85.

Elias, George Skaff, Richard Garfield & Karl Robert Gutschera (2012), *Characteristics of Games*, Cambridge (MA) & London: MIT Press.

Evans, Caroline & Susannah Frankel (2008), *The House of Viktor & Rolf*, London: Merrell.

Fanning, Colin (2018), 'Building Kids: LEGO and the Commodification of Creativity', in: Brandow-Faller, Megan (ed.) (2018), *Childhood by Design: Toys and the Material Culture of Childhood, 1700-Present*, London: Bloomsbury, pp. 89–109.

Fanning, Colin & Rebecca Mir (2014), 'Teaching Tools: Progressive Pedagogy and the History of Construction Play', in: Garrelts, Nate (ed.) (2014), *Understanding Minecraft: Essays on Play, Community and Possibilities*, Jefferson: McFarland, pp. 28–56.

Flanagan, Mary (2007), 'The Sims: Suburban Utopia', in: von Borries, Friedrich, Steffen P. Walz & Matthias Böttger (eds) (2007), *Space Time Play: Computer Games, Architecture and Urbanism—The Next Level*, Basel, Boston & Berlin: Birkhäuser, pp. 150–151.

Flanagan, Mary (2009), *Critical Play: Radical Game Design*, Cambridge (MA) & London: MIT Press.

Frenken, Caspar, Sereh Mandias & Eileen Schreurs (eds) (2015), *Studio: Dolls' House*, Delft: Chair The Architecture of The Interior, Technical University.

Friedman, Alice T. (1995), 'Model Homes and Dream Houses', in: Canadian Centre for Architecture (ed.) (1995), *Dream Houses, Toy Homes*, Montreal: Canadian Centre for Architecture, pp. 7–27.

Fuchs, Mathias (2006), *PlastiCity: A Multiplayer Urban Planning Game*, unpublished manuscript.

Garrelts, Nate (ed.) (2014), *Understanding Minecraft: Essays on Play, Community and Possibilities*, Jefferson: McFarland.

Gekker, Alex (2016), '(Mini) Mapping the Game-Space: A Taxonomy of Control', in: The Playful Mapping Collective (ed.) (2016), *Playful Mapping in the Digital Age*, Amsterdam: Institute of Network Cultures, pp. 134–155.

Gilberg, Mark, Alison Walker & Richard Sandomeno (2018), 'Fast and Furious: Operation, Maintenance, and Repair of Chris Burden's Metropolis II at LACMA', in: Rivenc, Rachel & Reinhard Bek (eds) (2018), *Keep it Moving? Conserving Kinetic Art*, Los Angeles: The Getty Conservation Institute, pp. 26–47.

Goldfarb, Bruce (2020), *18 Tiny Deaths: The Untold Story of Frances Glessner Lee and the Invention of Modern Forensics*, London: Endeavour.

Gordon, Eric & Steven Schirra (2011), 'Playing with Empathy: Digital Role-Playing Games in Public Meetings', in: Kjeldskov, Jesper & Jeni Paay (eds) (2011), *C&T '11: Proceedings of the 5th International Conference on Communities and Technologies*, Brisbane: ACM & International Institute for Socio-Informatics, pp. 179–185.

Grisebach (ed.) (2019), *Bauhaus forever!*, Berlin: Grisebach.

Groat, Linda N. (2020), 'The Sorting Task: Its Versatility and Adaptability in Research, Teaching, and Practice', in: Brković Dodig, Marta & Linda N. Groat (eds) (2020), *The Routledge Companion to Games in Architecture and Urban Planning. Tools for Design, Teaching, and Research*, New York: Routledge, pp. 203–220.

Gugerell, Katharina, Martina Jauschneg, Mario Platzer & Martin Berger (2017), 'Playful Participation with Urban Complexity—Evaluation of the Co-Located Serious Game Mobility Safari in Vienna', in: Schrenk, Manfred, Vasily V. Popovich, Peter Zeile, Pietro Elisei, Clemens Beyer & Gerhard Navratil (eds) (2017), *Panta Rhei—a World in Constant Motion. Proceedings of the 22nd International Conference on Urban Development, Regional Planning and Information Society*, Wien: Competence Center of Urban and Regional Planning, pp. 413–420.

Gugerell, Katharina, Mario Platzer, Martina Jauschneg, Cristina Ampatzidou & Martin Berger (2018), 'Game Over or Jumping to the Next Level? How Playing the Serious Game "Mobility Safari" Instigates Social Learning for a Smart Mobility Transition in Vienna', in: Bisello, Adriano, Daniele Vettorato, Pierre Laconte & Simona Costa (eds) (2018), *Smart and Sustainable Planning for Cities and Regions. Results of SSPCR 2017*, Cham: Springer, pp. 211–224.

Gugerell, Katharina & Christian Zuidema (2017), 'Gaming for the Energy Transition: Experimenting and Learning in Co-Designing a Serious Game Prototype', in: *Journal of Cleaner Production*, no. 169, pp. 105–116.

Haney, James A. (1971), 'Games, Simulations and Learning', in: *Research News—Office of Research Administration, The University of Michigan, Ann Arbor*, vol. 21, no. 9, pp. 3–11.

Hebert, Budd (1972), 'The New Town Game: An Evaluation Based on Instructional Experience', in: *Simulation & Games*, vol. 3, no. 3, pp. 349–360.

Hensel, Thomas, Robert Eikmeyer & Eva Kraus (eds) (2019), *BAU [SPIEL] HAUS*, Wien: Verlag für moderne Kunst & Nürnberg: Neues Museum.

Hodge, Brooke (1990), 'Introduction', in: Canadian Centre for Architecture (ed.) (1990), *Buildings in Boxes: Architectural Toys from the CCA*, Montreal: Canadian Centre for Architecture, pp. 5–8.

Hofmann, Susanne (2014), *Partizipation macht Architektur: Die Baupiloten—Methode und Projekte*, Berlin: Jovis.
Hofmann, Susanne (2020), 'Room for Play in Architecture: Participatory Games and Game-Like Tools in Architecture Developed by die Baupiloten', in: Brković Dodig, Marta & Linda N. Groat (eds) (2020), *The Routledge Companion to Games in Architecture and Urban Planning. Tools for Design, Teaching, and Research*, New York: Routledge, pp. 17–31.
Hollein, Max & Gunda Luyken (eds) (2004), *Kunst—ein Kinderspiel*, Frankfurt am Main: Revolver Archiv für aktuelle Kunst.
Holopainen, Jussi & May Stain (2014), 'Dissecting Playfulness for Practical Design', in: Walz, Steffen P. & Sebastian Deterding (eds) (2014), *The Gameful World: Approaches, Issues, Applications*, Cambridge (MA) & London: MIT Press, pp. 419–438.

Ivković, Milena (2015), *Delft Campus Urban Game: Strategic Planning Workshop—Results*, unpublished manuscript.

Jacobs, Ko (2017), 'Werelden van overgave', in: Brand, Jan & Minke Vos (2017), *1:12. Verbeeldingskracht in zorgarchitectuur*, Arnhem: ArtEZ Press, pp. 13–66.
Javid, Ali (2020), 'Design as Crossword-Puzzle Solving: The Role of Game in Merging Research and Design', in: Brković Dodig, Marta & Linda N. Groat (eds) (2020), *The Routledge Companion to Games in Architecture and Urban Planning. Tools for Design, Teaching, and Research*, New York: Routledge, pp. 140–149.
Jenkins, Henry (2004) 'Game Design as Narrative Architecture', in: Wardrip-Fruin, Noah & Pat Harrigan (eds) (2004), *First Person: New Media as Story, Performance, and Game*, Cambridge (MA) & London: MIT Press, pp. 118–130.
Jenkins, Henry (2007), 'Narrative Spaces', in: von Borries, Friedrich, Steffen P. Walz & Matthias Böttger (eds) (2007), *Space Time Play: Computer Games, Architecture and Urbanism—The Next Level*, Basel, Boston & Berlin: Birkhäuser, pp. 56–60.
Juul, Jesper (2013), *The Art of Failure: An Essay on the Pain of Playing Video Games*, Cambridge (MA) & London: MIT Press.

Keslacy, Elizabeth (2015), 'Fun and Games: The Suppression of Architectural Authoriality and the Rise of the Reader', in: *Footprint: Delft Architecture Theory Journal*, vol. 9, no. 2, pp. 101–123.

Lahoud, Christelle (ed.) (2021), *The Block by Block Playbook: Using Minecraft as a Participatory Design Tool in Urban Design and Governance*, Nairobi: United Nations Human Settlements Programme (UN-Habitat).
Lantz, Frank (2007), 'Big Urban Game: A Playful Connection of the "Twin Cities"', in: von Borries, Friedrich, Steffen P. Walz & Matthias Böttger (eds) (2007), *Space Time Play: Computer Games, Architecture and Urbanism—The Next Level*, Basel, Boston & Berlin: Birkhäuser, pp. 390–391.
Lauwaert, Maaike (2007), 'Challenge Everything? Construction Play in Will Wright's SIMCITY', in: *Games and Culture*, vol. 2, no. 3, pp. 194–212.
Lauwaert, Maaike (2009), *The Place of Play: Toys and Digital Cultures*, Amsterdam: Amsterdam University Press.
Leinweber, Ulf (ed.) (1999), *Baukästen: Technisches Spielzeug vom Biedermeier bis zur Jahrtausendwende*, Wiesbaden: VMA Verlag, Drei Lilien Edition.
Leorke, Dale (2019), *Location-Based Gaming: Play in Public Space*, Singapore: Palgrave Macmillan.
Lingens, Peter (1999), 'Bausteine. Einleitende Betrachtungen', in: Leinweber, Ulf (ed.) (1999), *Baukästen: Technisches Spielzeug vom Biedermeier bis zur Jahrtausendwende*, Wiesbaden: VMA Verlag, Drei Lilien Edition, pp. 12–33.
Luyken, Gunda (2004), 'Kunst—ein Kinderspiel', in: Hollein, Max & Gunda Luyken (eds) (2004), *Kunst—ein Kinderspiel*, Frankfurt am Main: Revolver Archiv für aktuelle Kunst, pp. 24–51.

Maerkle, Andrew & Harry Perlmutte (2006), 'Building Asia Block by Block: A Collaboration between ArtAsiaPacific, Lego and Nine Leading Architects', in: *ArtAsiaPacific*, no. 49, pp. 54–63.
Martin, Gareth Damian (2017), 'Memories of a Broken Planet', in: *Heterotopias*, no. 002, pp. 22–54.
Marwaha, Parvinder (2014), 'It's a Doll's World', in: *Mark—Another Architecture*, no. 52, pp. 130–135.
McKenzie Wark (2015), 'Capture All: *SimCity*, Gamespace, and Play', in: *The Avery Review*, no. 6.
Medendorp, Clazien (2008), *Kijkkasten uit Suriname: De diorama's van Gerrit Schouten*, Amsterdam: KIT Publishers.
Metzger, Wolfram & Jutta Tremmel-Endres (1996), *Traumwelten der 50er Jahre: Puppenwelt und Wirklichkeit*, Karlsruhe: Info Verlag.
Millar Fisher, Michelle (2018), 'Work Becomes Play: Toy Design, Creative Play, and Unlearning in the Bauhaus Legacy', in: Brandow-Faller, Megan (ed.) (2018), *Childhood by Design: Toys and the Material Culture of Childhood, 1700-Present*, London: Bloomsbury, pp. 153–172.
Miller, Laura J. (2005), 'Denatured Domesticity: An Account of Femininity and Physiognomy in the Interiors of Frances Glessner Lee', in: Heynen, Hilde & Gülsüm Baydar (eds) (2005), *Negotiating Domesticity: Spatial Productions of Gender in Modern Architecture*, London: Routledge, pp. 196–212.
Montola, Markus (2009), 'Games and Pervasive Games', in: Montola, Markus, Jaakko Stenros & Annika Waern (eds) (2009), *Pervasive Games—Theory and Design: Experiences on the Boundary between Life and Play*, Amsterdam, Boston et al.: Morgan Kaufmann, pp. 7–23.
Montola, Markus, Jaakko Stenros & Annika Waern (2009), 'Designing Spatial Expansion', in: Montola, Markus, Jaakko Stenros & Annika Waern (eds) (2009), *Pervasive Games—Theory and Design: Experiences on the Boundary between Life and Play*, Amsterdam, Boston et al.: Morgan Kaufmann, pp. 77–90.
Morris, Mark S. (2014), 'Dimensions of the Mass-Produced Doll House: Fisher-Price versus Playmobil', in: Lasansky, Medina (ed.) (2014), *Archi.Pop: Mediating Architecture in Popular Culture*, London & New York: Bloomsbury, pp. 61–74.
Mourão Pereira, Carlos, Teresa Valsassina Heitor & Ann Heylighen (2017), 'Exploring Invisibility through Multisensory Spatial Research Methods', in: Hannes, Karin, Ann Heylighen, Bernadette Dierckx de Casterlé, Frederik Truyen & Anja Declercq (eds) (2017), *Quality and Reflexivity in Qualitative Inquiry: European Congress of Qualitative Inquiry 2017 Proceedings*, Leuven: KU Leuven, pp. 9–18.

Olsberg, Nicholas (1991), 'Preface', in: Canadian Centre for Architecture (ed.) (1991), *Potential Architecture: Construction Toys from the CCA Collection*, Montreal: Canadian Centre for Architecture, pp. 5–6.
Olsen, Chelsea (2017), *The Stettheimer Dollhouse: A Life and Salon in* Miniature, unpublished manuscript.
Orbanes, Phil (1989), 'Where Did They Move Square Mile?', in: *Games International: The Journal of Fun and Games*, no. 3, pp. 20–21.

Papadakis, Andreas (1983), *Dolls' Houses*, London: Architectural Design & Academy Editions.
Pasierbska, Halina (2015), *Dollhouses from the V & A Museum of Childhood*, London: V & A Publishing.
Pearson, Luke Caspar (2019), 'Video Game Urbanism: How We Design Virtual Game Spaces to Engage New Audiences with the Architecture of Tomorrow', in: Gerber, Andri & Ulrich Götz (eds) (2019), *Architectonics of Game Spaces: The Spatial Logic of the Virtual and Its Meaning for the Real*, Bielefeld: Transcript, pp. 293–312.
Pedercini, Paolo (2019), 'Invisible (Game) Cities: Andri Gerber in Conversation with Paolo Pedercini, January 25, 2019 (E-mail)', in: Gerber, Andri & Ulrich Götz (eds) (2019), *Architectonics of Game Spaces: The Spatial Logic of the Virtual and Its Meaning for the Real*, Bielefeld: Transcript, pp. 47–57.
Perry, Gill (2013), *Playing at Home: The House in Contemporary Art*, London: Reaktion Books.
Pijzel-Dommisse, Jet (2000), *Het Hollandse pronkpoppenhuis: Interieur en huishouden in de 17de en 18de eeuw*, Zwolle: Waanders.
Pinos, Jan, Vit Vozenilek & Ondrej Pavlis (2020), 'Automatic Geodata Processing Methods for Real-World City Visualizations in Cities: Skylines', in: *ISPRS International Journal of Geo-Information*, vol. 9, no. 1, pp. 1–18.
Platzer, Mario, Hannah Stowasser, Martina Jauschneg, Oswald Devisch, Teodora Constantinescu, Jeremiah Diephuis, Georgi Kostov, Cristina Ampatzidou & Katharina Gugerell (2018), *Play!UC: Playing with Urban Complexity*, Vienna: Green City Lab.
Poplin, Alenka (2011), 'Games and Serious Games in Urban Planning: Study Cases', in: Murgante, Beniamino, Osvaldo Gervasi, Andrés Iglesias, David Taniar & Bernady O. Apduhan (eds) (2011), *Computational Science and Its Applications—ICCSA 2011, Part II*, Berlin & Heidelberg: Springer, pp. 1–14.
Poplin, Alenka (2014), 'Digital Serious Game for Urban Planning: "B3—Design Your Marketplace!"', in *Environment and Planning B: Planning and Design*, vol. 41, no. 3, pp. 493–511.

Rugoff, Ralph (ed.) (2008), *Psycho Buildings: Artists Take on Architecture*, London: Hayward Gallery.

Sanchez, Jose (2015), 'Block'hood: Developing an Architectural Simulation Video Game', in: Martens, Bob, Gabriel Wurzer, Thomas Grasl, Wolfgang E. Lorenz & Richard Schaffranek (eds) (2015), *Real Time: Extending the Reach of Computation—Proceedings of the 33rd International Conference on Education and Research in Computer Aided Architectural Design in Europe, Volume 1*, Brussels: Education and Research in Computer Aided Architectural Design in Europe & Vienna: Faculty of Architecture and Urban Planning, TU Wien, pp. 89–97.
Sanchez, Jose (2016), 'Massive Re-Patterning of the Urban Landscape', in: *Architectural Design*, vol. 86, no. 5, pp. 48–51.
Shubert, Howard (1993), 'Toys and the Modernist Tradition', in: Canadian Centre for Architecture (ed.) (1993), *Toys and the Modernist Tradition*, Montreal: Canadian Centre for Architecture, pp. 17–32.
Siret, Daniel, Ignacio Requena-Ruiz & Arnaud Dercelles (2020), 'Jouons (enfin) à la Ville Radieuse!', in: Prévot, Maryvonne, Éric Monin & Nicolas Douay (eds) (2020), *L'urbanisme, l'architecture et le jeu*, pp. 117–130.
Somers, Dirk (2015), 'Epilogue', in: Frenken, Caspar, Sereh Mandias & Eileen Schreurs (eds) (2015), Studio: *Dolls' House*, Delft: Chair The Architecture of The Interior, Technical University, pp. 49–51.
Somers, Dirk, Bart Verschaffel & Maarten van den Driessche (2019), *Bovenbouw Architectuur. Living the Exotic Everyday*, Antwerpen: Flanders Architecture Institute.
Speidel, Manfred (2006), *Stadtkrone und Märchenpalast. Zum Glasbauspiel von Bruno Taut*, unpublished manuscript.
Stals, José Lebrero (ed.) (2010), *Toys of the Avant-Garde*, Málaga: Fundación Museo Picasso.
Stenros, Jaakko (2014), 'Behind Games: Playful Mindsets and Transformative Practices', in: Walz, Steffen P. & Sebastian Deterding (eds) (2014), *The Gameful World: Approaches, Issues, Applications*, Cambridge (MA) & London: MIT Press, pp. 201–222.
Stock, Karin & Katherine Wheeler (2018), 'Reconstructing Domestic Play: The Kaleidoscope House', in: Brandow-Faller, Megan (ed.) (2018), *Childhood by Design: Toys and the Material Culture of Childhood, 1700-Present*, London: Bloomsbury, pp. 193–211.
Strouhal, Ernst & Manfred Zollinger & Brigitte Felderer (eds) (2012), *Spiele der Stadt: Glück, Gewinn und Zeitvertreib*, Wien & New York: Springer.
Suits, Bernard (2005[1978]), *The Grasshopper: Games, Life and Utopia*, Peterborough: Broadview Press.
Summers, Luis H. (1979), 'Operational Games in Architecture and Design', in: *Journal of Architectural Education*, vol. 33, no. 1, pp. 2–7.
Sutton-Smith, Brian (1994), 'Does Play Prepare the Future?', in: Goldstein, Jeffrey H. (ed.) (1994), *Toys, Play, and Child Development*, Cambridge: Cambridge University Press, pp. 130–146.

Tan, Ekim (2017), *Play the City: Games Informing the Urban Development*, Heijningen: Jap Sam Books.
Tan, Ekim (2019), 'Play the City: Dungeons and Dragons for Cities', in: Gerber, Andri & Ulrich Götz (eds) (2019), *Architectonics of Game Spaces: The Spatial Logic*

of the Virtual and Its Meaning for the Real, Bielefeld: Transcript, pp. 265–276.
Temkin, Ann (ed.) (2014), *Robert Gober: The Heart Is Not a Metaphor*, New York: The Museum of Modern Art.
Tóth, Eszter (2015), 'Potential of Games in the Field of Urban Planning', in: Bártek, Tomáš, Jan Miškov & Jaroslav Švelch (eds) (2015), *New Perspectives in Game Studies: Proceedings of the Central and Eastern European Game Studies Conference Brno 2014*, Brno: Masaryk University, pp.71–89.

Vale, Brenda & Robert (2013), *Architecture on the Carpet: The Curious Tale of Construction Toys and the Genesis of Modern Buildings*, London: Thames & Hudson.
van der Hoorn, Mélanie (2012), *Bricks & Balloons: Architecture in Comic-Strip Form*, Rotterdam: 010.
van der Hoorn, Mélanie (2015), 'TAM Associati: Ideals Put into Practice', in: Berre, Nina, Mélanie van der Hoorn & Anne Marit Lunde (eds) (2015), *Arkitekturstriper: Architecture in Comic-Strip Form*, Oslo: Nasjonalmuseet for kunst, arkitektur og design, pp. 88–93.
van der Hoorn, Mélanie (2018), *Spots in Shots: Narrating the Built Environment in Short Films*, Rotterdam: nai010.
van Gerrewey, Christophe (2016), 'Dirk Somers: Poppenhuizen en geschiedenis', in: *De Witte Raaf* no. 180, pp. 8–9.
Venhuizen, Hans (2010), *Game Urbanism: Manual for Cultural Spatial Planning*, Amsterdam: Valiz.
von Borries, Friedrich, Steffen P. Walz & Matthias Böttger (eds) (2007), *Space Time Play: Computer Games, Architecture and Urbanism—The Next Level*, Basel, Boston & Berlin: Birkhäuser.
von Wilckens, Leonie (1980), *The Dolls' House: An Illustrated History*, London: Bell & Hyman.

Wasiuta, Mark (2009), 'The Persistence of Informational Vision: World Game 1969, 2009', in: *Journal of the Society of Architectural Historians*, vol. 68, no. 4, pp. 590–593.
Wheelwright, Peter (2000), 'Peek-A-Boo Views', in: *A Quarterly of Interiors*, no. 10, pp. 120–125.
Woods, Stewart (2012), *Eurogames: The Design, Culture and Play of Modern European Board Games*, Jefferson: McFarland.

Yagou, Artemis (2013), 'Modernist Complexity on a Small Scale: The Dandanah Glass Building Blocks of 1920 from an Object-Based Research Perspective', in: *Deutsches Museum Preprint*, no. 6.

Zinguer, Tamar (2015), *Architecture in Play: Intimations of Modernism in Architectural Toys*, Charlottesville: University of Virginia Press.

Donau
U-Bahn
Simmering

+1
0
+1
−1